JunkBots, BugBots, and Bots on Wheels:

Building Simple Robots with BEAM Technology

JunkBots, BugBots, and Bots on Wheels:
Building Simple Robots with BEAM Technology

Dave Hrynkiw and Mark W. Tilden

McGraw-Hill/Osborne

New York   Chicago   San Francisco
Lisbon   London   Madrid   Mexico City   Milan
New Delhi   San Juan   Seoul   Singapore   Sydney   Toronto

The *McGraw·Hill* Companies

McGraw-Hill/Osborne
2600 Tenth Street
Berkeley, California 94710
U.S.A.

To arrange bulk purchase discounts for sales promotions, premiums, or fund-raisers, please contact **McGraw-Hill/Osborne** at the above address. For information on translations or book distributors outside the U.S.A., please see the International Contact Information page immediately following the index of this book.

JunkBots, BugBots, and Bots on Wheels:
Building Simple Robots with BEAM Technology

1234567890 FGR FGR 0198765432

ISBN 0-07-222601-3

Publisher
  Brandon A. Nordin

Vice President & Associate Publisher
  Scott Rogers

Acquisitions Editor
  Marjorie McAneny

Project Editor
  Jennifer Malnick

Acquisitions Coordinator
  Tana Allen

Technical Editor
  Wilf Rigter

Copy Editor
  Robert Campbell

Proofreaders
  Paul Medoff, Jennifer Malnick

Indexer
  David Heiret

Computer Designers
  Carie Abrew, Jean Butterfield

Illustrators
  Michael Mueller, Melinda Moore Lytle

Cover Series Design
  Jeff Weeks

This book was composed with Corel VENTURA™ Publisher.

Contents at a Glance

Contents

Preface

Fast-Tracking the Robot Dream

You've seen it.

Every January, for many Januarys now, on TV, radio, and in print, come predictions by qualified futurists that "sooner than you think" we'll have vacations on the moon, orbiting space cities, flying cars, free electricity, immortality, rocket belts, clones of our own, artificially intelligent computers, and most prominently of all, the long sought after but elusive Home Robot Butler—a cheap, reliable mechanism to vacuum and clean, allowing us a carefree suburban existence without guilt. Many of these same futurists will (off season) also predict a dire long-range future for mankind where technology overwhelms us. Machines will rule while humans are caged in museum dioramas involving Laz-E-Boy recliners.

Well, for those of you waiting fretfully for when the robots take over, take heart. It's not going to happen. There's no evidence for it.

Today we can understand why we don't have the other things promised by the science fiction dreams of old. Space travel is too expensive, flying cars too complicated, the moon is a barren rock in plaster of paris, and talking computers are great in movies but unmarketable in real life. But what about that butler? You would think, with the advances that have been made, that surely it can't be too hard to make a cheap, self-contained trashcan that could do chores around the house. If you could buy one for $49.99, wouldn't it be the best Mother's Day gift you could give? Wouldn't you want a dozen for home and office? How hard can it be to make a device that moves around doing the little things so that you could concentrate on larger issues, like the color of your Laz-E-Boy recliner?

The short answer is that it's very hard, but not according to popular mythology. The problem is that the apparent ease of making a "living" robot is a deception fostered by over three thousand years of fictional stories reinforcing the Pygmalion dream—the functional animation of an artificial creation with the properties of life. The oldest "robot" references we have are the fictional bronze maidens from Homer's "The Odyssey," and later the animated statues of golems and gargoyles. Throughout history, there have been stories of machine-like dragons, demons, ghosts, and creatures called forth to do some task, because whatever is summoned always has some extra-human quality making it ideal for the job: great strength, mindless devotion, horrific visage, strange powers, or, after Mary Shelley made her contribution, the echo of human pathos.

You know it. Loner mad scientist creates mindless robot minion to do evil megalomaniacal bidding and/or satisfy deluded scientific goals. Robot comes to life but (shock) acquires will of its own. Scientist loses control, and the next thing you know, the robot's running through a forest with a heroine in its arms with herds of angry villagers in tow. Such plot lines always left me asking two prominent questions: Why would a robot show any interest in the spindly Fay Wray character and not the cool lab equipment, and where do villagers get so many flame torches at a moments notice?

Alas, unlike in the movies, and despite all wishes to the contrary, the ability to make a conscious robot creature doesn't happen by just throwing electronic bits together. Even the best minds and budgets haven't managed it outside the usual nonclassroom biology. True, sophisticated computer characters have been made that appear to have some aspects of life (they're a prime seller of the video game market), but their responses are limited. Even real goldfish show more life than the best screensavers made in their image. However, the general mass-belief in "automatic consciousness" is a problem for robotics researchers because popular media keeps implying it's not a problem.

It's not just a problem, it's one of the biggest mysteries: Why is it so hard for us to do artificially what mother nature appears to do automatically?

The answer is that it's not easy for nature either. Out of approximately twenty million living species on this planet (a good half of which are beetles), nature has only seen fit to evolve one with a precision soul. We overestimate the importance of being sentient because everything we do is so anthropocentric (by the human, for the human, to the human). The fact is that we aren't the only thinking creature on the planet, but we are the only species to believe our own press about the value of the phenomenon.

The point is, if monkeys, rats, and raccoons (to name just a few) have seen no reason to acquire our level of society despite their having thumbs, advanced brains, and three billion years of similar evolutionary breaks, why should machines take the initiative? Why would your toaster want to plot against you even if you do abuse its handle during breakfast? Why do we believe the movies when they say the robots will get us, when we don't believe a park bench when it says "wet paint"?

Fortunately, we don't have to worry. Today the most threatening thing a robot might do is fall on your foot. There is no volition allowing robots to do anything more than avoid you, at a speed far too slow to be the least bit threatening, and with a battery life that would make any "war against the robots" the shortest documentary in history. There is always a frightening first impression made by self-starting mechanical equipment, but it's something people get used to quickly. After working with them for several decades, I'm used to them popping about, but in the beginning, it was a different story.

I remember that, as soon as I was able and, being fairly lazy about housework, I tried to build a robot butler of my own. While a student in the 1980s, I bought a footstool-sized radio-controlled "Omnibot" and cracked it open. To my delight, it was mostly empty inside and I proceeded to load it up with all the machinations my student mind could imagine. Ultimately, after hours I shouldn't have wasted spending money I didn't really have, I finally had a robot that could push a suped-up dustbuster around under computer control. I then sat down to what I'd anticipated would be the "fun" part, building a mind for my new robot friend.

It took hours—hundreds, if not thousands, in fact—before the robot was capable of performing even the most basic of survival tasks, such as reliably returning to its home base for recharging. But I persevered, knowing that not only would this satisfy my own interest but would probably cinch my eventual Ph.D. (Yes, you make rationalizations like that in science, just as in many other dysfunctional relationships.)

It was tough. Programming the machine in Lisp, I quickly found that I couldn't just let the device make generalizations about my apartment space. I had to feed in specifics about width, dimensions, and areas of interest that I wanted it to patrol for security, cleaning, and even how it was to act as an answering machine and alarm clock. It got so bad that for a while I was dreaming in code (a nasty trip I wouldn't recommend for anyone).

Ultimately, though, after concessions and repeated redundant recursive reprogramming (repeatedly), I had a machine that could methodically vacuum its way about with a few friendly features like saying "Good Morning" or "Good Afternoon" when it actually was. It had friendly features and moving arms. I was proud, for maybe a week, before the problems began.

The first thing to go was the voice. I put a lot of time into that voice, but hearing the same tinny statements from the robot got highly annoying, so out it came. The second instant was when I tripped over it in the middle of the night while going to the bathroom and learned another sad truth about my "friend." If you trip over a dog or a cat in the middle of the night, it's usually not a big deal—they're soft, they'll heal, and they will ultimately forgive you. When you trip over a mobile machine, however, you break a toenail, swear like a dockyard worker, and are invariably in for a long and involved robot repair the next day, if only to wash the blood off.

Okay, okay, no problem. Change the programming to come out only when there is no one about. It was getting annoying with it constantly underfoot anyhow.

The next problem came to light as I lay in bed on a calm Sunday morning, hearing the robot come into the bedroom on its rounds and suck up a sock that had missed the laundry hamper the night before, immediately stalling the vacuum motor. I had to spring up immediately to clear the problem or risk the robot burning out its motor (as on many other occasions). Hack again. Trying variations on the programming didn't help, so ultimately the simple fix was just to restrict it from going into the bedroom.

The day also came when an incredible rattling sound came from the kitchen, and I looked in to see the robot sucking up dry kibble from the cat bowl. My cat glanced from the robot and shot me the unmistakable interspecies message "get this human thing out of my *face.*"

More hacking. More frustration. The kitchen went off-limits.

I won't detail the toilet-paper incident, but needless to say, it was soon banned from the bathroom. That left it to roam only the carpeted area in front of the TV, and after a month, it was removed even from there.

I came home from work to find the robot spinning uselessly in the middle of the carpet. Resigned now to its failings, I switched it off, broke it open, checked everything, but found it fine. However, it did this repeatedly, day after day. Took a while to find out what was happening. When the robot was coming out to vacuum, my cat had learned to move play furniture in front of it, systematically making the poor robot think it was completely surrounded by impassable objects until all it could do was spin. The cat then went back into the bedroom to sleep while the robot's battery ran down.

The last straw: five-dollar cat beats five thousand–dollar robot. Every change to the robot's software had taken considerable effort, and as problems had escalated, my enthusiasm had rapidly died. The device was switched off and remains today as a hat rack: the last useful thing it was good for.

Twenty years later, I still cannot throw it away, but I still have no interest in ever restoring it. Go figure.

It was only much later that I found out how common my disillusionment story was. If you ever have occasion to visit other roboticists around the world, I recommend that you take them out for a beer and ask them their stories (be prepared to pay for a keg). What you'll likely get are various humorous retrospectives on the death of a long-standing dream, and why many enthusiasts rarely build more than one robot in their entire lives.

The stories are many, but this one shows some insight into our flawed assumptions: A nameless American national research center replaced its security guards with complex roving robots but had to go back to security guards again after a year. The problem? People kept on breaking in, not to steal stuff but to empty their gun clips into the roving security machines, apparently just for kicks. It cost the center over two million dollars to develop machines to replace one hundred thousand dollars a year worth of humans, and they had to go back because they'd forgotten (or perhaps never understood) why human security is so effective in the first place: Namely, humans are not just the cheapest form of self-contained scanning system that can be reproduced with unskilled labor, they also have an implied status that keep them from getting shot. Without status, a robot is just a target. Home robot vacuums will never become popular because as soon as they remotely annoy the humans or household pets, it's garage-sale time for Robbie. The machines can't escape the Frankenstein trap we've dug them into. We want everything from them but will concede them nothing.

So what does a machine have to have before it can go from "tolerated" to "accepted" to its own 1-800 help line? As they stand now, robots don't stand at all. The dream of a home vacuum cleaner will never get off the shelves until we can find a way to put them on the same social level as household pets, or at least beanie babies. The problem has been justifying a market that can bridge the gap between the robot myth and the real world. The home robot does not sell, and many other conventional routes have been tried and fried. Not because the robots weren't capable, but because machine-human racial disparity is at an all-time high. What could close the distance between what we dream robots could do and what we would actually buy? Maybe toys or pets, maybe intelligent toasters, maybe self-driving cars.

Maybe none of these. It's not important what you'll eventually do with your robot. Don't sweat applications unless you need to. It's fun just experimenting, especially if you can get results and experience without the necessity of a NASA budget, and especially if you remain motivated enough to build more than just one.

That's what this book is about. Enclosed are some cool tricks to help work on devices with no focus at all other than existence. I like to think these tricks don't just help build better robots, but better roboticists (we have enough hat racks). Survive and rework. It's the same method nature uses. Seems to work fine. Why not for machines?

Years ago, I made the assumption that one could evolve better robots if they were made selfish and not servile. What I found, several thousand robots later (Must. Get. A. Life), is that there are minimal elegant solutions to building capable devices so long as they spend their energies on themselves and not their "masters." Small, elegant, solar-powered, almost perpetual, they can live in home and lab as a form of "robot ecology" without benefit of computer brains or battery. Initially, I studied them as they roamed about; now I just have to remember to put them in the dishwasher once a year to get the dust off. A different approach, still fledgling, but these "living machines" are quiet, careful, small, out of the way, and very easy to live with.

Think of it as the first specification for something to share your world—quiet, unassuming, amusing. Perpetual motion machines can be really annoying unless you build well. This book shows some ways how. What robots will become eventually is anyone's guess, but answers come faster by observing robot reality than simulation or fiction. The great thing about living robotics is that most of the neat stuff hasn't even been tried, and it won't be until skills are developed that we can share and show.

You gotta build. Simple, elegant solutions. Enjoy.

Mark W. Tilden
T.S.T., Hong Kong
August 14, 2002

Acknowledgments

A simple list of thanks to some of the people behind the production of this book:

Cheryl Hrynkiw—For understanding the importance of this project, and taking on much, much more than what was fair to her. Much more is owed to her than can be listed here. Suffice it to say that she has far exceeded her role as wife, friend, and companion. Also for her concise first-edit hack and slashes that gave focus to this book.

Grant McKee—His skilful implementation of BEAM technology made many of these projects simpler and more robust. Grant is also chiefly responsible for most of the photographs in the book as well as the construction of each project.

Wilf Rigter—Our technical editor and master of the electronic arts who watched over our projects with incisive, and often frustratingly brilliant, feedback.

Julianna Hrynkiw—For being as patient as a three-year-old can be, understanding that "When Daddy's done the book, we're going to the ZOO?!?"

Darcy Dueck—For assisting in the day-to-day management of Solarbotics and drafting all the pretty 3-D schematic illustrations in this book.

Glue, the Dog—For the nightly "Take me for a Frisbee toss!" pestering that pried this weary author away from the computer at ungodly hours of the morning.

Additional thanks to:

The folks at McGraw-Hill/Osborne for bringing this book concept to light. Special thanks to Jenny Malnick and Margie McAneny for the constant good-natured e-mail abuse (given and taken!).

Derek Mah of Attoboy Graphics (www.attoboy.com) for his creative vector-artwork illustrations that helped explain the technical concepts in this book.

The "SG" group of hard-core BEAMers that created the core of BEAM technology and the laws of BEAM Robotics.

Ted and Fran Hrynkiw, for saving the best for last!

—Dave Hrynkiw

Introduction

Junkbots, Bugbots, and Bots on Wheels: Building Simple Robots with BEAM Technology is intended to fill a void in the robotics community—how to actually construct a simple robot out of next to nothing. BEAM technology has proven to be a very effective way to build a simple, effective robot with easily accessible parts. If there's a book to make it easy for a robotics newcomer to actually build his or her first robot, this is it!

This book doesn't pretend to be an all-in-one resource for a new roboticist, but it certainly offers information and techniques not offered anywhere else. The purpose of *Junkbots* isn't to teach you everything about robots but to get you up and running in robotics with simple techniques, parts, and projects.

The audience for *Junkbots* includes absolute beginners, roboticists not familiar with BEAM techniques, and educators/club-leaders looking for simple robot-related projects they can use in the classroom. Experienced electronics hobbiests will also be pleasantly surprised by some of the simple and clever designs.

Junkbots is organized into three main categories. The first is the introduction to electronics, mechanics, and assembly techniques, which will be an especially valuable read to a new roboticist. Veteran roboticists shouldn't skip too much of this section, as there's some interesting practical insights worth reading.

More experienced readers can jump straight into the second portion, starting with Chapter 7, the "heart" of the book—the projects! Not all projects turn into full-fledged robots, as some projects are warm-ups that demonstrate principles that can be used in other robot designs. Each project grows in complexity, so start at the beginning and allow your expertise to grow with the book.

The last portion of the book contains the appendices that detail additional resources, technical schematics, and special materials and techniques. BEAM-style robotics occasionally requires unusual materials and procedures, which are detailed here. For those who can read technical schematics, they're included in Appendix C to augment the "wiring diagram"–style schematics used in each chapter. And for further research, a listing of useful BEAM-related resources is in Appendix A to help round out the reader's experience with BEAM robotics.

Thanks for Picking *Junkbots* Up!

We hope you find *Junkbots* an enjoyable read and that you actually sit down at the workbench to create your own robotics. We'll be continually supporting the book at http://junkbots.solarbotics.com, so drop by occasionally to see what's up!

Figure I
(left to right, top row)
Mark W. Tilden,
Wilf Rigter,
Dave Hrynkiw,
Cheryl Hrynkiw,
Grant McKee,
Darcy Dueck,
(bottom row)
Glue, and
Julianna Hrynkiw

Chapter 1

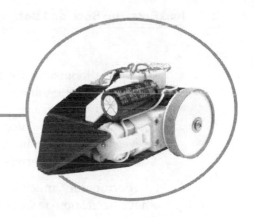

Welcome to the World of *Simple* Robotics!

For a long time, robotics has been the domain of universities, industrial laboratories, and car-production assembly lines. The robots you would find were usually large, slow, garbage-can-sized devices, or incredibly specialized manipulator arms anchored to an assembly-line floor. If these devices interested you, you needed considerable schooling, because there's no way that you'd otherwise be allowed near these robots.

Fortunately, much has happened in the last ten years to change this. There have been some *really cool* advances in robotics, bringing the technology out of the laboratory and into the garage of the interested builder. Microprocessors have become cheaper and more powerful, motors are smaller and stronger, and *knowledge* has become easier to access. Thank the founders of the Internet for that wire connecting the world's computers together!

The simple advancement of technology isn't the only reason for the explosive growth in robotics—a few new ideas that have popped out of the heads of some brilliant people have made this all possible. Rodney Brooks (director of the MIT Artificial Intelligence Laboratory) and Mark Tilden (recently of the Los Alamos National Laboratories and toy consultant with Wow Wee / Hasbro) changed the way people think about building robots. Hold on, we're going to have a quick history lesson on where the robots you will be building came from.

The Start of the Simplified Robotics Revolution

Back in 1948, Mr. William Grey Walter constructed some amazingly simple yet behavior-rich robots using *vacuum tube* technology. (Figure 1-1 is a striking example. For more information, check out the online resource at http://www.plazaearth.com/usr/gasperi/walter.htm.) These were *not* like robots that had to sit and calculate for incredibly long periods of time before making a few inches of progress. This new style of robot flailed about, and took immediate input from whatever it interacted with, and learned from those interactions. These simple "tortoise" robots are in many ways the grandfathers of the devices you'll be working on.

Rodney Brooks reinitiated the simple robot revolution by analyzing what other roboticists had tried, and turned it on its head. Rather than trying to design and program a central robot "brain" that takes care of all of the decisions (an immensely difficult task), he created a new system called "subsumption architecture." Subsumption architecture is a technique where the behavior of a robot is managed in layers, each layer controlling a single aspect of the robot's

Figure I-I
William Grey
Walter's
"Turtle" robot,
which uses
vacuum tube
technology
(Image
courtesy
of Owen
Holland and
the University
of the West of
England,
Bristol)

operation. For example, a low-level layer could be "Walk Forward," which the robot will happily do until it bumps into something. At this point, the slightly higher level "Lift Leg Higher" kicks in, overriding the "Walk Forward" layer until the robot successfully climbs over the obstacle, at which point "Lift Leg Higher" stops, and the low-level "Walk Forward" takes over again.

Brooks also made the radical decision *not* to try his concepts out in a computer simulation first. Although the computational power and programming were available to him to do so, he came to the realization that *if you can't accurately model every aspect of a robot's intended environment, then **don't do it**. Use the real thing instead!* What you and I may consider to be a minor, insignificant detail that isn't worth inputting to a computer may in fact drastically affect how the robot would work in real life. Take dust for example: In a computer model, dust behavior isn't the simplest thing to model, as it is affected by air currents, static electricity, and moisture levels in the air. But to a solar-powered robot, several weeks of dust on the solar cell will cause a noticeable change in robot performance. That same dust may also settle on the optical sensors, or (in the case of animal hair) cause electronic circuitry to misbehave. Brooks' decision to test his ideas with *real robots* in the *real world* is an important part of the evolution of BEAM-style robotics.

Of course, I'm simplifying the concepts of subsumption architecture greatly, but if you want more information, Brooks has many published papers and books on the concept. Remember that Internet thing I mentioned earlier? Great stuff online.

Brooks has a very complete Web site at MIT containing his papers; the address is http://www.ai.mit.edu/people/brooks/index.shtml.

In 1991, Brooks produced some very innovative robots by the names of Genghis and Attila, which demonstrated some *very* impressive behaviors using only a fraction of the computational power that other "traditional" robots used. There was a huge surge of media interest in these "bug-brained" robots who could do so much with so little. Brooks went on a speaking tour, with one of his stops being the University of Waterloo, where Mark Tilden was in attendance. As Brooks was championing building robots with little computational power, Tilden wondered, "Well, how about practically none?" And thus, BEAM robotics was born!

Figure 1-2
Brooks'
Genghis robot:
The first
"bug-brain"
robot

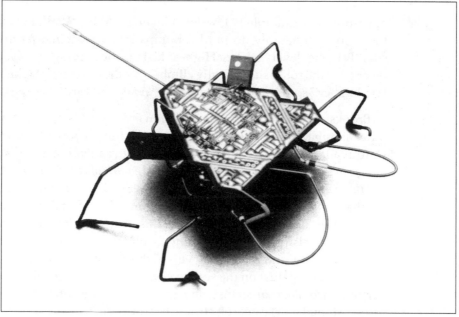

Figure 1-3
Tilden's _Unibug_
robot: Built on
the foundations
laid by _Genghis_
(© Peter Menzel
Robosapiens)

BEAM Robotics

BEAM is an acronym, which stands for

❏ Biology
❏ Electronics
❏ Aesthetics
❏ Mechanics

Mark Tilden chose these words to summarize the concepts he thought were the most important to building a successful autonomous (self-guiding) robot. Let's step through each word:

B: Biology

There is considerable inspiration to be had from studying Mother Nature; after all, who can argue against a laboratory running millions of simultaneous experiments for millions of years? Limb shapes (like your hand), optimized mechanics (like a kangaroo's leg), vision and hearing systems (owls and bats)—there's stuff here that somebody should be working on figuring out. Maybe even two people. But keep in mind that we humans have invented some technology _rarely_ found in nature, like wheels, rotating bearings, and some really _excellent_ glue.

Another way "Biology" is exploited in a robotic manner is that _we_ are the way the robots evolve and improve on themselves. Rather than depending on the long, messy process of letting animals reproduce newer and slightly improved versions of themselves, robots use *us* to create new generations of themselves. Tilden assists BEAM robot evolution by encouraging events such as robot workshops (http://workshop.solarbotics.net) and robot competitions (http://www.robotgames.com). After roboticists meet and pit their devices against each other, they go back to the drawing board with fresh inspirations combining the better characteristics of their own designs with what they've seen in competition. This is why the one-meter solar drag racing event "Solaroller" has evolved from a 21-minute snail race into a 11-second drag-race!

E: Electronics

Well, this is pretty obvious, isn't it? What else are we supposed to use to build robot brains? Do *you* have the skills to perform microsurgery on animal parts? Besides, nobody wants the SPCA on his case. Trust me; stick with silicon-based electronics until somebody else figures out neural gel-pack technology.

BEAM electronics also prides itself on clever, minimalist design, with the frequent twist of using a chip designed to do "X" to do a few other things too! This is one of the reasons that you won't find many microprocessors in a BEAM design, as they're usually overkill for the application. We can trick a chip designed to pass eight parallel signals in a computer (a *simple* common chip called a 74AC240 Octal Buffer Transceiver) into being a circuit to track light; drive motors; compare signals; reverse signal paths; and act as a clock circuit. *None* of these functions were part of the original specifications for the chip, but through some clever, simple electronics, we make it do things the chip designers *never* imagined.

Using clever, efficient BEAM electronics means saving the microprocessor computer brains for the *really* tough stuff.

A: Aesthetics

This word isn't something you run across every day. It essentially means "having the quality of looking *cool.*" You may think this is a bit frivolous, considering the daunting challenges you'll have collecting, assembling, and testing your robot, but think of it in terms of robot *life span.* A robot that looks good has been constructed with attention to detail. No wires sticking out means no wires to get snagged and *ripped out.* A shell on the robot protects the guts from the hostile poking of a kitty-cat (believe me, I've seen it).

Another case is where "form follows function," meaning that a design properly done has its own natural beauty. Think of a fighter airplane (the P-51 Mustang leaps to mind): it looks clean, sleek, and aggressive because those are the characteristics it needs to fulfill its role as a military aircraft. In nature, a shark has a similar clean, sleek, and aggressive appearance to make it an effective hunter. In the field of robotics, a clean, colorful robot attracts the attention of *other* roboticists, which leads back to the "Biological" aspect of evolving your robot design. If your design looks good and performs well, it's most likely to be the inspiration for other roboticists, making *your* design the mother of these other devices.

Aesthetics will ensure the long life of your robot. After all, how often do you see a forest creature wandering around with a spleen hanging out and a leg duct-taped on? Mother Nature does it right....

M: Mechanics

Mechanics is a pretty straightforward word; I'm not referring to the guys who fix your car, but to the secret of many successful BEAM robots. With a clever mechanical design, you can lessen the amount of work the electronics have to compensate for. This is also why BEAM robots look the way they do, and not like small garbage cans with wheels and a laptop computer balanced on top.

Too often, roboticists will take great pains to build the electronic brains of their device but take shortcuts with the mechanics. With a walking robot, a limb that hits the surface 1/2" further ahead than the others will make the robot take a curved path rather than a straight one. If you don't catch this slight error, you will find yourself trying to fix it in the programming, when in fact all you need is a pair of snips and the knowledge of what leg to trim down.

Analog and Digital: Robot Brain Fundamentals

There are two major families of electronic circuits: *analog* and *digital*. What makes them different is how they process data. Digital is easy to explain—it's 1's and 0's; on and off; True and False. There's no gray area with digital—it's either a yes or no signal that gets processed. Digital electronics are responsible for the huge boom in the cheap, inexpensive devices in you house. VCRs, computers, calculators, and digital cameras all use digital calculations.

Analog electronics is a bit harder to wrap your brain around. It's older than digital, and if you remember vacuum tubes glowing in a radio or TV set, you're remembering analog electronics. Where digital uses only 1's and 0's, analog uses 1's and 0's *and everything in between*. Think of it this way: if digital is like a light switch (on or off), analog is like a light dimmer (on, off, and all the levels of illumination in between). Digital is like a staircase; analog is like a ramp. A button is digital; a steering wheel is analog (see Figure 1-2). Most video-game controllers have digital button inputs, along with wheels or joysticks for smooth analog control.

Figure 1-4
Digital
versus
analog vectors

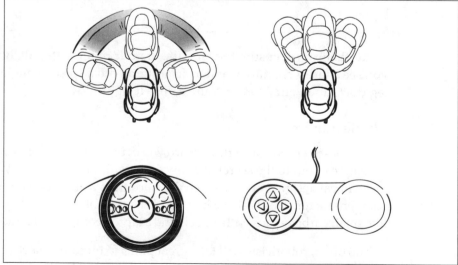

Practically all the electronic devices you use today are mostly digitally based, and for good reason—they're small, powerful, reproducible, and programmable. When solid-state silicon ("chip") technology came on the scene in the form of transistors many moons ago (well, 1947, about 660 moons ago), the analog-style vacuum-tube technology was quickly eclipsed, because transistors used much less power, space, and money. Digital logic (the 1's and 0's) is well suited to being jammed into an inexpensive single little chip with many decision-making circuits packed together. This is the main advantage of digital over analog, as an analog circuit needs more space and power to perform the same functions as a digital one. But in the *real world*, we don't operate in a strict digital manner; we see things in shades of gray, move at continuously varying speeds, and behave differently from each other. So should our robots.

The Concept of "Appropriate Technology"

Before the hand-held calculator (yes, there was such a time), most calculations were performed with something called a *slide rule.* A slide rule, which looked like a ruler with another, sliding ruler inside, could give you a pretty good idea of what the results of some pretty complex mathematics were. Since it was just a ruler with numbers printed on it, you had to approximate the answers, but in many cases, that was good enough. A digital calculator would chew up the numbers and give you an answer to practically infinite decimal places (like the value of π as 3.14159...etc., etc., etc.). A slide rule would show you that your result was near 3.14. By comparing the complexity of each device, you have a pair of sliding sticks that gives you a pretty good idea of the results you need, versus a much more complex machine with batteries, buttons, and hundreds of circuits (and thousands of transistors) that gives you the same results to absurd accuracy.

In some respects, this is a lame comparison. If slide rules are so good, why aren't they used anymore? Digital calculators offer so many more options, such as memory, advanced math functions, and graphing ability, in a small, tidy package. But for fundamental mathematical functions, slide rules are easily the match for a calculator at a tiny fraction of the complexity.

BEAM seeks a similar simplicity in robot technology by promoting *appropriate* technology for the task at hand. You *can* use digital systems to perform the same functions as a simple BEAM circuit, but why? Save the digital systems for the more complex mathematics that they're good at, and use the more adaptive analog solutions for the real-world work. Electronically, you'll find

BEAM solutions will be much less expensive, easier to find, and simpler to tune than digital microcontroller solutions.

Robot Brain Essentials

Brooks had done his experiments using a tiny network of digital-powered microcontrollers (a microcontroller is a small, optimized computer) mounted in the robot body; literally one for each limb of the robot, all taking cues from each other on how to make their next move.

Tilden took this one step further, and substituted well-tuned analog circuits for the microcontrollers.

Mark Tilden thought that replacing the programming and 1's and 0's of microprocessors with robust analog control electronics would result in an even simpler control mechanism for a mobile robot. Considering that analog electronics hadn't been seriously used in robots in quite a while, and the associated parts and pieces had come way down in price, he was onto an *old* way to build robot brains. He was getting back to basics.

Brooks' technology processed sensor input, converted it to a digital quantity (so the microcontrollers could work with the input), and then applied a change to how the robot behaved. The thing about digital electronics is that it works in *discrete steps*, which means it has to be broken down into a number. For example, if you are measuring the light levels on a sensor, a microprocessor will most likely assign it a number from 0 to 255 (this just happens to be a convenient number for microprocessors). Yes, 256 levels of brightness may sound like a lot, but actually your eyes perceive *millions* of levels of illumination. We're discarding a lot of information by boxing it into just 256 levels.

Tilden wanted sensors to directly affect the way his robots interacted with the world, so instead of preprocessing the sensor information digitally, he simply fed it directly into the analog control circuitry, getting a desired response that took into account the whole of the sensor input—not just 1 of 256 levels.

Tilden's Laws of Robotics

Not being content to stop with just removing the computer from the robot body, Tilden started assessing the rules and assumptions most people were making in their attempts to build a mobile, autonomous robot. If I say, "State the Three

Laws of Robotics," you *most likely* will recall some elements of Isaac Asimov's "Three Laws," from "Runaround" (*Astounding Science Fiction*, 1942).

The Three Laws of Robotics

1. A robot may not injure a human being, or, through inaction, allow a human being to come to harm.

2. A robot must obey the orders given it by human beings except where such orders would conflict with the First Law.

3. A robot must protect its own existence as long as such protection does not conflict with the First or Second Law.

Like Brooks and all other innovators, Tilden discarded existing presumptions and created his own laws.

Tilden's Laws of Robotics

1. A robot must protect its existence at all costs.

2. A robot must obtain and maintain access to a power source.

3. A robot must continually search for better power sources.

Or otherwise more informally known as

1. Protect thy ass.

2. Feed thy ass.

3. Move thy ass to better real estate.

His justification was that given present and foreseeable technology, Asimov's laws make for incredibly *boring* robots. Heck, if an Asimovian robot has enough power to push a vacuum cleaner into your toe (assuming if it could even recognize the difference between your toe and a toy lying on the floor), it'd be too nervous to get any practical work done. By turning these rules written for fictional robots with Asimov's Positronic brains around, Tilden laid out the guidelines for constructing robots that would consider you just as hostile to it as your cat Fluffy. That makes for a robot with some useful behavior!

Let's take a closer look at these rules:

1. A robot must protect its existence at all costs.   Make the robot resistant and well suited to its environment as much as possible. There's no sense sending a flat, wheeled robot into a grassland prairie, when a legged machine would be much more suitable against tall grass and uneven terrain. Don't make your robot out of paper if it's going to be exposed to rain or a dog's wet tongue. Also, your robot shouldn't be scared of its surroundings—what good is a robot if all it does is cringe in the corner, hoping it doesn't get stepped on?

2. A robot must obtain and maintain access to a power source.   More fundamentally, the second rule means that the robot must be able to keep power flowing. Any robot that can't sustain itself will simply die and become useless. A huge number of so-called autonomous robots don't have the ability to self-recharge, and after a few hours they turn into expensive toe-stubbing bricks.

3. A robot must continually search for better power sources.   The robot should have the capability to actively scout out its environment and procure the best energy source it can. If a solar-powered BEAM device runs under the bed and dies, does anybody hear it scream? The robot *must* have the ability to use sensors to keep itself alive.

If any of these rules disturb you and makes you think one day your solar-powered robots will evict you from your home and make you sleep in the garage, remember this: *shut off the lights and start bot-stomping!* You can always build more, and keep this second generation in a cage.

Why These Projects Are Made the Way They Are

Enough of the history on where BEAM technology came from. Let's move onto what it *is,* a collection of techniques using (relatively) simple electronics to build devices that can live on their own. More than that, how can it be implemented without needing the high-precision, high-cost parts usually associated with robots? *Boy,* you're lucky to be reading this book—we're going to show you the cheap'n'dirty techniques to building cool robots!

Power Sources for BEAM Devices

Autonomous robots *should* live on their own. That "on their own" part is a big challenge to many roboticists; the vast majority of robots eat batteries like a kid eats french fries, so what good is an autonomous robot if you have to hunt it down in three hours to recharge it again? So unless you've perfected the low-weight, micro-thin power extension cord, think about using some clever BEAM circuitry to power your device with solar energy. The heart and soul of many BEAM creatures is a circuit called a *solarengine,* which concentrates the relatively weak power output of a solar cell to a point that it can power a much larger device than the solar cell could by itself. This simple way to make your robots autonomous is one of the main reasons BEAM robots have become so popular.

Tilden turned to solar power in frustration at having to replace batteries on a regular basis. What practical good was a robot if it needed its batteries changed as often as a baby's diapers? Although one of the "larger" solar cells used in BEAM devices (37×33 mm or 1.45×1.3") supplies a small fraction of the power available from a battery, it will go on providing power for tens of years, versus the few hours available from a battery.

Solar cells are a technology where light is converted directly to electricity. (I bet you didn't know that, did you?) Unfortunately, they're not very good at their job. The sun beats down on us with about 1,000 watts per square meter—immense amounts of energy, considering that it takes only 100 watts to run a handsomely loud stereo. Ah, but our solar cell is capable of turning only about 3.4 percent of this energy into usable power; the rest is turned into heat. Although it's much easier and cheaper to find a battery than a solar cell (ever see a solar cell hanging next to the batteries at your local "Mr. Hardware" store? Didn't think so...), solar cells offer some *very* nice advantages over other power supplies:

❑ **No moving parts** Unlike a gas engine, there's nothing to physically wear out.

❑ **Long life** You'll exhaust the battery's chemistry much quicker than a solar cell's. Consumer-grade small solar cells have a lifetime of decades.

❑ **Light weight**   This means better survivability. Ever see a bug fall off the ceiling, bounce twice, and carry on? Imagine doing that yourself!

❑ **Renewable, nonpolluting power**.

The disadvantages to solar cell technology:

❑ Power output is low, which means we need many cells to get usable power (but we have solarengine circuits to help—stay tuned for details).

❑ Glass tends to break, but you *can* get flexible plastic solar cells.

❑ Some *nasty* chemicals are used to manufacture solar cells, depending on the exact type. Mind you, this is true of many batteries, but chemical advances are making both more environmentally friendly.

❑ Solar cells are difficult to find.

If you are intrigued by the idea of extremely long-lived robots, it is worth your while to hunt down the necessary parts to make them work. Compared with battery power, solar robotics requires more finesse in part selection and assembly. You can't use the power-hungry motors from most toys; you can't use large slabs of plastic for the body; you can't afford to waste the milliwatts of power usually available from a battery. Solar-powered robotics teaches efficient design, in both electronics and mechanics, but more important, it lets you build robots that can continue operating for many, many years without human intervention. Think of building a device that will carry on doing what it's designed to do, as long as there's enough light to read a newspaper by.

Admittedly, solar-powered BEAM robots *are* slow to watch, but you will be surprised by the progress they make over the hours and days when you leave them alone. This, in itself, is a hidden feature of a solar-powered robot. A quick-moving, active robot is intrusive with its motion, noise, and size. On the other hand, a slow, persistent, quiet robot working in the background will not bother you with its needs.

This is not to say that battery-powered robots are evil—not at all! Battery-powered robots have enormous energy, offer immediate reward value, and are easier to tune and troubleshoot. Some of the projects we'll be working on work best with batteries, so if you can handle the necessary recharging or battery replacement tasks that come with building a robot like that, *enjoy!* You may find that the battery pack from a dead cell phone will make an ideal power source.

The designs we are going to work on are simple, elegant, and efficient. Some are powered by batteries, some by solar cells, some by both. What makes the robot projects in this book different from those you'll find in most other books is that they're designed to be constructed out of common and not-so-obvious materials that you will most likely have around your house or find in a quick shopping trip.

Parts and Construction Materials

Serious robot research usually starts on the back of a napkin, or on a pad of paper. Then it progresses up to a drafting table, or a computer-aided drafting system. After that, construction drawings are developed and sent out to a machine shop. Can you see the need for a team of university grad students? This is all very acceptable technique if you have the resources and money, but for the average garage-roboticist, it is a far-off dream.

Fortunately, we live in a high-tech, "conspicuous consumer" society where lots of neat stuff has a built-in expiration date. That's the reason you most likely have a kitchen drawer entombing a dead Walkman, a remote control for a long-discarded VCR, and spark plugs (really—I just checked my kitchen drawer). With little effort, you'll have accrued the parts for building the body for your creation. Building the framework will be more like experiments in artwork than robot building, as you'll be modifying existing junk rather than machining it from scratch. But if you are in the enviable position of owning a lathe and mill, don't make it your first line of attack—play with the materials on hand first, as you will find arrangements that you would never have thought of.

If you have a box of dead Walkmans or technojunk in the corner of the garage, this book is ideal for you. You'll *finally* have a reason to pull them out and start disassembling them! Before we get to the fun part, though, let's shift gears and talk about an important topic for aspiring robot builders—safety.

Chapter 2

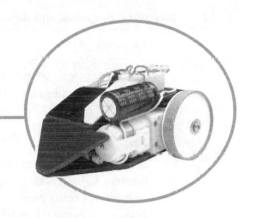

BEAM Safety: Read This Before Building a Robot

Yes, safety sounds boring, but the truth is, life with only one eye is too. Remember all that stuff your mom told you about safety back when you were a kid? I'm sure you'll remember this one the best:

"Stop that! You'll poke your eye out!"

Well, it's time to call up Mom and thank her for that very important piece of advice. Constructing your robot involves working with some potentially dangerous tools and substances, and if you do not take the proper precautions, you can get seriously hurt. This chapter will show you how to stay safe while building your bot.

The Safety Geek Says

Eyes

Your eyes are going to be open to the most serious risks if you do not take the proper precautions. So among all the points of safety we'll be covering, rank this among the top of the list: *Protect your eyes*.

Basic Safety Considerations

It's overkill to wear a lab coat and insulating gloves to build robots, but if you follow a few basic safety principles, you'll be able to identify when you should be using particular care in a process. We've put literally thousands of students through BEAM workshops by teaching safety around the following three principles:

What Can the Tool I'm Using Do?

Pretty simple question, but give it a bit of thought. Think about what the worst thing a tool can do to you or your workspace, and keep it from even getting near to that point. For example, a hammer…hits things. That means put it away when you're done, so it doesn't fall off the table and hit your foot. This scenario might sound like a cartoon, but the only thing that'll be funny will be the way you'll be walking for the next few hours after the accident.

A soldering iron…gets hot. Keep flammable things away from the soldering station, and never let it touch anything but what *needs* to get hot. I've got a page of scorched schematics because it was carelessly placed *on top* of the soldering iron holder, with the soldering iron still on!

Snips…cut things. That in itself isn't very dangerous, but the little clippings it shoots when it clips sure are! Hold the snips so that the clippings shoot down and away from your (or anybody's) eyes. Having pieces ricochet off the ceiling and land pointy-side up on the carpet to embed themselves into my foot isn't something I want to do twice!

Before you use a tool (especially a new one), give some thought to what it's capable of doing to you and the space around you. Read the instructions it comes with, so you *know* what it can and can't do.

What Can the Part I'm Working on Do?

You won't be using a tool without a part, so parts are equally important to think about. Examples from my own personal history:

A large copper wire will get *hot* when you're trying to heat it up to the point that you can solder to it. So holding it in your fingertips is a very good way to burn your fingerprints off. Try using a proper holding device, like a vise.

Screwing a screw *through* a piece on your lap is a good way to puncture your clothing (and skin), especially if the screwdriver slips off. Clear off some space on your table, and use a proper (puncture-proof) surface.

Gluing two pieces together with cyanoacrylate (super glue)? Don't use your fingers to hold the parts together, unless you want to rip your fingerprints off when you pry your fingers off the newly glued part. Better to use the same holding tools you used to solder the large copper wire; human skin bonds very well to most anything with super glue.

What Can the People Around Me Do to Me?

This won't apply to you unless you're working with a partner, but since we recommend working in teams (which is immensely more productive and fun), give this some thought. If the previous two safety rules *aren't* being followed by absolutely everybody, you have to watch out for your safety by watching out for their safety. Your friend may not realize that he has the snips pointed so you're the target for the clipping about to launch at your face. Don't just sit there—make him aware of the danger. If you can't warn him in time, make sure you're set up to handle the problem. Nobody is more responsible for your own well-being than yourself!

Basic Safety Equipment

Among your first purchases should be a decent set of *safety goggles.* If there's anything to spend a few bucks on to get quality, it's these! There's nothing more irritating than a poor-fitting, scratched-up set of goggles. And what happens if something irritates you? You stop using it! Pay the $20 for a decent set—you'll appreciate it.

Please, if this is the only thing you learn and do in this whole chapter, make it this: *Get and use a set of goggles.* By "use," I mean use at all times while you're at the workbench. Threats to your eyes include flying wire clippings; solder splashes; molten solder spatter; solder flux fumes; spring-loaded mechanisms you're dismantling; slipped tools; exploding light bulbs (I personally survived this); and exploding electronics (rare, but can happen). Seem like a long list? It's far from complete. Get the goggles. Use the goggles. Do it, or I'll send Guido the killer garden-slug to beat some sense into you. Goggles come in various qualities, some of which are shown in Figure 2-1. All will do the job, but you may find that the slightly more expensive ones are more comfortable and will most likely be used more often.

Figure 2-1
Goggles: Get them! Wear them!

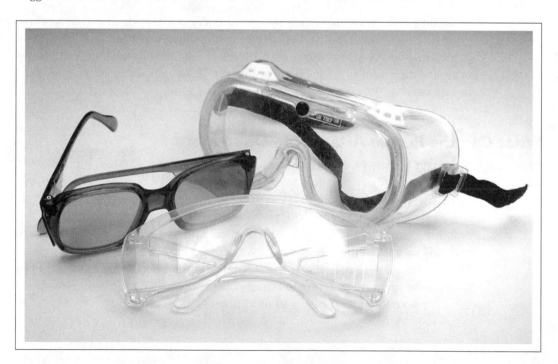

A good quality *utility apron* is not as important as goggles, but it sure can be appreciated after it catches that hot soldering iron that just rolled off the bench and protects your crotch and legs. An extra layer of fabric goes a long way in giving you enough time to correct an otherwise painful situation. Besides, the apron does double-duty as a small components catcher. Go ahead and borrow your mom's/wife's old ultra-flowery kitchen apron—I won't tell...but I may sell the photos!

Dangerous Things to Be Aware Of

As we've already discussed, the materials you work with can cause just as much damage as a tool, drill, or soldering iron. When constructing your robot, you need to be aware of certain materials that can prove to be dangerous. Numero Uno on this list is lead.

Lead

Yup, one of the oldest known hazardous materials to man is back in the field of robotics. Did you know that the Roman Aqueducts used lead sheeting as the channelways? Until the water mineralized the channel walls, those Romans had some nasty stomach aches.

Lead is very common in solder, which is the material you'll be using to make your electrical connections. You can buy lead-free solder (a tin/silver compound rather than a tin/lead compound), which is safer to use but not quite as easy to use. Regardless of your choice, you won't be able to totally escape exposure to *some* lead, as it is still the most widely used type of solder by far in the electronics industry. When you pop and pry apart those dead electronic carcasses, you'll have no choice but to deal with it if you want that cool part inside. No matter what type of solder you decide to use, it will most likely come in a package like one of those shown in Figure 2-2.

Figure 2-2
Solder, in its various packages

The Safety Geek Says

Working with Lead-Based Solder

✖ Wash your hands with soap and water after a construction session. Handling solder transfers lead to your hands, and if you touch food and eat without washing, you'll be ingesting lead.

✖ Don't inhale the fumes from the soldering process. That smoke is from the burning of *flux*, which is a paste inside each strand of solder. The purpose of flux is to clean the soldering surface and make the solder joint strong and pure. As a rule, the fumes from burned solder aren't very pleasant, in neither smell nor what they do to your lungs.

✖ Don't use solder as dental floss, or chew it like gum. Brain damage is a *very* undesirable trait in roboticists.

Hot Stuff

There's lots of opportunity to get burned doing electronics. Like pain? Be careless, and you'll have all you want.

Soldering Irons

Your soldering iron will be your tool of choice while putting your projects together. Respect it. Appreciate it. Take care of it. It is most likely the single most potentially nasty piece of equipment you'll be using.

The tip of a standard "pencil"-style soldering iron heats up to approximately 600 degrees Fahrenheit, or 315°C, which is plenty hot to leave an impressive burn. Even when it is cool, treat the tip with respect—it looks *exactly the same* as when it's nasty hot. One year at a robotics workshop, we caught two kids poking each other with cold soldering irons. Think they lasted more than 30 seconds at the workshop after this? *Not a chance.* It was a situation where there *could* have been very serious injury.

Figure 2-3
Hot soldering irons: Love them, but don't kiss them.

Hot Glue Guns

Glue guns are a pretty popular hobby-craft tool, and come in two varieties: hot glue, and low-temperature glue. In both cases, they're still *hot tools*. The low-temperature is somewhat safer to use, but at the cost of less ability. The *hot* hot glue gun is really quite good, but it is also *very nasty*. Unlike when you're being burned with a soldering iron and you just jerk your hand away from the iron, hot glue sticks to your skin and keeps burning. I've received worse burns from one of these tools than a soldering iron—beware!

Batteries

You don't traditionally think of batteries as something dangerous, or even hot for that matter. But *if improperly handled,* they are a terribly nasty source of heat and fire. Now, this is not an invitation to perform an experiment—just trust me on this. If you short out a battery by running a wire directly across its terminals, even a small "AAA" 1.5-volt cell, you can

- ❑ Cause the wire shorting the battery out to melt its insulation off
- ❑ Make the same wire glow red-hot
- ❑ Make the battery crack open and leak

True story: I once accidentally shorted the contacts of a 9-volt battery with my metallic wristwatch band and got a stinging burn from the heat generated. Imagine my delight in discovering how hard it was to unclasp a hot watch from my wrist while dancing around the room....

Additional to the heat-danger of a battery, be aware that some types actually use some fairly unhealthy elements in their construction (like Nickel-Cadmium rechargeable batteries). Do the right thing and read the packaging that comes with the batteries, and use and dispose of them as directed.

The Safety Geek Says

Working with Hot Things

- ✘ If there's any possibility that it *might* be hot, treat it like it always is (e.g., soldering irons).
- ✘ The components you were just soldering? They're just about as hot as your soldering iron. Give them half a minute to cool down before you even think about touching your circuitry.

✖ Review first-aid procedures, especially the parts about burns. It's a good idea, because you eventually will get a burn. My latest boo-boo was putting a soldering iron down on the rail of a vertical lift I was on, and then putting my hand down on top of it—not smart. Glad I had water to cool it with.

✖ Got burned? First, stop the hot thing (unplug iron, etc.). Second, run cold water over the burn. Third, run more cold water over it. Fourth, seek the necessary medical attention you need!

✖ Don't store your batteries in a big bag or box where 9-volt batteries can short out against other batteries.

✖ Always have a small water bottle nearby to cool off burns or extinguish small fires. You'll need it for making the solder-sponge damp anyway. Also have some baking soda nearby for electrical fires.

✖ When you shut down your workbench after a bot-building session, scan it for a few seconds looking for smoke or anything potentially dangerous. Like that piece of paper that's lying on top of your soldering-iron holder—is it *really* a good idea to leave it like that?

Things Better Left Alone

As much as I would like to say that we could rescue all the electronic junk that will come your way, *it simply ain't so.* There are some items that shouldn't even be looked at twice. Identify the dangerous ones, leave them alone, and move to the next potential victim of your hacking. Here's a list of some things to avoid.

❏ **Televisions** Unless if you *really* know what you're doing, there's not much worthwhile in a television. The circuitry can generate well over 20,000 volts, and the storage capacitors can hold their power for quite a long time—longer than you might think. You don't want to be digging around with a screwdriver when there's that sort of voltage ready to bite you. Besides the voltages, the cathode-ray tube (the glass viewy, watchy thingy) contains some materials that aren't exactly healthy. Let's stay away from televisions, shall we?

❏ **Computer monitors** See the reasons just listed for "Televisions."

- ❏ **Really old electronic appliances**   I'm referring to things like vacuum tube radios and antique stereos. This is mostly because of changes in the way electronic parts are manufactured—anything that old (even if still functional) will most likely not be built to the rigorous standards we have today.

- ❏ **Smoke detectors**   These life-saving devices actually use small amounts of radioactive material in their smoke-sensors. Radio isotopes are *not* of any use to you at this early stage in your robotics career, so steer clear of them, okay?

- ❏ **Egyptian cobras coiled around unexploded World War II bombs labeled with "Atomic Waste" stickers**   You just have to know that something like that isn't worth the hassle.

Do use some common sense when evaluating items you want to tear into. "Danger—High Voltage" and "Hazardous Materials Within" are among the phrases that should trip the common sense centers in your brain. Listen to them—better safe than crippled and blind!

Given that warning, you shouldn't be *too* scared off by labels like "No user serviceable parts inside" or "To be opened by qualified technical personnel only." Now that the item is junk, it's fair game to rip into it to see what makes it tick. If you're not an adult, *make sure* you are doing this under the supervision of an adult. Hate to lay these heavy warnings on you, but we'll be intentionally tearing apart things that were never meant to be violated.

The Safety Geek Says

Familiarity

Please take care when opening up unfamiliar devices. Only *you* are ultimately responsible for your own protection and safety when ignoring these warning labels.

Your Work Environment

It would be nice if we could all have our ideal workspace. My father has a nicely converted small garage to do his woodwork; my father-in-law has a full auto-body shop. When I started with electronics, my workspace was a surplus door mounted across two sawhorses at the foot of our bed. My wife was not amused when I cut a stiff wire and sent the clipping ricocheting off the ceiling and onto the pillow beside her (this was before I knew better about safety). Shortly thereafter, we moved to larger accommodations, with a room just for me and my robots.

Besides being a story illustrating the hazards of clipping wire (are you wearing your safety goggles yet? Didn't think so. Expect Slug-Guido soon), it does illustrate that you can set up a workstation nearly anywhere. There are a few safety considerations that should always be in place at any workstation.

Lighting

I'm growing older, and my eyes need more light to focus accurately. If you're young, with laser-sharp vision, I'm envious. Otherwise, I suggest lighting your workbench with *at least* two swing-arm lamps. This will give you the ability to use one for general lighting, and the other for lighting up that specific project you're working on. Besides, if a bulb in one lamp goes, you won't be totally left in the dark.

An additional inexpensive $10 fluorescent lamp unit gives off nice, soft light and can be mounted directly in front of you, above your work surface.

Power

It's a *really* good idea to run all your workstation appliances from a single power bar, especially a reasonably good-quality one with a quick-interrupt circuit breaker. It gives you a "Panic" stop point, where if there's suddenly smoke, the first thing you do is hit the power bar switch, shutting off all your tools. This is the way I have my own workbench set up, as shown in Figure 2-4.

Figure 2-4
Workstation power bar installation with central shutoff

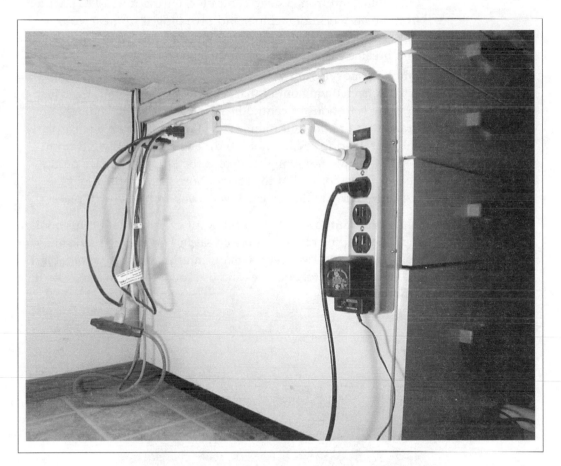

Second, the circuit breaker built into most power bars will be quicker than the breaker in your house fuse box. If something causes a short, it won't cause the whole room to go dark. If you find that you are tripping your power bar more than once or twice a year, you really should spend some time figuring out which faulty tool is causing the problem.

Ventilation

As mentioned previously, solder flux *does* give off a mildly irritating smoke. Inhaling it or getting it in your eyes can sting and cause irritation. Plan on having two types of ventilation:

❑ **Smoke removal from your face.**   This is as simple as yanking an old cooling fan from a dead computer, wiring it to a DC adapter from an answering machine, and propping it up near your soldering iron so that it blows the smoke away from your face. You breathe easier, and the cool breeze feels nice.

❑ **Smoke removal from your room.**   An open window is a good start. A fan blowing out of that window is even better. Even just running your house's central heating on "circulate" mode will draw fresh air into your room. When I'm planning on a particularly smoky soldering session, I use a dryer-vent hose I wired up to a high- volume fan (bought surplus for $10) that I place on my bench. The other end of the 15-foot hose gets dropped out the window, dumping the exhaust well away from my workplace.

In conclusion, I want to say that I *really* want every reader of this book to have a good time building his or her projects *safely*. Having run workshops for over a thousand students, I've seen too many injuries that were avoidable. Do me a favor—wear your safety goggles and use some common sense. I'd hate to send Guido after you.

Figure 2-5
A $15 solder fume extraction setup

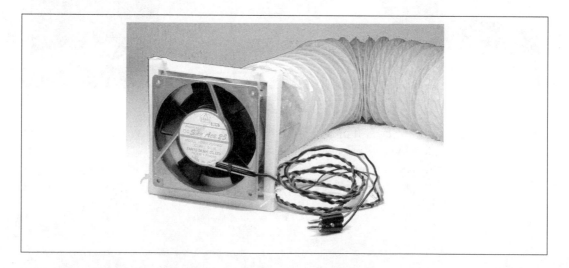

Chapter 3

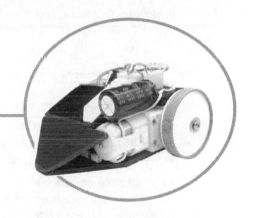

Identifying Electronic Bits

There are many, many types of electronics bits, and every bit usually comes in two or three shapes. Some parts look the same but perform different functions. Or have opposite functions. Treat electronic bits just like food spices—just because it looks like salt doesn't mean it *is* salt. And using salt when you're expected to use sugar will make for a funky tasting donut....

The purpose of this book is to get you up and running with some simple robot projects, so we're not going to delve too deeply into electronics theory. There are a *huge* number of books on the market (and Web resources) that already do an excellent job at this, some of which are listed in Appendix A. We suggest you select one or more of these books to learn the nitty-gritty details on electronics, and keep them near your workbench.

Basic Component Types

We won't beat you over the head with too many technical terms and definitions. (Do you *really* need to know the difference between "active" and "passive" components? Didn't think so.) Instead, let's focus on the parts and pieces you'll most likely be tripping over as you dive into the wonderful world of electronics.

Resistors

Resistors are likely to be the single most common component you'll come across when prying open dead electronic devices. They're the small, cylinder-like things with (usually) four color bands. They come in several physically different sizes, but for the most part, you can tell a resistor by the color bands, which reveal what value the resistor has.

Figure 3-1
Resistors as found in an answering machine's circuit board

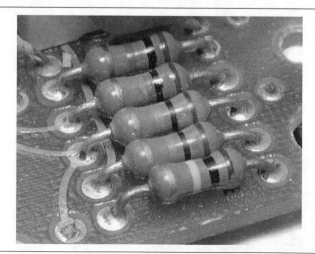

Resistors are measured in the unit "ohms" (symbol: "Ω"), usually with the prefix "k" or "M"; "k" is the standard prefix meaning "thousand," and "M" stands for "million." So when somebody refers to a 1.0k resistor, they mean 1,000 ohms. And 2.2M is 2.2 million ohms. You should also be aware that some people (especially those with military backgrounds) write these values as "1k0" and "2M2." By placing the multiplier value where the decimal point is, they leave no chance of mistaking a 10k resistor with a 1.0k (or 1k0 resistor).

The purpose of a resistor is to resist the flow of electrical current in a circuit. Great name, huh? If electricity is compared to a flow of water, a resistor is like a narrow neck in the hose.

Remember that resistors come in different sizes? That's because when resistors resist, a by-product of the process is heat, and the bigger the resistor, the more heat it can handle. Different-size resistors have different power ratings (measured in watts). The inexpensive small resistors used in BEAM circuits have a 1/4 watt or 1/8 watt power rating and aren't much longer than 8 mm (3/8").

As mentioned before, the resistor's four color bands determine its value. The system is a bit strange at first, but the more you use it, the more natural it will become. For your reference, we suggest that you photocopy Table 3-1 and use your niece's crayons to color in the boxes appropriately for easier color identification.

Band Color	First Band	Second Band	Third Band (Multiply by...)	Fourth Band (Tolerance)
Black	0	0	×1	–
Brown	1	1	×10	1%
Red	2	2	×100	2% (rare)
Orange	3	3	×1,000 (or "1k")	-
Yellow	4	4	×10,000 ("10k")	-
Green	5	5	×100,000 ("100k")	0.5% (rare)
Blue	6	6	×1,000,000 ("1M")	0.25% (rare)
Violet	7	7	×10,000,000 (10M) (rare)	0.1% (rare)
Grey	8	8	-	-
White	9	9	-	-
Gold	-	-	-	5%
Silver	-	-	-	10%

Table 3-1
Resistor Color Codes

The first three stripes set the value of the resistor, and the last sets the tolerance. Tolerance is the range that the resistor is manufactured to. Most resistors you'll find will have the gold stripe, meaning that they're manufactured to fall within 5 percent of their stated value.

Let's go over this with an example or two, shall we? Let's start simple—if you are faced with a resistor colored red/red/red/gold, what is it? According to the chart, red is the number 2, so it's a 2...2...×1,000 ohms = 2,200 ohms (more commonly known as 2.2kΩ). The gold stripe means it's within 5 percent tolerance (between 2,090 to 2,310 ohms).

Figure 3-2
A 2.2k resistor example

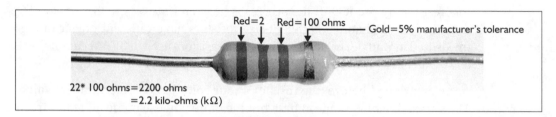

That was easy. Let's try something harder, and in reverse. What are the colors for a 470k resistor? Four is a yellow stripe...seven is a violet stripe...let's see, 47×10,000 (yellow stripe), plus the tolerance stripe (gold or silver). That'll be yellow/violet/yellow/gold.

Figure 3-3
A 470k resistor example

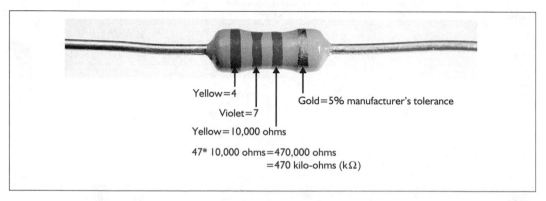

If there is something you will eventually have to commit to memory, it will be the resistor color code. Ah yes, tiny Grass-hoppa, you will learn the resistor color codes.... Some people prefer the *mnemonic* method (where the first letter of each word in a phrase matches the letter of the color), but we prefer using a color-coded little placard kept with the resistors. It took a while, but the colors-to-values translation finally sunk in, and it isn't needed much anymore.

If you still want a mnemonic, try this:

```
Black Beetles Running On Your Grass Bring Very Good Weather
(Good = Gold tolerance; Weather = Silver)
```

or

```
Bad Beer Rots Our Young Guts But Vodka Goes Well
```

The last one doesn't give the appropriate image to young, budding roboticists, but strangeness seems to stick in the mind. Choose your mnemonic, ladies and gentlemen...

Capacitors

If resistors are the bread to the electronics world, capacitors are the butter! You will find capacitors to be as common as resistors, but they *do* come in a much wider variety of packages and types. Using our flowing water analogy again, a capacitor would be the equivalent of a water balloon, able to take in and spit out water without (ideally) any leakage.

Capacitors are measured in a unit called "farads" (symbol: "F"), but in truth, a farad is a tremendous amount of capacitance. You will see that most capacitor values are measured in millionths of a farad, using the "micro" (symbol: "μ," called a "mu") in front of the F. For example, you will most likely see a 0.22μF or 4700μF capacitor, but rarely a 0.47F capacitor (note the lack of the "μ"). Also be aware of the less-often used "picofarad" (pf), which is yet 1000 times *smaller* than a microfarad (billionths of a farad).

Most capacitors will also have a listed maximum voltage rating. This voltage is the *absolute maximum voltage* a capacitor should be exposed to; otherwise, it may fail. If you are using 9 volts in your circuit, you can use a 10V, 16V, 25V, or higher capacitor, but definitely *not* a 6.3V capacitor. Pay attention to the capacitor labels, as the maximum voltage rating is easily overlooked. A recent mistake happened when a 6.3V capacitor (a common value around here) was used in a robot powered at 18 volts. When I turned the robot on, it ran for about five seconds, slowed down, then started smoking! What a dumb mistake!

Since there are so many types of capacitors, let's quickly go over them before expanding on how to read them.

You will run into three major types of capacitor: electrolytic, monolithic, and tantalum (see Figure 3-4, but ignore the candy, as it's just a size reference). Table 3-2 lists each capacitor's characteristics, which *must* be respected; otherwise, you can seriously screw up your circuit and potentially cause damage to your robot and you.

Figure 3-4
The three major types of capacitor

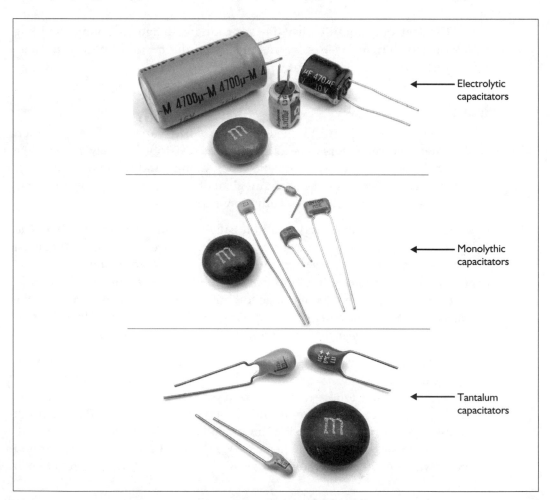

Electrolytic capacitors

Monolythic capacitors

Tantalum capacitors

Capacitor Type	Shape	Voltage Range	Common Capacitance Ranges	Special Qualities
Electrolytic	Metal can with stripe on one side. Usually have full ratings printed on case.	3–600V	4.7–10,000µF	Polarity sensitive! Can have low maximum voltage. Tend to leak stored energy. *CAN EXPLODE!*
Monolithic	Miniature "Chicklet" in bright colors. Use numeric code for ratings.	35–100V	0.001–1µF	*Not* polarity sensitive. Apt to break if physically abused.
Tantalum	"Gum-drop" appearance in bright colors. Usually have full ratings printed on case. Stripe indicating polarity near one leg.	6.3–50V	0.1–150µF	Polarity sensitive—don't install backward!

Table 3-2
The Major Capacitor Types and Their Personality Quirks

Electrolytic and tantalum capacitors usually have their maximum voltage rating and capacitance value printed right on them, with no sneaky codes to interpret. The thing about these types of capacitors is that they are *polarity sensitive*, just like a battery. This means they have to be installed the proper way around—not just stuck in any old way. With these capacitors, you have to look for a mark near one of the legs of the component. Large electrolytic capacitors have a large stripe down the side of the body near one leg that identifies "negative"—think of the large stripe as a *large* "–" symbol. Most tantalum capacitors have a little bar with a "+" sign near it running down near one of the legs, identifying "positive." Another tip for most capacitors is to look for the *longer* lead—that one is *positive* (+).

Figure 3-5
Polarity, capacitance, and maximum voltage ratings for electrolytic and tantalum capacitors

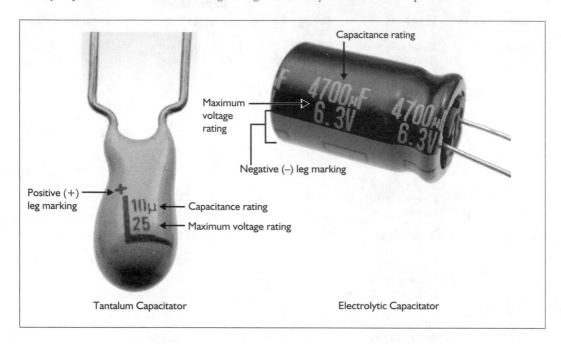

Tantalum Capacitator   Electrolytic Capacitor

Your TV remote won't work if you put the batteries in backward, and the same applies to electrolytic and tantalum capacitors, except that they are a bit more dramatic in the way that they stop working—they *can literally go "poof."* When you kill a capacitor, the effect can be as minor as a small "pop" and a wisp of smoke, or as catastrophic as a loud "BANG" and a small fire. This sort of behavior *probably won't* happen with a solar-powered circuit, but if you're using batteries in your design, *please* be careful when using this type of capacitor.

Monolithic capacitors are *not* polarity sensitive and don't care which way they get plugged into your circuit. Unlike electrolytic and tantalum capacitors, most monolithic capacitors are labeled in a numeric fashion that's just a *little* easier to read than resistor color codes, but there is a curve ball to be aware of. Monolithic capacitors *can* have numbers on both sides, with one side being the size code (good), and the other side being the date-of-manufacture code (bad). It *can* get pretty confusing when you're looking at a capacitor labeled "104" on one side and "941" on the other.

Here you have to use some common sense until you get the hang of the codes. The "941" refers to the year and week of manufacture (1999, week 41). As a size value, it would come out as 0.000094μF (a small value, not making much sense). If we try that with the "104" number, it would mean the capacitor was manufactured in 2001, week 04. Not impossible, but just unlikely enough to get confusing. You probably won't care when your capacitor was manufactured, so it's more of a nuisance code than anything else to you.

The capacitance number code usually includes three numbers, with the first two representing the value of the capacitor (in picofarads, 1/1,000,000 of a microfarad), and the third being the 10 multiplier (or the number to multiply the first two numbers by 10 to what power).

Time for an example: Given a monolithic capacitor labeled 474, how many microfarads (μF) is it?

The first part is easy: **47** picofarads. What's the multiplier?

Hmmm. **4**. That means multiply 10 picofarads by 10 to the fourth power (10^4), which is $47 \times 10,000 = 470,000.0$ picofarads, or (by shifting the decimal point left six places) 0.47μF. Keep in mind that there are a million (1,000,000) picofarads in a microfarad.

Figure 3-6
Monolithic capacitor code-breaking

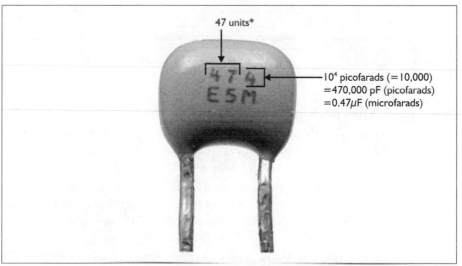

47 units*

10^4 picofarads (=10,000)
=470,000 pF (picofarads)
=0.47μF (microfarads)

It won't take you long to get the hang of it. You'll be able to read the first two numbers and know that if they're followed by a "4," the capacitor is in the 0.XXµF range, whereas a "3" means it's in the 0.0XXµF range. If there is no third number to the code, that means the value given is the value of the capacitor in picofarads. Just in case, Table 3-3 is a chart to help you decode the numeric capacitor code.

Third Digit	Multiply the First Two Digits by This to Get Microfarads (µF)	Example
0	0.000001 (or divide by 1,000,000)	47 = 0.000047µF
1	0.00001 (or divide by 100,000)	471 = 0.00047µF
2	0.0001 (or divide by 10,000)	472 = 0.0047µF
3	0.001 (or divide by 1,000)	473 = 0.047µF
4	0.01 (or divide by 100)	474 = 0.47µF
5	0.1 (or divide by 10)	475 = 4.7µF
6	(not used)	
7	(not used)	
8	100 (or divide by 0.01) Note: *rarely* used	478 = 4700µF
9	10 (or divide by 0.1) Note: *rarely* used	479 = 470µF

Table 3-3
Capacitor Number Codes

Rare and Special Capacitors

BEAM circuits, especially the ones that use solar power, often use a rare style of capacitor called a supercap. Supercapacitors store many, many times the energy of the standard capacitors you'll find most of the time. These supercaps use a special chemistry to store lots of power at low voltage, and because of this chemistry, they're usually somewhat more expensive than a regular electrolytic capacitor. The purpose of these supercaps is to act as power backups for the memories in many devices, including PDAs (personal data assistants), computer configuration memories, digital clocks, and portable stereos. When you turn off the power or yank the main batteries out of any of these devices, the supercap keeps the data in memory alive until the next time you power up.

Physically, supercaps are usually quite small, usually smaller than a regular 4700μF 6.3V capacitor. It's that special chemistry that lets them hold so much more power, even when they're physically smaller in size.

Figure 3-7
Three are supercapacitors, one is a tasty treat: Don't mix them up!

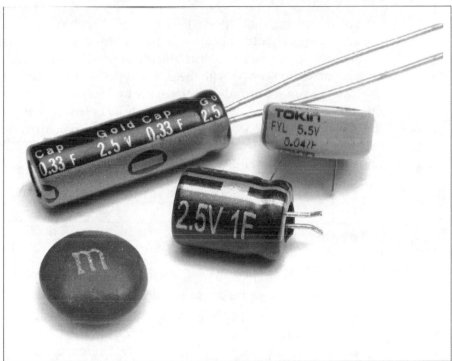

Supercaps are usually measured in full farads or fractions of a farad, at a low voltage. It's not uncommon to find supercaps rated 0.047F, 0.33F, or even 1F at 2.5V maximum voltage. When a regular 4700μF capacitor would charge in five seconds of direct sunlight, a supercap would take one to three minutes, but the trade-off in time is gained back in that you'll have much more power to give to your BEAM device in one burst. Properly used, these supercaps do allow you to make your devices run quite actively between charging periods, but there is the characteristic of *internal impedance* you have to watch out for.

Internal impedance is the property of a capacitor that governs how quickly it can charge and discharge. The chemistry in a normal electrolytic capacitor lets it charge and discharge almost instantaneously, but this is not the case with all supercaps. Some can't push their energy out fast enough to keep a motor turning, which simply means your device will stand still because its motors are being starved of the power they need to turn. It's as if you had a great big water tank that you wanted to use to put out a fire, but you were forced to use a hose the diameter of a drinking straw. You have lots stored up, but you can only pull out so much at a time!

With a supercap that is powering a memory backup chip, high internal impedance doesn't matter much, as memory chips draw very little power. But motors *love* power, and want it as quickly as possible, and need a *low* impedance capacitor to keep up with them. The types of supercap you will want to keep an eye out for include *aerogel* (made by Maxwell or PowerStor, among others) and *gold* chemistry capacitors (made by Panasonic). If you can find the datasheet to a questionable supercap, you want to look up the *internal impedance* number, and hopefully it will be only a few ohms. Over 10 ohms is nearly unusable for driving a BEAM device that uses motors, but you can always use high-impedance supercaps in motorless devices.

The Robot Geek Says

Capacitors

✖ If the capacitor has a polarity marking, *respect* it.

✖ Make sure you don't expose the capacitor to more voltage than it can handle.

✖ The lower the capacitor's rated voltage; the smaller it is—useful to know with small robots.

✖ Electrolytic capacitors store a lot of energy and are best for storing and smoothing power.

✖ Supercapacitors store the most energy and are often used as a substitute for small batteries.

✖ Tantalum capacitors store little energy but have low leakage and are best for setting longer time values.

✖ Monolithic capacitors store very little energy but are the quickest at charging and discharging rapidly; they are best for setting timing values and filtering high-frequency electrical noise. These caps are used in BEAM circuits for their low leakage and small size.

✖ Monolithic labeling shortcut: If the number is *XX*4 (like "474") it's a 0.*XX*μF capacitor (0.47μF). *XX*3 (like "473") is 0.0*XX*μF (0.047μF). If there is no third number, the value is in picofarads, plain and simple (47 = 47 picofarads).

✖ The most common factor values for capacitors are 1, 22, 33, 47, and 68. This means you will often see a 0.1μF, 10μF, 100μF, or 1000μF capacitor, but rarely *(if ever)* a 0.12μF, 12μF, 120μF, or 1,200μF capacitor. Common capacitor values start with numbers like 0.1μF, 2.2μF, 0.33F, 470μF, and 6,800μF. Get used to seeing those factor numbers times their multiplier, and you'll know that a "120" code on a monolithic capacitor is *most likely* a date code, not a value code.

✖ If you find a capacitor marked 0.047F, 0.22F, 0.33F, 0.47F, or 1F, *save it like it was gold.* You have found a fairly rare supercapacitor, which can be used to create devices that will run in bursts many seconds long, rather than for just fractions of a second. The drawbacks? They take long to charge up from a solar cell, might not be able to dump power fast enough to run a motor, and are usually rated for only 2.5 volts maximum.

Diodes

Diodes are very common parts you'll find alongside resistors and capacitors. Although they're about the same shape and size as resistors, it's easy to tell these from the others, simply because they're usually made of glass or black plastic with a single line around one end. Using our water analogy, a diode has the function of a one-way check valve, letting power flow through, but not back again.

Most of the time, you will be using *signal* diodes, which are small and designed to pass only light power loads. These are usually made of glass, with a black or yellow band near one end. You may trip over the occasional power diode, which is about double or triple the size, made of a black material, with a silver band near one end. These bigger diodes can handle much, much more power, but these big boys won't be used in our projects.

Figure 3-8
Diodes,
diodes,
diodes, and a
candy for size
(not taste)
comparison

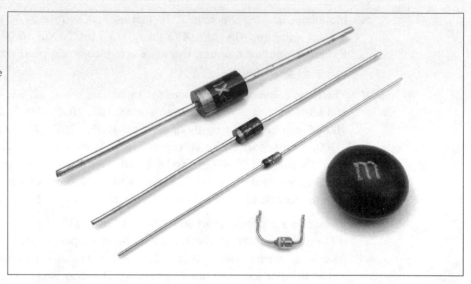

A standard diode has two ends: the *anode* and the *cathode*. For power to flow through a diode, the anode has to have a more positive voltage than the cathode. In other words, anode = positive side; cathode = negative side. To remember which is which, I have to invoke a phrase that my high-school physics teacher gave me. "I feel negatively toward cats" (*cat*hode = negative). It's the cathode that is also marked with the band, both on the part and on the symbol.

Diodes are (in our opinion) among the *worst* marked parts in the electronics industry. My suggestion is that when you buy a diode, make sure you keep it in the bag it came in so that you know exactly what type it is when you install it.

Transistors

Up until this section, all the parts described have been of little ability. With the transistor, we can start doing some *really cool stuff.*

There are two ways of using a transistor, as a *switch* or as an *amplifier of a signal.* Most of the circuits we'll be using implement the transistor as a simple switch, that is, as a way to have a wee bit of power toggle on much more substantial amounts of power. Think of it this way: when you flip a light switch on, you use *very little* power to actually flip the switch that passes the substantially greater power to the light bulb—a transistor works in a similar way.

There are two main flavors of transistor—chocolate and vanilla. Well, okay—I admit to stretching the truth. In fact, the two main flavors of transistor are *Neopolitan* and *Pistachio.* (Can you tell what I'm craving?)

Silliness aside, there actually *are* two main types of transistor—*NPN* and *PNP*. The N stands for "negatively doped silicon" and the P for "positively doped silicon." If you want to learn more about the physics of semiconductors, check the list of recommended reading at the end of the book. The important thing to know is that because of their mirror-arrangement to one another, these two types do essentially the same thing, but using inverse signals to do so. Here's another way to think about it: In North America, most light switches are set up so that an up-flick passes power to the lights. In India, it's much more common to flick down to turn on the lights. Same effect, reverse technique. NPN and PNP work (simplistically) much the same way.

Technically, an NPN transistor turns on when the base (the "control" pin) has a high signal (+) applied to it. The PNP version turns on when the base has a *low* (−) signal applied to it.

Unlike the resistor, capacitor, or diode, a transistor has three leads coming out of it. These are the power input, the power control, and the power output (respectively the *emitter, base,* and *collector* leads—see Figure 3-9). The ability of a transistor to take a tiny control signal on its *control* or *base* lead and let vastly higher amounts of power run through the other two leads makes it the fundamental "good stuff" in practically any electronic device you've ever seen.

Figure 3-9
Transistor pin
identification

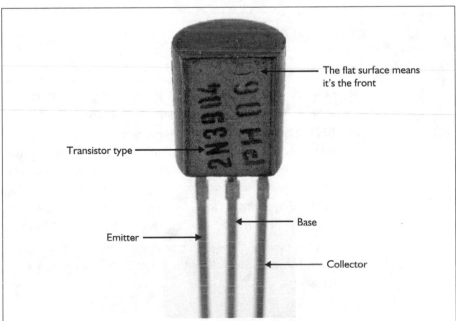

The flat surface means
it's the front

Transistor type

Base

Emitter

Collector

Unlike the other components, transistors come in a wide variety of shapes and sizes, but fortunately for you, we'll be using one of the most common plastic packages, called a "TO-92"(probably stands for "transistor outline"). Can't tell you why it's got such a peculiar name, but you'll probably think of this shape when somebody says the word "transistor." As mentioned previously, the transistor has 3 leads; the *emitter*, the *base*, and the *collector*. When holding a transistor, flat-face to you, pins down, that's the order the pins are, left to right.

This description applies to *most* transistors, and definitely to all the transistors we'll be using in our projects. When you strike out on your own and find a strange transistor, make sure you do the appropriate research before using it in your own circuit.

It's usually pretty easy to identify a transistor, as it will usually have a flat spot with writing on it. There's usually a manufacturer's logo and a part number marked on it. One of the tricky things about transistors is that the number that *actually tells you what it is* can be buried in the number. Example: a PN2222A offers the same sort of performance as a 2N2222 transistor housed in the more expensive metal TO-18 package. Obviously, the "2222" designation is the key to figuring out what the transistor can do for you. The other numbers usually refer to the way they've been packaged or manufactured.

 The Robot Geek Says

Transistors

✶ Learn to keep an eye open for the following transistors, as they're among the most useful, inexpensive, and popular types:

✶ **PN2222/PN2907** These are general-purpose NPN/PNP transistors that can drive some good amounts of power. They're listed together because they're *complementary* transistors, sort of like brother and sister—equal, but opposite.

✶ **2N3904/2N3906** These are also very common transistors (NPN/PNP), but with not as much "drive current" as the PN2222/PN2907 transistor.

✶ Don't let minor changes in transistor labeling throw you off—a PN2222A transistor offers the same performance of a 2N2222A transistor.

✖ If at all possible, avoid buying "like" transistors. Those are the ones labeled in blister packages as "3904-*like* transistors," containing transistors with *totally* different identification codes (these are called *house numbers*). If you can't find the part you need with the proper part labeling, look elsewhere.

✖ To contradict the previous point, *you can* usually find suitable replacement transistors, but get them from a knowledgeable source that can assure their performance. Here's an example: You can substitute a PN2222 transistor for a 2N3904 in practically all BEAM applications.

✖ Transistors are *very* sturdy devices. It is very difficult to damage them by overheating them when soldering. If (or most likely "when") your circuit fails to work, don't immediately blame the transistor, as *very few* bad transistors have been seen in my many hundreds of circuits we've had to troubleshoot. If you kill them in-circuit, they usually let you know by letting out a puff of smoke, or cracking a bit (*very rare* in solar-powered circuits).

We have to touch base on a variation of the transistor called a *field effect transistor (FET)*. If a transistor is a plow horse, a FET is a twitchy, high-strung racehorse. It offers better performance if you're willing to properly set it up and pay the extra money for it. We won't be using FETs in our designs, as they're not as nearly as common or robust as the transistors we'll use.

Integrated Circuits

We're into a whole new kettle of fish with integrated circuits (otherwise known as "ICs" or "chips"). The IC brings together all the components described in this chapter, but munged into one package. The actual elements of transistors, resistors, diodes, and (small) capacitors are *quite* small, so combining them into useful arrangements and sealing them up in a larger package makes designing more complicated circuits *vastly* easier and quicker.

Imagine you need a timer circuit in your robot to make it kick into reverse when it bumps into something. With the individual parts, you'd need about 22 transistors, 10 resistors, and 4 capacitors to get the same performance you'd get out of a single 555 timer chip. Whoops—you forgot that you have two touch sensors, each needing its own timer. Do you *really* want to do all that over again? You barely have space left to mount a battery, let alone another whole timer circuit. Fortunately, the 555 timer chip comes in an easy-to-use, bite-sized, dual-timer version called the 556, which is only marginally larger than a dime. *Now* can you see the advantage of using an IC?

Identifying an IC is a pretty easy task. They're usually a black rectangle, with a bunch of silver legs shooting down out of the sides. Some are smaller than others, or have leads coming out of all four sides, but they are all *integrated circuits.* Each pin (or leg) is how the IC talks to the rest of the circuit; leads may be power connectors, inputs, outputs, or means for tuning the behavior of the IC. Each IC is usually identified with an alphanumeric code on the top of the chip, with the manufacturer's logo, and a date-of-manufacture code. Unlike with resistor and capacitor markings, there is no way to tell what the purpose of the chip is just by looking at it. Up until just a few years ago, anybody getting into electronics would have to invest some time and space in collecting the necessary *manufacturer's data books* just to be able to identify what chip they had, or wanted to use in a design. Fortunately for you, this whole internet thing descended on mankind like a huge data fog, so now all you have to do is find and ask the appropriate Web site for the information you need.

Remember when we mentioned how slight differences in codes in transistor markings usually *don't* affect the expected performance of a transistor? Unfortunately, this does not apply to ICs. An IC labeled "74AC240" *looks* like a "74LS240," but they have vastly different characteristics. We call them both "240 chips," and they both "think" the same way, but that's where the similarity ends. The "AC" and "LS" designations describe the *family* that they belong to. One family may do the same job faster, with more power, or both. Or they might have slightly different ways of doing the same job.

Note that if you find a bazillion-legged chip in a trashed VCR, it will *most likely* be of absolutely no use to you. This is an IC that has so much packed into it, it is only good for being the brains of a VCR, and nothing else. I don't recommend spending much time trying to figure out what these custom "house-brand" chips are.

So now you have a chip, and the data that tells you what it does and what the different legs do, but you have *no idea* which pin is #6. There are a few basic rules in identifying the chip and its pins.

The first thing you have to know is that most circuit diagrams showing the IC package outline are drawn "live bug," which is with the IC sitting there with the legs pointing down. Next, you'll notice that there's a little half-circle notch out of one side of the chip—that identifies the front and top of the IC. Another indicator of which pin is the first is the little dimple next to one of the pins (usually the *top-left corner*). By counting down the side of the chip from this pin, you identify pins 2, 3, 4, etc. The geeky thing about ICs is that you *don't* read the pins like a newspaper column, which is when you get down to the end, you jump up to the top of the other side—that is *incorrect*. Continue counting pins by scooting around the corner over to the other side and counting up the other side. Think of it as like reading a clock *backward* starting from the 12 o'clock position, to 11, 10, 9, and all the way back around to 3, 2, and 1.

Figure 3-10
Using chips: Identifying dead bug, live bug, what kind of bug!

The Robot Geek Says

Integrated Circuits

Our projects will be using most of these chips—keep an eye peeled for them:

* **74(AC/ACT/H/HC/HCT)240—*Octal Buffer Inverter Chip*** A *very* versatile chip, often used in BEAM circuitry. Its original purpose is to invert and direct "eight lanes" of data traffic back and forth in a computer-type device.

* **74(AC/ACT/H/HC/HCT)14—*Hex Schmitt Inverter*** One of the original chips to be used heavily in BEAM technology. A simple chip, it takes a signal input, reverses it, and dumps it out again (high in, low out, and vice versa).

* **74(AC/ACT/H/HC/HCT)245—*Octal Driver Chip*** Versatile for driving loads (such as motors). Much like the 240-type chip, it directs "eight-lane traffic" in a computer, but *without* inverting the signals.

* **555—*Multipurpose Timer*** This chip is probably the most widely used IC of all time. *Well* worth keeping in your parts bin. To find out more about the 555, try the online tutorial at http://www.uoguelph.ca/~antoon/gadgets/555/555.html. Not *too* many BEAM applications, but it's a great chip for further exploration.

* **LM386—*Audio Power Amplifier*** A good chip to trick into a brain and motor driver. Originally used to make sound signals louder.

* **LM324—*Quadruple Operation Amplifier*** Another amplifier, but with four in a single package. This chip is gaining in popularity in the BEAM community because it is quite versatile.

* **7805—*Positive 5V Voltage Regulator*** Comes in different voltage flavors; the last two numbers indicate the output voltage This chip is very useful for converting up to 40V down to 5V to safely power your BEAM circuit. Keep an eye out for the 78L05 (they're less common but come in the small TO-92 package).

As a rule, *never* expose an IC to more than 6 volts, unless if you're *darn sure* it can handle it. This means no hooking your circuit up to a 9-volt battery without a way of reducing the voltage!

Do not sit on an IC, especially if it's "dead bug" (pins up). Those pins are *quite* sharp. And they leave a very embarrassing set of bite marks.

You are now officially armed with just enough information to be dangerous. If you find components that puzzle you, don't be scared to do a bit of reading and research. The Internet has some great resources to determine what chips do what, for instance at http://www.solarbotics.net/library/datasheets/. Solarbotics.net is sponsored by Solarbotics Ltd. (http://www.solarbotics.com) as a free community Web server, hosting data and free Web sites for practically anybody who wants to put up a BEAM-related Web site. Another excellent site to search for electronics data sheets is http://www.digikey.com. Digikey is a very good mail/Internet order company that has a *very* complete inventory of parts. Punch the part number in question into their search engine, and if it finds it, it will present you with product ordering information and a link to the datasheet for that part.

Chapter 4

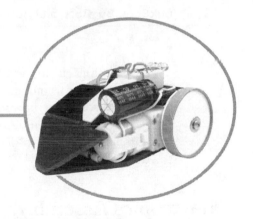

Electronics Assembly Techniques

Putting electronic bits into something that's going to become a robot requires a combination of talents—like how *not* to superglue your finger to your nose; how *not* to use hot glue to solder components together; how *not* to permanently glue a solar cell to a countertop. These are all *just as important* as the proper "how to" lessons you'll be learning. Keep that in mind, and you'll do just fine.

Electronics Assembly

Metal is the preferred conduit of choice when it comes to connecting electrical components together. Iron and copper are plentiful, easily turned into wire, and operate over wide ranges of conditions. The trick to connecting these wires together effectively is that you need to merge them together with another metal to get a good connection. The most common way is by using a technique called *soldering*. Soldering is heating up a metal so that it melts into and around the other metals touching it. This binding metal is usually a mixture of several metals, such as tin, lead, and silver, plus a compound called *flux* that helps clean the connection and ensure a good joint. Tin and silver by themselves are pretty unthreatening, but you *should* be careful with flux and lead. If you don't know how to be careful with them, you skipped over what the Safety Geek had to say in Chapter 2, didn't you? I suggest a quick review is in order—I'll wait here while you go back and reread that chapter….

Now that you know how to safely handle solder, let's review the basic tools you'll need and use.

Solder

Solder is obviously the stuff that makes everything electronic "stick" together. It comes in different packages, but it almost always looks like a thin length of shiny, silvery wire. Please keep in mind that there are two main types of solder—*electronics solder* and *plumbing solder*. The difference is that plumbing solder uses a stronger flux that can eat away at the connections you'd make if you use it in electronics. *Make sure what you're using is specifically for soldering electronic parts, not for installing a sink!*

In general you can solder to the following metals: copper, nickel, tin, lead, silver, gold, and *some* steel if you prepare the steel by cleaning and scuffing it up well. Other materials *may* solder if properly prepared, but this list is of the materials you'll find most common.

The Soldering Iron

You've got the solder; now you need the "make hot" tool, also known as the *soldering iron*. Solder melts at around 400 degrees Fahrenheit (around 200 degrees Celsius), so your soldering iron will have to be able to heat the parts to *at least* that temperature. There are many types of soldering irons, and *most* will work. You want to avoid the big *pistol grip*–type soldering irons that are rated 100 / 140 watts. They have their uses, but soldering small electronics isn't one of them. Save yours for building robot bodies later.

Keep your eye out for a simple *pencil-grip* soldering iron, which is about the size of a large marker and plugs directly into the wall. Most hardware and electronics retailers will have these available in the $20 range. I used my original Radio Shack soldering iron kit (part #64-2802—$7.99) for two years before I was finally sure I was going to be serious about robotics and invested in a *much better* Weller soldering iron (the WTCPT Controlled Output Soldering Iron, for around $90—shop around). The pen-type soldering iron takes a minute or two to heat up and doesn't pack quite the same "heating" punch as the Weller brand, but we fully recommend using the inexpensive one until you're sure you will be using a soldering iron enough to make it worth the extra cash.

Figure 4-1
Different types of soldering irons: Use the proper tool for the job!

Soldering Iron Accessories

There are a few accessories that are pretty much necessities if you want to do the job right, and since they're inexpensive, there's no reason *not* to have them on your workbench.

Wire Strippers / Cutters

You will most *certainly* need to make connections with wires, and when you do, you'll need to cut and strip those wires. You remember wire—that metallic noodle in a plastic sleeve, right? The whole point of the sleeve is to protect the wire from shorting out against anything it's *not* supposed to be touching, but to solder to it, you have to first cut off a bit of the insulation without damaging the wire inside. Fortunately, the proper tool to do this is inexpensive and effective.

Figure 4-2
Wire strippers: Better and cleaner than chewing!

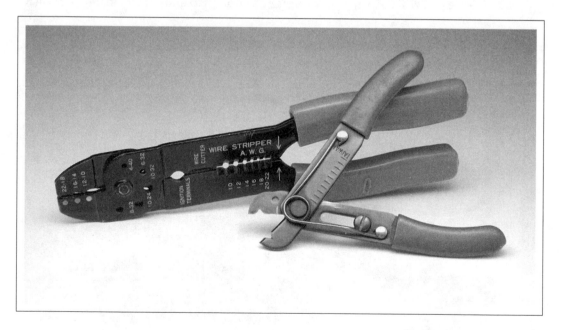

The tool I'm referring to is *not* your teeth. As tempting as it may be to try to chew the insulation off, you'll get a very strange groove in your tooth from repeatedly gnawing on wire—*don't do it*. Go spend the few dollars on a simple grooved wire cutter, and it will last you for years, and protect your dental work. Place the wire in the V-groove, gently pinch down on it until you feel the wire (trying *not* to nick the wire), and then pull the insulation off. That's it!

The wire stripper also has a set of cutting surfaces a bit farther behind the V-groove for snipping wire—again, a *much* better solution than gnawing through it.

Soldering Iron Stand

Whichever type of soldering iron you buy, make *sure* you also get a holder-stand as part of the deal. You'll need a safe place to put your iron when it's hot—there's nothing like having a hot soldering iron rolling off the table and into your lap (it's a bad thing). Some irons come with a little metal cradle—this is *not* good enough, as it's too easy for the iron to be pulled or knocked off the cradle. Make sure you find a full wire-coil type holder-stand

Figure 4-3
Don't mess with a 600°F chunk of metal on your desk; store soldering irons properly.

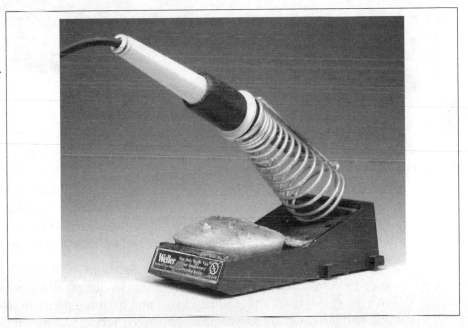

Soldering Sponge

As you use your soldering iron, the tip will get covered in flux, oxides, and other crud. Have a damp sponge on hand to give your iron a quick wipe on just before every solder connection you make. You don't want it to get *too* wet—if you hear a boiling, bubbling noise when you wipe your hot soldering iron on it, your sponge is much too wet. The sponge should be made of cellulose—not that plastic, rubbery stuff used for cleaning dishes, as it will burn and melt when you wipe it with a hot soldering tip. Better to use a damp paper towel than a fake plastic sponge.

Figure 4-4
Solder sponges: For keeping soldering tips clean, not for blotting spilled Coke!

Helping Hands

This is an ingenious tool that makes electronics assembly a much happier process for that special somebody in your life. You may ask, "Why happier for the other person, and not me?" Easy: You won't be burning *their* fingers when you solder the two pieces together that they're holding for you.

Helping hands can be bought at many locations, including hobby shops, surplus stores, hardware stores, and electronics outlets. Some come with one, two, or three claws, a magnifying glass, and high-temperature soldering surfaces built right in. If you want to build one on the cheap, simply buy a packet of "alligator clips" and find some heavy copper wire and an old chunk of 2×4 lumber. Solder the clips onto the wire, staple the wire onto the wood, and you have your own ultra-deluxe *helping hands*. On the other end of the scale, you can buy jeweler's quality, constant-pressure versions for upward of *$60 a claw.*

Figure 4-5
Helping
hands:
Assisting
lonely
roboticists
for decades

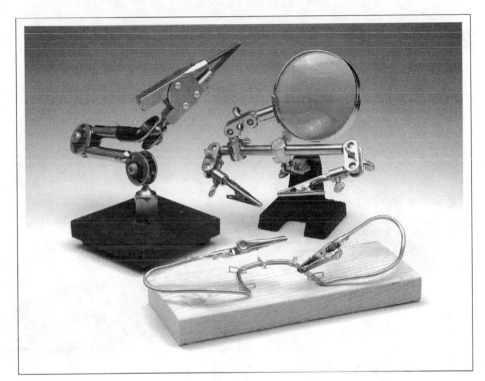

Desoldering Tools

Skip this paragraph if you know you won't ever make a mistake. Everybody still here? Good—glad to see you're all being realistic.

Desoldering tools are an essential part of your toolkit, especially if you're planning on "acquiring" parts from old or dead electronics. All the techniques require you to heat the solder back to its molten state and get rid of it somehow. Here are your options.

The Desoldering Pump (Also Known As the Solder Sucker)

This is my tool of choice, as it's reliable, strong, and makes a satisfying "shhhLUCK" sound. It's easy to use, too. Push the spring-loaded plunger down, heat up the solder, put the solder sucker's tip to the molten solder, and hit the release button. The plunger springs back up, sucking the molten solder into it. Repeat as needed! I personally recommend the ERSA Soldapullt 140, as it's small and effective for only $25. A less expensive alternate is the Radio Shack #64-2098 "Vacuum Desoldering Tool" for $7.99.

Figure 4-6
Solder removal tools: Featuring the solder sucker and the solder wick

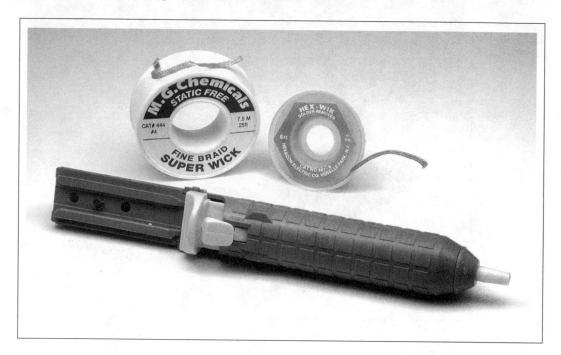

The Desoldering Bulb

This works on a similar principle as the solder sucker, but I find it doesn't have the same vacuum "pull" as the rapid suck of the desoldering pump.

Solder Wick

This is a braid of fine copper wire, with solder flux. You place the braid down on the offending solder, heat it up by pressing down on top of the braid with your soldering iron, and let the solder melt and wick into the braid. Pull it off, let it cool down, snip off the part of the braid with the absorbed solder, and you're done!

The "Whack-It" Technique

This technique requires that you

- ❏ Wear safety glasses and an apron (you're wearing them anyway, aren't you? Or do I have to call Guido again?)
- ❏ Have a work surface you're comfortable with abusing slightly
- ❏ Are in an area where there is *no chance* of injuring somebody else

Heat up the solder connection with your iron, then rapidly smack it down against the work surface. The molten solder will fly out, hit the surface, and harden into a metallic splatter mark. *Never* do this directly in front of your face—hold it off at an angle so that there is no chance that back-splash might come back at you (in fact, use a full-face shield for this procedure). Although potentially the most dangerous technique, if done properly, it's the quickest and cleanest method to get rid of unwanted solder. Use it as a last resort if you don't have a solder-sucker.

Figure 4-7
The "whack-it" technique: Use with caution!

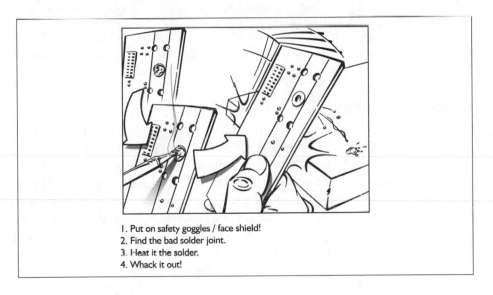

1. Put on safety goggles / face shield!
2. Find the bad solder joint.
3. Heat it the solder.
4. Whack it out!

It may be strange to hear, but you can sometimes do a better job of getting rid of solder *by adding more.* If you're having trouble removing solder from a circuit (especially from the holes in circuit boards), *add* some to the connection first. This will give your soldering iron a better chance to properly reheat *all* the solder in the area you wish to make solder-free.

Wire

When soldering a wire to another wire or component, you have to take into account *what type* of wire you're using. There are essentially two types of wire—*solid* and *multistranded*, each having its own application.

Figure 4-8
Solid-core and stranded wire

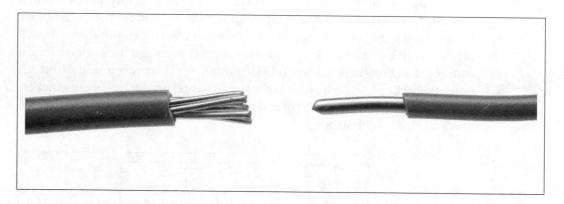

Solid-Core Wire

Solid-core wire is exactly that—a solid, single core of wire surrounded by a plastic or rubber insulating coating. Solid wire is rigid, meaning it doesn't bend very easily, and when it does bend, it tends to stay bent. Unfortunately, if you bend it too many times, it will eventually fatigue and break. It doesn't matter how frequently or quickly you bend it, but after *X* amount of bends, it *will break* at the point where it's bending. Solid wire is best used in applications where you have to push a wire into a socket (as in a prototyping breadboard), or where it won't be moved much. An *okay* source for fine solid wire is telephone cable (the stuff that runs in the walls, not to the phone itself). Heavier stuff that is *much more* usable is called *22 gauge* (gauge is a way of measuring its size). It's definitely worth buying a spool or two of this single-conductor solid wire in different colors in the 20–24 gauge range. Look at Radio Shack or Future-Active stores for spools you can buy off the shelf.

Multistranded Wire

Multistranded wire has many very fine wires at its core, which makes it much more flexible than the solid-core wire. Multistranded wire is like a wet noodle—it flops over *very* easily. Although the fact is not of immediate importance to you, this kind of wire can carry more power than an equivalent gauge of solid-core wire. It's commonly used in applications involving a lot of movement, like the wire that connects your computer to your mouse (an *excellent* source of *very high quality* multistranded wire). You'll also find it in extension cords, headphone lines, and ribbon cables, as well as attached to practically any connector in a computer or VCR. As you can tell, manufacturers *love* multistranded wire because it is so much more robust than solid-core wire. When dissecting these appliances, don't overlook the wire—a box full of different types of wire is a *good* thing to have.

The Magic That Is Soldering

Soldering requires heating up the wires you want to join, and then melting solder around them to join the wires together. Sounds simple, but let's look *carefully* at the procedure, so you'll know how to do it correctly:

- ❑ **Prepare the connecting wires.**   If you are joining two wires, the process is as simple as stripping off enough insulation that you can twist the two wires together. With multistranded wire, roll the wire between your fingertips to make it a nice, compact bundle—there's nothing harder to solder than a messy pile of strands.

- ❑ **Tin the wires if necessary.**   Tinning is simply melting solder onto the exposed wire. This is useful when you don't have an easy way to *mechanically* attach the wire to its mate. Look at it this way: If you have a loop you can wrap the wire around, you don't need to tin. If you're soldering to a component leg, tinning will make life easier. It's a pretty easy process—simply heat the exposed wire on one side with the soldering iron while pushing solder onto the other side. When the wire gets hot enough, the solder will melt right into it.

- ❑ **Put the parts to be soldered together.**   If you can, twist the wires together, or use your helping hands (or the fingers of an unsuspecting ~~victim~~ assistant) to hold the parts right next to each other. *Warning: The parts will get hot!*

❏ **Wipe your soldering iron tip on the sponge.** Remember, you want a nice, clean soldering iron that will transfer the heat effectively.

❏ **Apply the heat.** Touch your soldering iron tip to the components. If your parts are tinned, all you have to do is reheat them with your soldering iron, and they'll melt together—done! If the parts *aren't* tinned, then you have the added task of using one hand to hold the soldering iron in place and the other to apply some solder. If the connections were *not* tinned, you can expect to use up about 3/8"–1/2" (10–15 mm) of solder per connection.

Figure 4-9
"See Dick solder": The whole soldering procedure in pictures

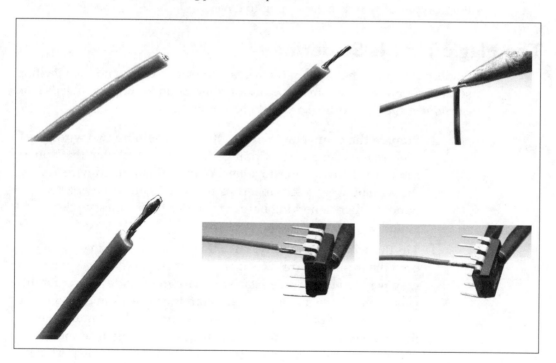

Soldering a component into a *printed circuit board (PCB)* is much the same process. You remember PCBs, right? They're those green or brown boards in most electronic appliances that the parts are plugged into. The neat thing about PCBs is that instead of your having to run wires from component to component, the PCB has a thin copper foil line running across its surface making the connections for you—all you have to do is solder the connection to the PCB.

Although you most likely *won't* be using any PCBs with these projects, you *can* get blank prototyping boards that you can solder your components to, and then run connecting wires. (Radio Shack strikes again, with the #276-150 "Multipurpose PC Boards" for a buck-fifty.) The process for soldering to a PCB is much the same as for soldering directly to other components, except you have to prepare the bare soldering surface of the PCB first. You have to prepare the surface because there can be oxides (rust), oils, and other miscellaneous crud on the surface you can't see. Best to give it a *gentle* scrub with a scuff pad, such as a 3M Scotch-Brite pad or some sort of steel-wool pad (*without* detergent). It just takes a bit of a scrub to make all the contacts nice and shiny, then wipe the surface off with a clean paper towel.

After you insert the electronic component in place, you might want to bend the legs a bit so that it stays in place while you flip the board over, where you'll do the soldering. The same sort of soldering procedure applies here as for wire: Heat up the components on one side and apply the solder to the other, using about 3/8" (10 mm) of solder for each connection.

Figure 4-10
Soldering to a circuit board

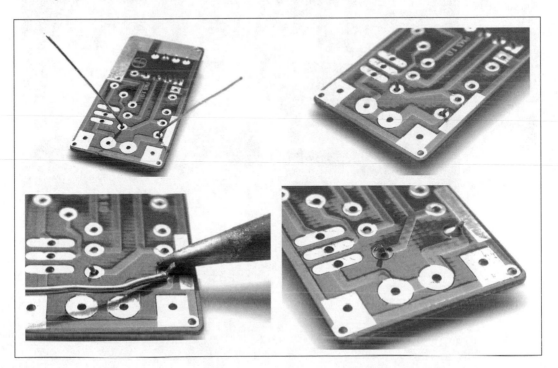

Now that you've made your solder connections, it's time to inspect them. A proper solder joint will look shiny and silvery, and it will easily pass what I call "the wiggle test." The wiggle test is performed by grabbing the component in question and giving it a firm but gentle wiggle back and forth. Do this while examining where the leg comes out of the solder joint on the other side, and look for movement. See any? If so, your solder melted to one component *or* the other, but not both. Simply reheat the connection, and *perhaps* add a bit more solder to make sure it takes this time.

If your solder joint looks "frosty" or has black bits on the surface of it, it is most likely a *cold-solder joint*. This is a solder connection that failed to heat and cool properly, and is a failure just waiting to happen. Again, the answer is to reheat and reapply a bit more solder. If it *still* doesn't look right, raise your solder-removal equipment over your head, and bellow, "Prepare to *meet thy doom*" while invoking the mighty power of your solder sucker. Then try it again. If you liked the bellowing portion, you can do that again, too.

Figure 4-11
Bad solder
joint

The Robot Geek Says

Soldering

✖ You are a *roboticist*, not a *painter!* This means you don't melt solder to the tip of your soldering iron and smear it onto the connection you're trying to make. You're *guaranteed* to fail.

✖ Heat the part, not the solder. The solder will melt and go to where the heat is.

✖ Stick it to the PCB! When soldering parts to a printed circuit board, poke the soldering iron tip right in the junction where the component lead comes out of the solder pad hole. This will heat *both* parts together, giving you a good solder joint.

✖ Having trouble getting the part hot enough to melt solder to? Melt just *a bit* of solder to the tip of your iron and push it into where you want to heat up. Molten solder transfers heat better in difficult situations.

✖ Get tip tinner and cleaner for your soldering iron! This amazing stuff will extend the life of your soldering iron tip by three or four times. Just don't breathe the fumes. Look for it at Radio Shack (part #64-020 for $5.99) or Future-Active.

✖ Keep a container of water at your bench, just for keeping your sponge moist. Just don't drink from it—you'd be surprised what can grow in it in a month's time.

If you're new to this whole soldering thing, take your time and develop your technique. After a few hours, you'll be able to tackle any of the projects in this book. Don't hesitate to get the part hot before applying solder (a common fear), keep the soldering iron tip clean, and everything else will fall into place. Enjoy the process—you can't build bots without melting some metal!

Chapter 5

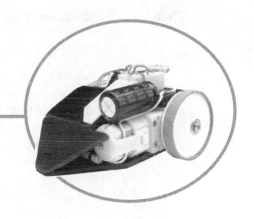

Tools and Mechanical Assembly Techniques

I f you're an at-home handyman, you'll have more than enough tools to put these devices together. If you're a poor student in a college dorm, you'll have adequate tools to put these devices together. If you're living in a cardboard box under a bridge, you *might* have a bit of trouble gathering up the necessary tools, but if you ask around, you may be surprised what you can find. Failing that, pawn shops usually have quite a variety of *very inexpensive* tools that will fill your need.

Mechanical Tools

You really don't need much to successfully build a BEAM device. To make your robot-building life easier, here's the list of tools you *should* have anyway.

❑ **Standard pliers**   Otherwise known as "grabber-nabbers," these are great for bending materials, and holding parts while somebody else solders to them. Pretty much any old set of pliers will do fine—no need to spend very much on these. Cost: under $8.

❑ **Needlenose pliers**   Also known as "fine grabber-nabbers," these are excellent for use in tight locations where the regular grabber-nabber won't fit. Although an inexpensive pair will serve the purpose, you'll find that the higher-quality versions found in good tool stores (like Future-Active) are much nicer. The better ones don't flex at the tip, don't rattle at the hinge, have better "teeth" for holding small parts, and are spring-loaded so that they always self-open. Cost: Anywhere from $5 to $30, depending on quality.

❑ **Screwdrivers**   This means both the heavy-duty type you use for prying open a paint can and the fine "fix-your-glasses" type. Get a big-handled "multibit" screwdriver, and treat yourself to a set of *quality* fine screwdrivers. I recommend a 5-pack of the "Wiha" or "Xcelite" brand. Cost: Around $25.

Figure 5-1
A *good* quality set of fine screwdrivers will be your next-best friend, right after the soldering iron.

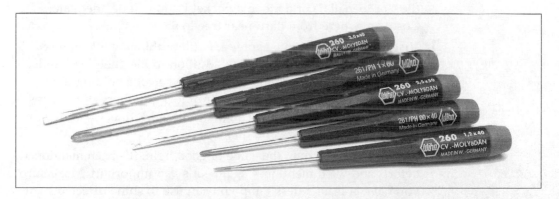

❏ **Heavy side cutters**   Heavy side cutters look like pliers but have a pair of tapered edges for cutting and snipping. They are great at cutting heavy-gauge wire and plastic, and are a *very* necessary tool for breaking apart techno-trash. A 5" long pair is about the smallest you should look at getting, and the more you spend, the better they get. Try to afford yourself a medium to expensive set, as the cheap ones have weak cutter jaws and will "notch" the cutter if you try to snip something too hard. Cost: $15–$25.

❏ **Fine cutters**   These miniature cutters should *only* be used to cut electrical wires and the leads that come out of electronic components. Using them for anything else will most likely result in their getting "notched" (a *bad* thing) and becoming near-useless. In a pinch, you can use them to cut toenails too.... Cost: $10–$65 (you get what you pay for!).

Figure 5-2
Fine cutters: Guess which one has tried to cut music wire?

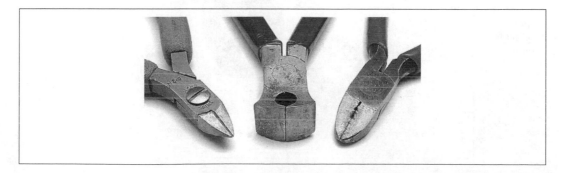

❏ **Fine file**   Use this for smoothing out sharp edges or cuts. You *can* spend quite a bit on files, but for our uses, a simple metal nail file (for toenails?) or a file in a pocket knife will be adequate. Cost: Anywhere from darn-near free to $5.

❏ **Vise**   As discussed in Chapter 4, holding things while you're soldering is pretty important. In addition to the "helping hands," you should acquire a small vise of some sort for holding items larger than wires. In a pinch, a pair of locking pliers (Vise-Grips come to mind) or something similar will work fine. Cost: free to $30, depending on size and quality.

❏ **Light**   Don't discount the value of good light. It's been mentioned before, and we'll mention it again—it's *that* important. Make sure you have at least a desk lamp you can use to shine directed light onto a part. It will also come in handy for testing solar-powered designs, especially if it uses an incandescent or halogen bulb (fluorescent lamps don't feed solar cells very well). Cost: Look up! That bright thing in the sky is free, but it doesn't work well at night. Spend $8 on a swing-arm lamp.

❏ **Magnifying Lens**   There *will* be times you will need to sneak a closer peek at something, either to identify it or to see if there's something wrong with it. A magnifying glass isn't bad, but for really getting a close look, try to find a *jeweler's loupe*. They can magnify very well and are worth between $10 and $25 at a jeweler's supply store. Inexpensive plastic loupes can be found for only a few dollars in bargain and surplus tool stores. Cost: In Canada, Princess Auto usually stocks them in their surplus department for only $1.99 each. Good-quality ones can run upward of $30.

Figure 5-3
Jeweler's magnifying loupes: *Excellent* for super-close inspection of parts

❏ **A hot glue gun**   Not the ideal tool for long-term, *permanent* robot construction, but it does the job in a pinch. The smaller types are easier to handle but take longer to heat up. If you're comfortable with tools, get the *regular-temperature* type, as the *low-temperature* models don't have as much "holding power." Don't forget extra glue sticks too. Cost: Raid Mom's craft drawer (free) or spend $5 on a small hobby glue gun.

❏ **Super glue (cyanoacrylate)**   Try to steer clear of the corner-store grade, and get yourself a small bottle of the *thin viscosity* (watery) variety at the hobby store. This stuff *rocks*. The "consumer" grade is not that good, as the chemistry isn't that pure, and who knows how long it's been sitting on the shelf? The glue you get from the hobby store has a shelf life, uses *very good* chemistry, and has fabulous holding power. Store it in the fridge for longer life, as it'll get gooey over the course of one or two years on a sunny shelf. Cost: About $5 for a 1/2 oz. bottle.

❏ **Five-minute epoxy**   This stuff complements cyanoacrylate very well, as when super glue doesn't work, the epoxy usually does. We've used the cheapest to some pretty expensive stuff, and they're all sufficient for our purposes (don't be scared of the cheapest, as you *should* be with super glue). Cost: $2 or $3 for the off-the-shelf five-minute formula.

❏ **Security bits**   A good set of these is less necessary but still useful. These are the end pieces that will fit into any multibit screwdriver, but match the many strange types of screw heads that are usually used in electronics assembly. We *want* to take apart the things the manufacturers *don't* want us to, so instead of using the brute-force "where's my bigger hammer" method, seek out a set of these bits. Although the "hammer" technique of dismantling works, spend the cash to dismantle *with style*. Cost: $7–$20 at automotive/industrial supply shops such as Princess Auto.

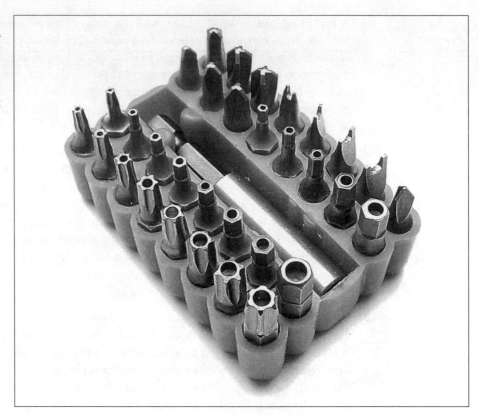

Electronics Tools

If you're going to get serious about doing robotics, you'll need a few more tools in addition to the soldering equipment discussed in Chapter 2.

❏ You're going to *need* a multimeter of some sort—something that measures voltage, resistance, and current. A digital meter is preferable for beginners, as you can't get much simpler than reading the number, and they're much more easily found than the analog-style meters (with the needle on a scale), which are rapidly disappearing. If you don't already have a meter, start by buying the least expensive one you can find. If you eventually find that it's lacking features you need, *then* buy a more advanced meter—believe me, you *will* eventually find uses for two meters at a time (this is coming from a man with more than five meters).

Radio Shack usually has a monthly special on meters, so if you're patient, you'll eventually find a meter in your price range. They have a simple digital meter (part #22-810) for $19.99, occasionally on sale for $14.99. Or scan the Internet—good deals on meters are fairly common. Cost: $15–$200.

Figure 5-5
Digital
multimeters:
Even the
worst of them
are useful.

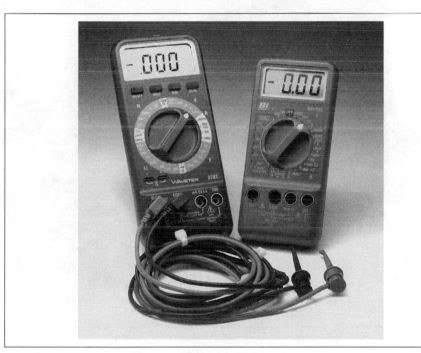

❏ Look for a variable-voltage DC power supply/adapter. You don't have to spend hundreds of dollars on a professional-grade power supply. Even experienced roboticists do just fine with the simple wall-wart type with the voltage-selector switch. Get one with the multiple tips so that you'll be able to use it for charging batteries, powering prototype circuits, and even powering a salvaged cooling fan. Expect to pay between $10 and $20 for a reasonably good adapter, *or* keep an eye on the DC adapters that accompany junked answering machines and the like. It won't take long before you find a nice 4.5 VDC (volts DC) adapter ideal for powering electronics, one at 6 VDC for charging batteries, or a 12 VDC unit for powering that cooling fan. Cost: $5–$10.

Figure 5-6
Multiple voltage adapter

❏ The electronics breadboard is a *fundamental* piece of equipment
you should use first before you even *think* about soldering a
circuit together. The breadboard lets you wire up a temporary
circuit quickly and easily, and lets you make changes quite
rapidly. It's the first place you should go to when you want to
start a new circuit, as you'll be able to assemble it without having
to make solder connections. Cost: ~$5–$15.

Figure 5-7
The
electronics
breadboard

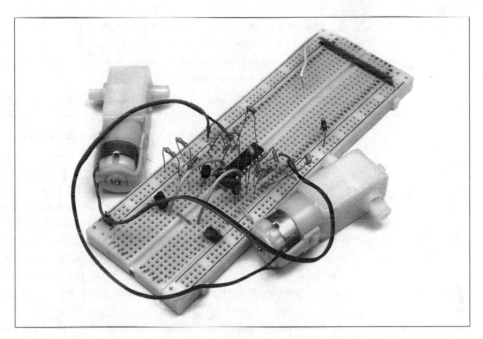

The breadboard is arranged in parallel strips of holes that are electrically connected, so to electrically connect two wires, you simply jam one end of each wire into the same strip. Breadboards prefer a particular *gauge* or *thickness* of wire—too small, and it doesn't make a good connection; too large, and you can damage the holders under the holes in the breadboard. Again, Radio Shack to the rescue, with their Jumper Wire Kit (part #276-173, $5.49), which is a collection of precut, prestripped, prebent wire specifically for use on a breadboard. If you're more "do it yourself," get yourself a small spool of solid-core (only one wire) wire, sized between 20 and 24 gauge, and use that to make your own jumpers. Future-Active also has similar wire kits and raw wire available in-store.

Support Tools

Support tools are much like the supporting actors in a movie—not up front in the spotlight, they nonetheless make the star (tools) perform better.

❏ **A *good* power bar**   As mentioned in Chapter 2, a good one will have a built-in reset breaker and an on/off switch. If you can, get something better than the ones you use for plugging in your Christmas lights. Cost: $10.

❏ **Drawers / Bins / Boxes**   You're going to start accumulating plenty of components, especially when your friends and family know that you're on the prowl for techno-trash. Within six months, you'll have more dead toys than Toys"R"Us after Christmas day. Gather some decent-quality boxes that will fit on your shelf, and cut the lids off. Or if you don't mind spending a few dollars, visit an industrial supply or box store and get an assortment of similar cardboard shelf boxes. If you don't mind spending more than a few bucks, get plastic, stackable bins for holding parts and partially finished projects. If you're a particularly good scavenger, a *printer's-type drawer* is an ideal tray to hold many, many small pieces in a single unit. Of course, there are the new-fangled plastic cases you can get at tool stores (Future-Active carries the "Lid-Storage Containers," #06-215, for about $14) that have lots of little compartments for parts. Figure 5-8 shows much of your range of options. Cost: Free to $50.

Figure 5-8
Organizing bins: A more well-thought-out way to lose things that are important to you

❏ **Freezer-grade resealable baggies**   These use heavy-duty plastic, some have neat zippers, and they all have a white space for writing descriptions on. When you have a box of capacitors, you *will* appreciate being able to grab a bag of 4700µF capacitors instead of rooting around in a big bin. Of all the storage solutions, this one is the cheapest and most effective. Don't turn into a pack rat that can't find anything—locating the right part for the right job is worth taking a few minutes to bag and ID the parts you dismantle. Cost: $2/box.

Figure 5-9
Freezer baggies, large and small: The most inexpensive and effective part filing system known to robot-junk collectors

Consumables

As you progress through the chapters, you'll be seeing complete part lists for the devices being built. Some of the designs *will* require some "free-form" work, meaning you'll have to build some parts absolutely from scratch. The following is a list of consumables (things you'll use up) you'll most likely find useful to have on hand:

- ❑ **Music wire of various diameters**   Visit your local hobby store and pick up a rod of the five smallest diameters. Although finicky to solder, music wire is *very* strong and resilient, and it makes for good axles, sensors, and support wire. Cost: 20–50 cents a rod.

- ❑ **Brass rod of various diameters**   Again, your local hobby shop is a good place to look for this material. But *don't* buy the smallest diameter stuff—it's much too weak to be of much use. Start with 1/16" diameter and grab yourself a few rods of various sizes up from there. Brass rod isn't as strong as music wire, but it *sure* is easy to solder together. Makes for pretty, golden frames. Cost: 50 cents to $1 a rod (it depends on diameter/length of rod!).

❑ **Toner cartridge wire**   This needs to be explained a bit. Back in the early days of BEAM robotics, it was discovered that the 2 mm shiny silver wire that supports the toner drum shield on HP brand laser printers is *unusually* stiff. Sometimes it solders well, sometimes not—we're not sure why. But when it does solder well, it's incredibly strong for its diameter, and worth ripping off the toner cartridge before you dispose of it (check with the office-supply manager). This material makes for an incredibly strong robot framework, at an excellent price! Cost: free, free, free!

Figure 5-10
Toner cartridge wire: Bizarre, but true, this stuff is *very* strong, but practically unobtainable from anywhere else!

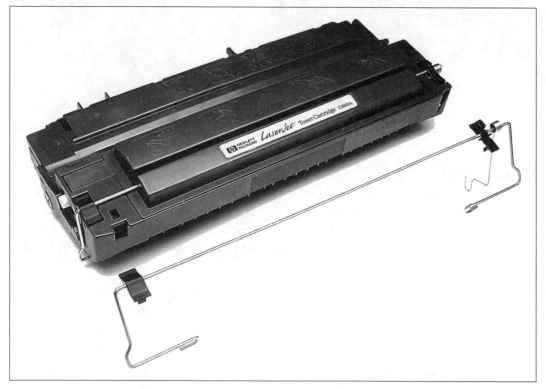

❑ **Sintra, or expanded PVC sheet**   This plastic sheet material is sold in a *very* wide range of colors and thicknesses, usually to sign-maker shops or trade-show booth builders. What makes it so useful is that is glues like a dream with both epoxy and super glue; it's easy to sand/file to shape; it's very colorful; and it's pretty strong for its density. To cut it, simply score a line on the surface with a sharp knife and flex it—it'll snap in two! If you approach your local sign maker or trade-show booth company, they may even have bins of small cut-offs that are useless to them, but *ideal* for you. Other than that, try Lynxmotion (http://www.lynxmotion) or Solarbotics (http://www.solarbotics.com) for their assortments. Cost: Free to ~$3–$5 per 8×10 sheet.

The Robot Geek Says

Tools

* Don't abuse your fine side cutter. Nothing's more frustrating than trying to cut a transistor wire when your cutters have been notched out.

* Get a digital multimeter. If you're a beginner, get the *cheapest one* you can find that'll measure voltage, resistance, and current

* Get the *good*-quality fine screwdrivers! Get the *good*-quality fine screwdrivers! Get the *good*-quality fine screwdrivers! Got them yet? Do I have to repeat myself?

* If you do nothing else to store your robot parts, buy yourself a box or two of the heaviest freezer-grade baggies you can find. Sort new parts into them *religiously!* Label the bags with a big, bold, black marker, and you'll save yourself much grief.

* Get your super glue from the hobby store. Avoid the supermarket/corner store stuff!

* Found some neat construction materials? Save them! If you haven't used them in a year, recycle or dispose of them! You'll soon learn what's worth keeping.

Now you know what you should have on hand (or what to look for in your neighbors' toolbox) when you sit down to start building. Don't worry if you can't find *everything* right away—as a good roboticist, you will be able to improvise your way around any lack of tools. Besides, there's always the last line of defense for any technogeek—duct tape, which spawned the roboticist's rule of construction:

"Pretty is nice, but ugly works!"

Chapter 6

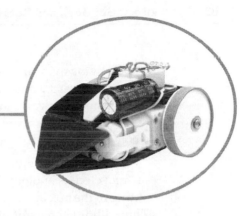

Dumpster Diving 101: How to Scavenge Robot Parts

Obviously, you won't be picking atoms and molecules out of thin air to construct your BEAM device, so let's get down to basic parts and materials you can use. You'll be surprised at what can be turned into robot construction material. Keep your eyes open—I'm sure there are things we've overlooked that won't be in our list!

One of the techniques we really try to promote in BEAM robotics is the use of "recycled technology." This is simply another way of saying "the neat junk sitting in the box in the corner of the garage because it's too cool to throw out." Think about the amount of electronic gadgetry you've discarded over the years. Remember that portable CD player you dropped while riding your bicycle? Or that Walkman that got stepped on when it was left on the steps? Or even that VCR your Uncle Stan drove over with the lawnmower? All these things have useful parts that can be used as components in your next device.

Figure 6-1
Electronic castaways, just waiting for a new home

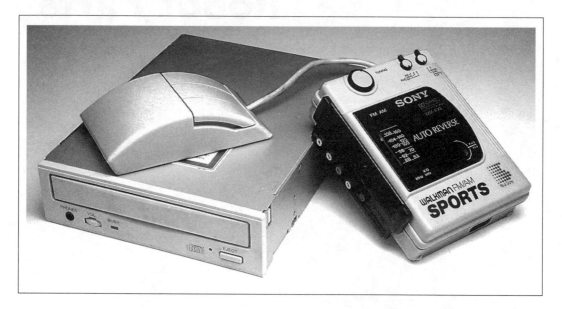

It is disappointing to see how much of a "throw-away" society most of the world has become. In most trash cans, you'll find equipment that no longer works due to the failure of a $0.25 component and yet contains other perfectly good things that can be reclaimed. By taking something apart, you learn more about how the things you use in everyday life work, without the guilt of wrecking it. (It's already from the trash, right?)

Once, when we hosted a workshop for some elementary school children, we asked them to bring in something broken and electronic from their home. One student arrived with an old electro-mechanical rotary telephone and was having a heck of a time getting it apart to see what made it work. We *thought* he was busy dismantling it, until the teacher looked out the window and commented to us, "What is Jimmy doing out in the parking lot?" Just as she asked that, student Jimmy raised the telephone over his head and smashed it to the ground, exploding it into many dozens of pieces. Upon his arrival back to the classroom, he remarked, "I've never had a class as much fun as this!" Although his technique was not very safe (uh, safety glasses?) and damaged a few of the parts he *could* have used in his BEAM device, his mindset was sound. It was neat; it was junk; it could be ripped apart by any method to get to the good stuff inside.

Even if you don't have much to start with, once your friends and relatives know you want their electro-junk, you'll be swamped in no time. By the time this happens, you'll have figured out what the really cool items to keep are, which ones have some neat salvageables, and which are truly crap. Be sure to start sorting your recycled technology early on, as the longer you let that pile grow, the harder it will be to remember where that neat cam-lifter-mechanism-thingy was.

New and Surplus Sources

When searching through your pile of techo-scrap doesn't turn up what you're looking for, it may be time to actually spend a little money *(GASP!!)*. Don't let this scare you too much, as a few well-spent dollars will go far in the construction of your robot.

Although you can salvage many components from discarded equipment, you may find it simpler to go out and stock up on the most commonly used items. Collect catalogs from the two major sources of robot parts—surplus and retail stores. Build your stockpile up from commercial electronics resellers like Solarbotics, Future-Active, Digikey, and Radio Shack, and surplus dealers, like The Electronic Goldmine (http://www.goldmine-elec.com) and All Electronics (http://www.allelectronics.com). The difference between the two kinds of sources is that commercial outlets get their supplies directly from the component manufacturers and usually have the latest and greatest devices, whereas surplus dealers get their stock from other sources, such as consumer electronic manufacturers that have excess stock of one part they no longer need. In short, you get as much as you want of the newest neat stuff from the commercial outlets, and (usually) limited quantities of neat stuff from surplus outlets, at reduced cost.

Figure 6-2
Catalogs: Remember how much fun they were when you were a kid at Christmas? That time has come again!

The commercial outlets should have the ability to get you almost anything you'll need, at practically any time. Surplus outlets will have an interesting variety of items at cheaper prices, but in limited quantities that may disappear. The most interesting surplus outlets are the types that specialize in electronics with electro-mechanical goodies as well. They'll occasionally have deals on neat gear motors and other items easily turned into a BEAM device. Good surplus outlets will have a printed catalog issued at least twice a year, with a Web site on the Internet. But be warned: When you find something *really* cool from a surplus company, be sure you buy as many as you think you'll use before sharing your find with the rest of the world. They'll sell out in no time, with only a slim chance of ever coming in again! One of the "unofficial" rules of being a BEAM roboticist is, "Find the cool stuff—and buy it all!" If you can manage this, you'll have more than enough for any projects you come up with, and you'll be able to trade with other BEAMers who subscribe to the same rule. Transistors and resistors definitely fall into this category, as they usually cost only pennies apiece, especially when bought in volume. At the time of this writing, surplus 2N3904 transistors can be purchased for approximately 10 cents each, or 100 for $7.00. With a little shopping around, 100 1/4-watt resistors can be had for a penny apiece. It's often a good idea to stock up on a part if it only costs you a bit more for a larger quantity, especially if the part is inexpensive to start with. Nothing is more frustrating than having a project come to a screeching halt because you ran out of a 10-cent part! But be warned: Most surplus purchases don't have the same sort of warrantees that come with retail-store purchases.

Garbage Reclamation

Even if you happen to have a reasonably decent stock of parts to build from, you should keep a pile of dead electronic devices to draw from. This shouldn't cost you much, if anything at all. Just simply keep an eye out for items other people may consider trash. Here are some things worth watching for:

❏ **Walkmans and other portable cassette players**   The better the cassette deck, the better the innards! These will have high-efficiency motors, gears, belts, pinch rollers, and pulleys.

Figure 6-3
Inside portable audio equipment, you'll find *ideal* raw robot material.

❏ **Portable CD players** For many of the same reasons listed for the Walkmans.

❏ **Pagers, especially vibration pagers** These vibrate to let you know you have a message. To make the vibration, a tiny motor spins an eccentric weight. These tiny motors have become practically the standard for making mobile BEAM critters.

❏ **Spent laser-printer cartridges** As mentioned in Chapter 5, these offer cool construction materials, like quality metal rods and plastic sheets.

❏ **Mechanisms that move** *slowly* This is usually an indicator of the presence of a *gearhead* motor (otherwise simply known as a "gear motor"). Gear motors turn much more slowly than regular motors because of a gear-reduction mechanism mounted on the motor. The gears in this mechanism convert the motor speed into *torque,* or the *ability to turn/twist a load.* If you have ever been in a car with a standard transmission, you know that you can't pull away from the stop light in fourth gear—that's like taking the engine shaft and tying it directly to the wheels. In first gear, it takes three turns of the engine shaft to turn the wheels once, trading rotational *speed* for rotational *torque.*

Figure 6-4
A gear motor versus a regular motor

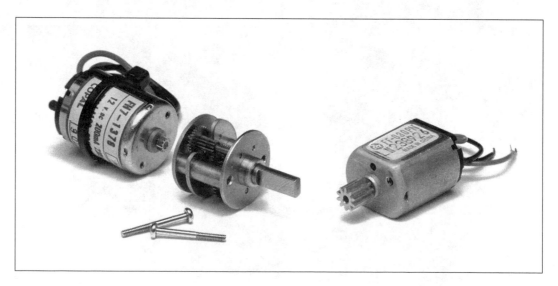

❑ In general, any portable battery-powered electronics or anything that has moving parts is something to watch out for. Being battery-powered means that the electronics *have* to be efficient; otherwise, they'll have an extremely short life. What good is a Walkman that plays for only 1/2 hour? Having moving parts means there should be mechanical parts you can scavenge. A digital clock has next to no useful parts, as all it does is beep and play the radio. But a wind-up toy will have all sorts of gears you can hack a motor into to make it BEAM-powered.

Where to Get This Sort of Stuff

Most computer repair centers have boxes of dead hard and floppy drives. These contain elegant springs, switches, and connectors, along with really cool magnets. Some large department stores have bins full of dead toys and portable cassette players that get returned after Christmas. These have motors, gears, and some really beautiful mechanics that would otherwise cost hundreds to buy. Cell phone and pager repair companies will have boxes of dead, crushed, and otherwise useless pagers that will have fully functional tiny vibration motors, LCD screens, piezo speakers, and switches you can reclaim. Now that you know *where* to get them, *how* do you convince them to part with their junk?

Figure 6-5
The high-precision innards of a pager

Most companies have policies regarding what they're supposed to do with the trash they generate. Many will not let anybody get near their trash, for fear of industrial spying. When you approach a company to ask permission to raid their dumpster, here are some guidelines to follow:

❏ Ask to see the manager of the repair department. This will get you in touch with the person most likely to know what sort of junk they produce, and most able to get you to that junk.

❏ If possible, bring along one of your BEAM creations, no matter how pathetic it may be. Use that as an excuse—"It'd be so much better if I could salvage a quality motor to use here instead of this big clunky motor." If you can prove to the person in authority that you're no commercial threat to them or a competitor's spy, they'll most likely call you when they've got another pile of goodies ready for pickup. After all, it's likely they suffer from the "Boy, that's really too cool to throw out" syndrome as well. And most techie-types appreciate neat electronic devices.

❏ Promise to keep it confidential. The last thing they want is every Tom, Dick, and Guido knocking on their door asking for the same thing. So if you do score big, share the wealth with your buddies with the understanding that they're not to pester your source of goodies. Also, some managers may get in trouble if higher-ups find out about their generosity. Keep it quiet, or you may lose your source when she loses her job!

❏ Take the bad with the good. If they offer you some really great parts, but they're only part of a larger pile of what is truly junk, don't pick and choose. They're going through the effort to get you this stuff, and being picky shows disrespect. You can always recycle/discard the useless stuff later.

❏ If you're gathering parts together for a workshop, *say so*. Free publicity for the company in exchange for some part they were going to toss out *anyway* is a good deal in their eyes! We've had some very nice photocopiers and other office equipment donated just by explaining they were for a group event.

❏ Show appreciation. If you do score it big with a neat stock of parts, build something for the person who made it possible for you. They'll appreciate the gesture, and it will have cost you only a few dollars in parts and some time.

Free Samples from Manufacturers

For another good source for parts, check out the manufacturers of electronic parts, especially those that make ICs (integrated chips). It's in their best interest to promote their product, so many companies have free sample programs, especially for new chips they're just releasing.

At first glance, it doesn't make much sense for a company to give away five or ten chips just because you ask for them, as it costs them staff time, shipping, and inventory. What *they* want to do is scatter their chips out to as many potential customers as possible. If their new chip proves to be useful to somebody, they hope it will turn around into a *huge* order when that chip gets used in a commercial product.

Don't feel too guilty asking for these samples. They may ask if you have a commercial application in mind, or they might not. Some even encourage hobbyists, as word-of-mouth can lead to their chip being used by an electronics engineer who happened to be at a robot club meeting where the hobbyist was showing off that chip in a robot. In short, it doesn't hurt to ask them for a sample—the worst they can say is "No."

 The Robot Geek Says

Scavenging

✖ If you see something that would be good for turning into a robot, it *had* to have been built *somewhere*. Write down part numbers, distinguishing marks, and company names for future reference!

✖ *Always* be polite when it comes to asking for somebody else's techno-trash. Sure, it's garbage, but it's *their* scrap, and they don't have to give it to you if they don't want to!

✖ Order the latest catalogs from surplus-supply companies about twice a year. Make sure you visit their Web sites for neat stuff that hasn't made it into the catalogs yet.

✖ It never hurts to contact chip manufacturers to see what sort of "free sample" program they have. For a few minutes on their Web site, you may be rewarded with a free package of goodies in the mail!

✖ Gear motors are *gold*. If you find a good gear motor supply, acquire as many as you can, as you will be able either to use them in the future or to trade/sell them to other roboticists with little effort. The best gear motors are made by Micro-Mo, Namiki, Maxon, and Nihon.

✖ When you find cool stuff, buy twice as much as you think you need (or more!). If there's plenty of it in stock, buy just a few, test them out, then get more if they *really* are "cool stuff."

A little patience and detective work will reward you with parts you couldn't otherwise find or afford. One of the most rewarding aspects of building these BEAM devices is watching a collection of totally unrelated parts merge into something brand new. Such is the world of robotics!

Chapter 7

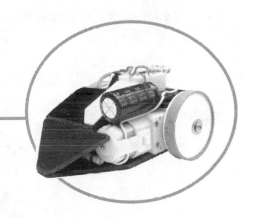

Project 1: The Symet: An Introduction to Solar-Powered Robotics

Parts List

- ❏ **1** × Motor
- ❏ **1** × Solar cell, minimum output of 3 volts
- ❏ **3** × Identical capacitors, sized between 470µF to 4700µF
- ❏ **1** × Resistor, between 1kΩ and 10kΩ.
- ❏ **1** × 2N3904 or PN2222 transistor
- ❏ **1** × 2N3906 orPN2907 transistor
- ❏ **1** × Flashing LED
- ❏ **1** × Metal paper clip
- ❏ **1** × 1" double-stranded fine electrical wire

The BEAM Symet

We're not going to attack a full robotics project until you've had some practice building a few simpler devices first, okay? Trust me, it's still a fun project, and worth doing. Besides, while you're too busy having fun, we'll sneak some useful info into your brain. It won't hurt…much.

The Symet is a solar-powered BEAM device that is *almost* a robot. Because the device looks the same from several sides, we've taken the name from the word "*Symmet*rical," but the extra "m" looks strange. "Symmet"—see? Doesn't that look bizarre? This device is about as simple and self-sufficient as they get.

The solar cell powers the motor; the motor moves the device; and when it bumps into something, it tilts in a new direction and keeps on going. That's the basic operation of the Symet.

The Solarengine: The Key to Solar-Powered Robotics

It's time to cover the solar aspect of BEAM robotics. As mentioned earlier, we'll use a solar cell to power this beastie. A tiny solar cell. At best, a solar cell provides only a small fraction of the power of a regular AA battery. In fact, of all the solar energy falling on the solar cell (as light), less than 1/20 of the power gets turned into usable electricity. You will *rarely* be able to attach a solar cell to a motor and expect it to do anything.

Fortunately, there is a family of electronic circuits that will let you convert the weak power output of a solar cell to drive the loads of a small robot. A *solarengine* stores the trickle of power from the solar cell, and releases it in bursts of *usable* energy. That means you have to wait a while until the power stores up to that usable level, but at least you're getting some movement when it would be impossible without the solarengine.

All solarengines work on the same principle:

1. Store the energy.

2. Decide when to dump the energy, then dump it.

3. Do it again, and again, and again....

The first step (store the energy) is pretty straightforward. You attach the solar cell to a capacitor or a rechargeable battery, and let it trickle the power in. If you use a small capacitor (say, 1000μF), it will take only a few seconds of lamp light to charge. If you're using a supercap (1F), you'll wait minutes; a rechargeable battery will take hours.

The second step is a bit more complex. A circuit has several ways to decide when to dump the energy, just as you have several ways to select a flavor of ice cream. Where you may use the qualities of flavor, color, or texture to satisfy your ice cream craving, a solarengine circuit can use time, voltage, or current to decide when it's time to activate. When the decision has been made to send the power out, a different part of the solarengine circuit blasts that power out to the rest of the robot, making it twitch, roll, walk, bleep, blink, or burp.

The last step sounds simple, but it can cause headaches. It's harder than it sounds to make sure a circuit restarts over and over and over again. You know when some days you *just don't want to get out of bed?* Well, sometimes electronics circuits misbehave that way too. Fortunately, this problem shouldn't bother you much, as the circuits we'll use are tried, tested, and true.

Solarengine Types

Most solarengines use a *voltage-based* activation circuit. That means the circuit watches the volts stored in the capacitor to determine when to activate, the same way you watch a pressure gauge as you pump up a bicycle tire. When it's high enough, you know you're good to go, and in the case of a solarengine, that means "time to dump power." Voltage-based solarengines are pretty simple to build, and they are quite efficient, meaning the voltage-monitoring circuit eats very little of the power coming in. This will be our solarengine of choice, and we'll try several sub-flavors (like covered with chocolate sprinkles, or nuts, or strawberries.... Whoops, wrong analogy!).

The second major type of solarengine uses a built-in activation timer. Timer-based solarengines will dump whatever power they've stored up over so-many seconds, whether the power-storage capacitor is 1/4 full, 1/2 full, or totally full for a while already. Like clockwork, they'll dump whatever they have at regular intervals. Solarengines of this type aren't much more complex than voltage-type solarengines, but they usually eat more power, as it takes energy to run the electronic timer accurately.

The third major type of solarengine watches the current flowing into the power storage capacitor to determine when to activate. It's like when you're inflating a bicycle tire: when the air pump can't push any more air into the tire, the airflow reduces to nothing. This sort of solarengine watches the flow of power into the capacitor, and when the solar cell can't push any more power into it, it dumps the power. This sort of circuit is somewhat complex, and not too many designs have been worth the difficulty of assembly. If perfected, this type of solarengine would give the best overall performance in all kind of light levels.

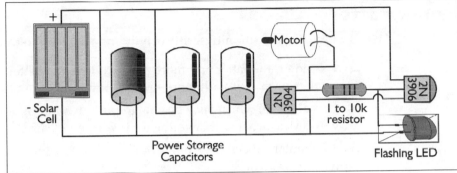

Figure 7-1
Flashing LED
solarengine
schematic

Symet Behavior

The Symet sits on the motor shaft and the edges of two capacitors, naturally sitting off-center like a toy top when it's not spinning. When the motor activates, it scoots the Symet forward a bit while the capacitors skid along. The neat thing about being symmetrical is that if it tilts over to a new side, the motor rotation will push the Symet in a new direction. The most important aspect of a successful Symet is proper balance. Try to make it as balanced to the center as possible, and your Symet will work equally well on any side it happens to rest on.

Figure 7-2
Symet motion explained

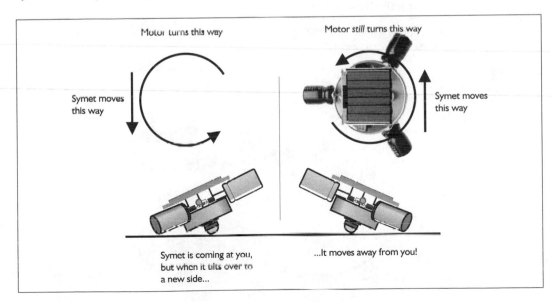

Symet Parts

Here's where we get to the nitty-gritty of building a device. First, get parts.

❏ **1** × Motor, the fatter and more pancake-like, the better. These rotate slower, but with more turning power.

❏ **1** × solar cell, which *must* be able to put out a minimum of 3.0 volts. Measure it with a voltmeter if you're not sure.

❏ **3** × Similar capacitors, from 470µF to 4700µF, with 1000µF being darn-near ideal.

❏ **1** × Resistor, 1k to 10kΩ. You remember your resistor color codes, right?

❏ **1** × 2N3904 or PN2222 transistor (either will do fine).

❏ **1** × 2N3906 or PN2907 transistor (again, either will do fine).

❏ **1** × Flashing LED. It *must* be a flashing or blinking LED—accept no substitutes. Get Active Components' KLF-336-HD red 3-pack or Radio Shack's 276-030/305/036 parts if you can't find this part. Red is preferable, as it will make your solarengine activate sooner than a green or yellow one, and it will be less prone to locking up (a bad thing).

❏ **1** × Chunk of stiff structural wire; a copper paper clip is practically ideal.

❏ **1** × Wee bit of electrical wire for making electrical connections to the solar cell.

Figure 7-3
Symet parts,
ready to go

Before you start actually soldering these parts together, it's a *good idea* to make *absolutely sure* that they work together. It's much easier to figure out a bug in a "plug in and play" circuit than it is to implement all your recently learned "desoldering" techniques. It's a plenty-good idea to get a hold of a breadboard, and temporarily hook up all the components you want to use, *just to make sure they work.* For the Symet, take a look at Figure 7-4, and copy how all the parts were put in. When you shine a light on it (a 60-watt incandescent light is good), the motor should take no longer than ten seconds to pulse.

Figure 7-4
The breadboarded Symet circuit

The Robot Geek Says

What Can Go Wrong with Your FLED Solarengine

✖ The flashing LED is sensitive to light! Most semiconductors that emit light have the bizarre side effect that they are also *sensitive* to light. A flashing LED *can* lock up and stop working if it's exposed to intense light (i.e., sunlight!), so keep the flashing LED covered by the solar cell or by some black tape to ensure reliable operation. If you don't, the Symet may pulse once, then stop working until you pass a shadow over it.

✖ If you hear a high-pitched whine from the motor (hold it up to your ear!), the solarengine is having trouble latching (turning on). Find a lower-value resistor and swap it into the solarengine.

✖ If there is no voltage in the power storage capacitor, you may have hooked up the solar cell *backward* to the circuit. This is a *very* common error.

✖ If your circuit charges your power storage capacitor up to only 0.6 volts and then stops, you most likely don't have the motor hooked up to the solarengine. It *needs* the motor hooked up to charge.

✖ If you see the FLED actually flashing, then the solarengine resistor is too low for the solarengine to trigger the latch. Get a higher-value resistor, and swap it into the circuit.

A typical trigger voltage for the FLED solarengine is about 3 volts for the green FLED and 2.6 volts for the red FLED. If the measured voltage on the power storage capacitor is *higher* than this, then the FLED is probably not getting power. If you don't have a multimeter to test this, you can do it with a single white or blue LED. Just put this LED in parallel with the power storage capacitor (the long leg of the LED goes to capacitor "+"). If the LED lights up, then there is probably more than 3 volts in the capacitor.

✖ There is a *slim* chance that the solarengine can become saturated by having *too much* power. It will trigger once, then no more. No simple solution for this—just use a smaller solar cell.

✖ The flashing LED solarengine is sensitive to what motor is used. If it isn't working with one motor, try a different one!

Building It!

The solarengine we'll use with this particular project is a "flashing LED solarengine." The two transistors and the resistor are arranged in what is called an "SCR latch"—which is the electronic name for a switch that when turned on, stays on. The flashing LED ("FLED") acts as the finger that flips the switch to turn it on, and once it's on, it stays on until all the power has run out. What makes a FLED such a convenient trigger is that it has a tiny, tiny chip inside that tries to make it light up every second, and every time it tries, it also tries to activate the switch circuit. Only when there's enough power stored up in the main power storage capacitor is there enough juice to let the FLED kick the circuit into operation. What makes a FLED particularly good at its job is the fact that when it's in the *off* part of its cycle, it draws almost no power, which means more power gets stored up in the capacitors

Since there isn't much to build as a body for the Symet, let's start by building the solarengine, as it's the trickiest bit to build. Everything else will be easy compared to this step, so let's tackle it first. We're going to take special effort with the steps in this first project, showing you the graphic of what do to, and a picture of the step showing how it should actually look like after the step is performed. Subsequent projects will have just the photos showing the result of each step.

The transistors we're using all have the same *pinout*. A pinout is the name and orientation of each lead coming out of the part. With our transistors, you can identify each of the leads by holding the transistor up, flat face toward you, pins pointing downward. From left to right, the pins are the *emitter*, the *base*, and the *collector*. What do those names mean? They describe the flow of "electron holes" through the component. The emitter and collector are like the input and output of a pipe, and the base is like the valve that controls the flow through the pipe. As for *electron holes*, that's a term best looked up in a beginner's guide to electronics, and is outside of the scope of this book.

Take your 2N3904/PN2222 transistor (remember, they do pretty much the same thing) and, starting near the transistor body, bend its left lead (the emitter) 90° out to the left side. Bend the right lead (the collector) 90° directly upward, so it's pointing up at you. Bending these leads will make it easier to solder other components later on.

Figure 7-5
Forming the 2N3904/PN2222 transistor leads

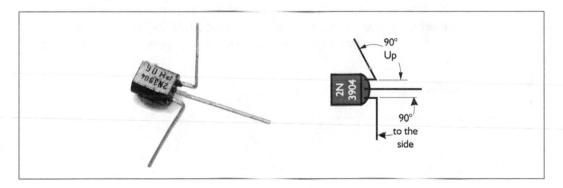

Take your 2N3906 or PN2907 transistor (again, they're functionally the same, so either will do) and, starting near the transistor body, bend the left lead (the emitter) 90° out to the left side. Bend the middle leg (the base) 90° directly upward so it's pointing up at you. Make sure your bends are looking like the ones in Figures 7-5 through 7-9!

Figure 7-6
Forming the 2N3906 (or PN2907) transistor leg

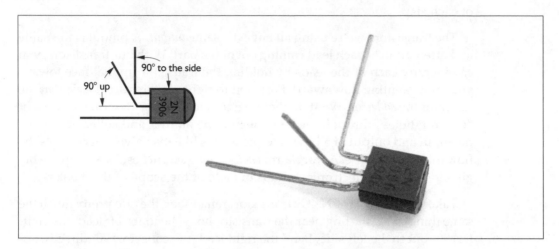

This is the first really tricky part to free-forming the circuit. We're going to solder the lead we *didn't* modify from each transistor together. That's the middle lead (the base) of the 2N3904/PN2222 and the right lead (the collector) of the 2N3906/PN2907. This is a good time to have a set of helping hands, be it a mechanical set or a friend's. Arrange the transistors so they're both face-up and their leads are overlapping so one almost totally covers the other. A bit of heat, a dab of solder, and they'll turn into the core of your solarengine circuit.

Figure 7-7
Joining the transistors together

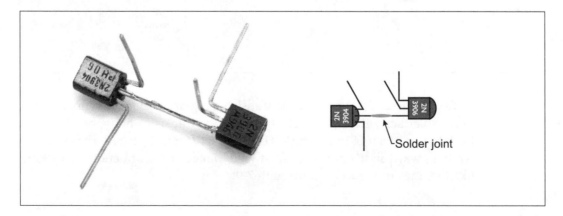

Adding the resistor isn't terribly hard if you tilt the transistor assembly slightly away from you. It's then a simple process to just lay the resistor across the two bent-up vertical legs and to solder where the resistor touches the transistor legs. Resistors don't have a front or back, so whatever way you put it in is fine.

When you're done soldering the two sides of the resistor to the transistor uprights, you can trim off the portions of the resistor that poke past the solder joints. Also trim off the excess vertical lead from the 2N3904/PN2222 collector, but *not* from the other transistor vertical leg—we need that for attaching the FLED.

Figure 7-8
Adding the resistor to the mix, and trimming the leads

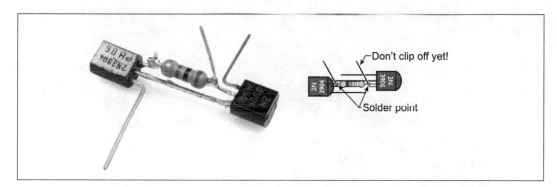

We're about to attach the flashing LED (FLED), but before we can do that, we need to identify the leads. Most LEDs have a flat spot near one of the legs that indicates the *cathode*, the lead where you hook up a negative power (–) or ground connection. The other side is called the *anode* and hooks to a positive (+) power connection. Locate the flat spot on the edge of the FLED, and make note of which lead is closest to it.

Figure 7-9
Identifying the cathode of the Flashing LED

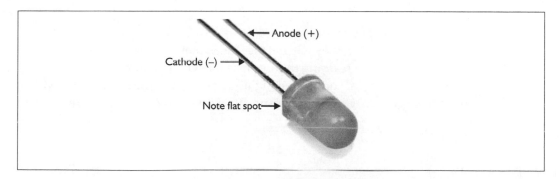

Take the FLED's cathode and bend it so you can solder it to the left lead (the emitter) of the 2N3904/PN2222 transistor. Then solder the other lead of the FLED to the upright middle lead (the base) of the 2N3906/PN2907 transistor, which is also soldered to the resistor.

Yeah, I know those directions seem clear as mud. Keep forging ahead and following the pictures, and you'll be fine.

There—you've officially finished your first FLED solarengine circuit!

Figure 7-10
Finishing the core circuit with the flashing LED

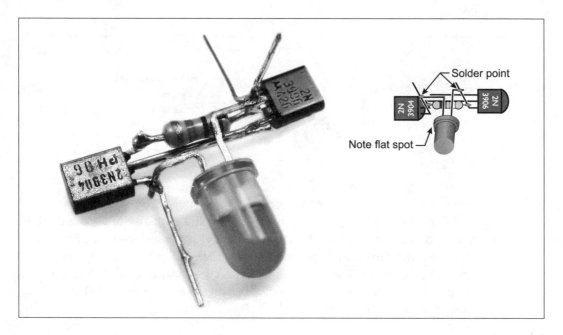

Time to find that big round shiny thing. Yes, we mean the motor, not your uncle's balding head.

Let's add the power storage capacitors to the motor. Spaced equally and soldered to the motor, they will balance the Symet while storing the power for the solarengine. We're doing this because the whole motor body will be used as one large electrical connection in the next step, and the motor body will be like one large convenient wire! Your capacitors will *most likely* have polarity markings (remember that the striped side is negative), so make sure you're connecting the capacitor's negative leg to the motor body. Bend the positive capacitor wires upward, just to get them out of the way, and clip the negative wires down so that they're just long enough to solder to the motor body. Soldering the capacitors on can be a bit tricky, because motors don't like to be soldered to. The metal body that covers the whole motor will have to be scuffed, sanded, or filed a bit to get through the dull surface to the shiny (solderable) metal below.

Figure 7-11
Soldering capacitors to the motor body

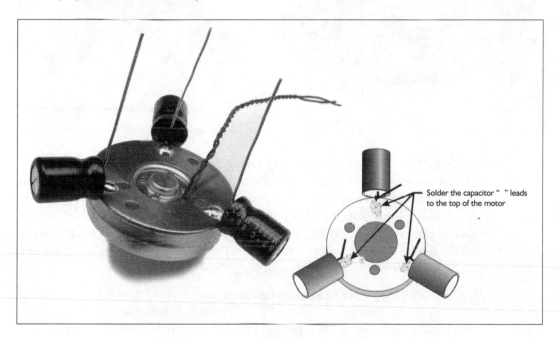

Solder the capacitor " " leads to the top of the motor

Now we'll mount the solarengine circuitry to the top middle of the motor. This is the place you will want to solder the left leg (the emitter) of the 2N3904/PN2222 transistor. Solder the left leg down to the motor, remembering to first scuff/sand/file a spot to solder to on the motor body before soldering, and you'll do just fine. Remember that since the motor is a large hunk of metal that absorbs lots of heat, you'll need to hold the soldering iron on somewhat longer before the solder will melt.

Figure 7-12
Attaching the solarengine circuit to the motor

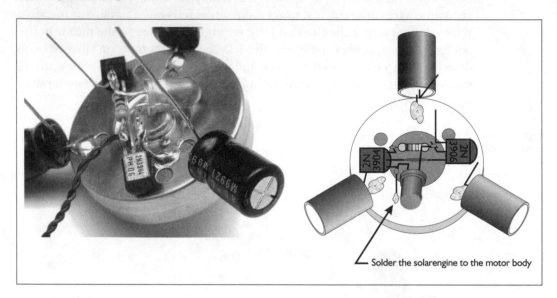

Solder the solarengine to the motor body

So let's recap: You've built a solarengine, attached it to the motor, and soldered three or four capacitors to the motor body. The next step is to finish making the electrical connections between all the "+" sides of the capacitors with a wire loop. This is called wiring the capacitors in *parallel*, which is connecting all the "+" leads together and all the "−" leads together to effectively make one big capacitor. If you have three 1000μF capacitors wired in parallel, they act as one big 3000μF capacitor.

This wire loop does more than just *electrically connect* the capacitors. It also acts as a bump-ring for the robot. When it bumps into something higher than the capacitor, it tips the Symet onto a new side, which makes it zoom off in a new direction.

Form the loop into as nice as a round ring as you can. Be patient, and massage it into a loop with your fingertips, and you'll be surprised how round you can make it. This task will be especially easy if you're the type of person who regularly mangles paper clips while talking on the telephone.

The next solder connection to make is from the left lead (the emitter) of the 2N3906/PN2907 transistor to the same ring that the capacitor "+" legs all share.

Figure 7-13
Soldering all the capacitor "+" leads *and* the left (emitter) lead of the 2N3906/PN2907 transistor to the metal ring

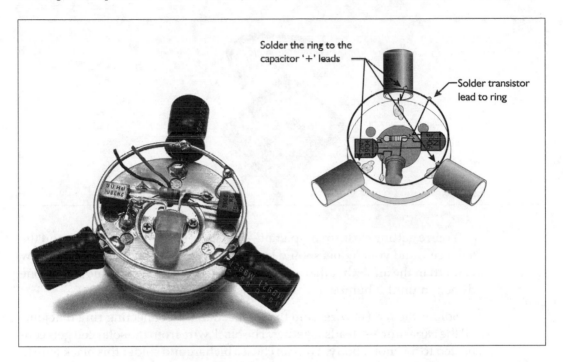

Solder short lengths of wire to the solar cell, one to each pad. If possible, use the common practice of using a red wire for positive (+) and a black wire for negative (−). Many, many years of research have shown that red wires conduct electricity best when attached to the positive terminal. If you don't have red wire, use the next-brightest color—it won't be as good as red wire, but it'll do.

If you just read that last paragraph and wondered "Well, where do I have some *red* wire?" don't worry about it—we're pulling your leg. Color-coding your wiring is simply a good way to identify what wire carries what sort of signal. Red and black are usually reserved for power wires.

Make *absolutely sure* you glue the wires down to the back of the solar cell after you're done soldering them on. The connections to the solar cell are usually quite fragile and will rip right off if an ant trips over them. Well, they're not *that* fragile, but still, the connections are weak enough you should make sure to glue the wire down after soldering. Use hot glue, or even tape, but use something to secure the wires down. It's a good procedure to follow on any solar cell.

Figure 7-14
Soldering and gluing wires to the solar cell

You're getting close to completion—just have to connect the motor and the solar cell, and your Symet should leap to life, do a song and dance, and throw confetti in the air. Either that, or it should occasionally twitch, moving in one direction until it bumps into something.

Solder the red (+) wire from the solar cell to the connecting ring that joins all the capacitor "+" leads together. The black wire from the solar cell gets connected to the motor body. You can cheat a bit here and solder this black wire to one of the same spots you did earlier for the capacitor "−" connections.

Figure 7-15
Soldering the solar cell to the Symet

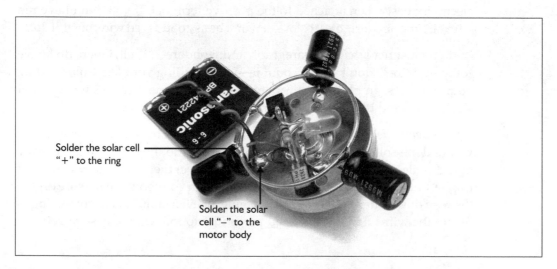

Solder the solar cell "+" to the ring

Solder the solar cell "−" to the motor body

One of the motor wires gets soldered to the left lead (collector) of the 2N3904/PN2222 transistor, and the other wire gets soldered to the capacitor connecting ring. It doesn't matter much which wire connects where, as it only will change the direction of motor rotation, and since this is a *symmetrical* robot, it doesn't have any effect on how the Symet moves.

Figure 7-16
Soldering the motor wire connections

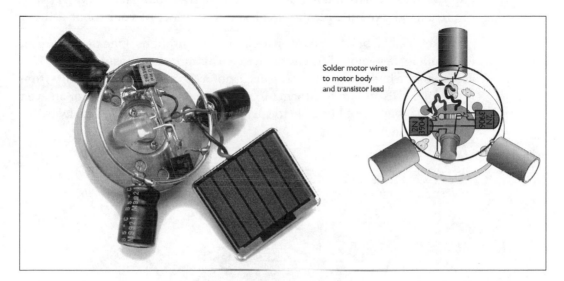

If your Symet twitches after lying in the light for a few seconds, you're ready to hot-glue the solar cell down to the top of the solarengine circuit. If it isn't...well, it's time to go back to the troubleshooting section to see what could be the problem. With "freeform" circuits, you run the risk of making accidental electrical connections because there are so many bare wires close together. Make sure you don't smoosh wires or component leads together accidentally!

Care and Feeding of Your Symet

Like most solar-powered BEAM critters, it's best kept in a pen with a hard, flat surface and walls high enough to keep it contained. Symets are cool little devices that love to ricochet around their environment, so they make great self-mobile plants for any robot display area.

If you find that your Symet isn't quite tipping over enough to keep it out of trouble, try adding a second, larger ring (it doesn't have to replace the one you already soldered in to the capacitors), and add a plastic sleeve to the motor shaft to add traction. At your local electronics outlet, you'll find neat material called *heat-shrink tubing* that once heated, shrinks down in size. This stuff is *ideal* for making friction sleeves on motors. In a pinch, cut a 1/4-inch slice of pencil eraser and press it on the motor shaft as a friction wheel. Another technique is to use a blob of hot glue on the end of the motor shaft. It works well but tends to leave little plastic streaks on the surface of your robot pen.

Symets can be built in many sizes and configurations. One of the largest ever built is "Behemoth," by Grant McKee. This monster measures 14cm (5.5") across, uses a high-quality cassette deck motor, is powered by 16.5 volts from three solar cells and travels 15cm (6") in a burst. McKee has plans for an even bigger one that should be able to survive outdoors in a grassy backyard!

Figure 7-17
"Behemoth," the monster Symet by Grant McKee

Another interesting Symet was built at a BEAM workshop in 2002 by Adam and Zachary Aronson. This Symet fits inside a computer mouse body, and has four coaster wheels on the bottom. By having the drive motor in the middle pointing straight down and two coaster wheels on each side, this Symet can move forward and backward. The paper clip on each end of the mouse is designed to tilt the Symet to its other side, making it scurry away from whatever hit the paper clip.

Figure 7-18
The Aronson mouse Symet

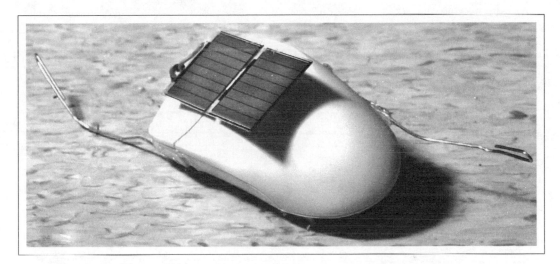

Experiment with your devices—since you built it, you're the best person to make modifications!

Chapter 8

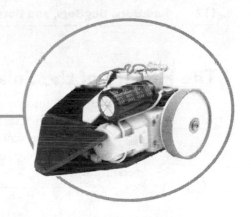

Project 2: The Solaroller: BEAM-Style Drag Racer

The History of the Solaroller

Dig waaay back into your memory and tell me what was the first competition you were ever in. Betcha it was a foot-race, when you were about 4. And when you had balance, did you have bicycle races? When your parents let you borrow the car when you were 16, you'd occasionally test the accelerator pedal from a green light, right?

The first BEAM robotics competition was Solaroller racing, as it was a way for competitors to have a simple platform to see who could build the best electronics and mechanics. In the early 1990s, it took over 15 minutes for one of these solar-powered dragsters to travel a meter (3.3 feet), but the winning time at the 2002 games was under 12 seconds! Competition encourages development of technology, and all the advances in making a Solaroller go faster were also used in the creation of many, *many* other BEAM devices.

Figure 8-1
Solaroller racing

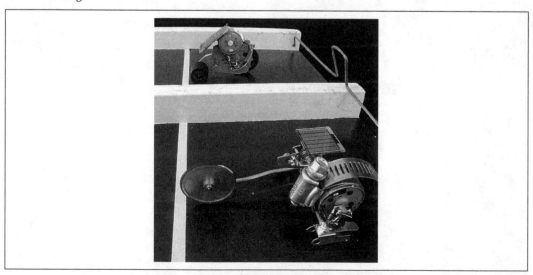

The Horsepower Under the Hood:
The Miller Solarengine

With any good race car, you start with the engine under the hood. With this Solaroller, we'll use a different type of solarengine than we used with the Symet. The Miller solarengine (aka the "Millerengine") was developed by Andrew Miller, one of the first serious BEAM-style roboticists. At the heart of the Millerengine is the "1381 voltage detector," which is a simple little device resembling a transistor that watches for a voltage to hit a particular level before sending out a signal.

The 1381 is a "watchdog" device, which means it's supposed to be installed in a battery-powered electronic device (like a cell phone) and watch the battery. When the battery can't run the electronics properly anymore, the 1381 tells the device to shut down. In the case of the Millerengine, we use it in a reverse function—it watches the power being stored up in the main power storage capacitor, and when that hits a preset level, it tells the circuit to activate and dump the power out. Figure 8-2 shows the complete schematic for the Solaroller.

Figure 8-2
The Millerengine schematic

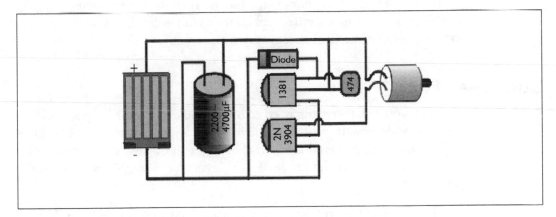

The Millerengine is a voltage-based solarengine, just like the previous FLED solarengine, but with a few differences. By design, the 1381 is a *very* power-efficient device, drawing 1/100 the power of a FLED. This means it will charge quicker than a FLED solarengine and run in much lower light levels because more power goes to be stored than is used up by the voltage-measuring circuitry. The other main difference between the two solarengines is in how they stay on. The FLED solarengine is designed to turn on, and stay on until all the power is gone. The Millerengine uses a little timer circuit to determine how long to stay on. This means you can configure it to run in many short pulses, or a single long pulse, just like a FLED solarengine. You'll most likely run your Millerengine in "long pulse" configuration, unless if you have a supercap as your power storage capacitor.

Solaroller Behavior

There's nothing too bizarre about a Solaroller's behavior—you give it light, and it scoots forward. With a 4700µF capacitor, you can expect a reasonably well-built Solaroller to move in 5–15 mm bursts (1/4" to 1/2") every few seconds, especially if you've got a decent solar cell powering it.

If you're a patient sort of person, get a hold of a supercap and wait for the action. A 0.33F capacitor on a Solarbotics SolarSpeeder Solaroller takes around two minutes to charge up, but then it zooms two–three meters (6.6–10 feet)! If you use a similar capacitor on your Solaroller, you'll get much more impressive bursts of energy.

Solaroller Parts

Although you can, there's no need to build a Solaroller out of space-quality solar cells and ultra-efficient motors. Your friendly solarengine circuit will let you build a solar-powered race car that will run off less-than-stellar solar cells, and in a much wider range of light levels too! Key things to be on the prowl for are:

- ❏ 1 × Dead tape-transport mechanism. That means something like a cassette deck, which will (most likely) have a decent motor and pulley, and two or three wheels we can salvage. We'll use a dead portable cassette player and a pinch roller from an old VCR with this Solaroller. Keep the other dead parts handy for structural materials.

❏   **1 ×** 2N39042N3904 or PN2222 transistor.

❏   **1 ×** 1381 trigger. This part won't be that easy to find, as *most* devices that use them use the ultra-tiny versions that aren't much bigger than the head of a pin. You may have to order one from Digikey (part MN1381-C-ND) or Solarbotics (part 1381C). You may get lucky and find a similar part from another manufacturer: Telcom's TC54VN20 looks the same and does the same thing as the Panasonic 1381-C. For your information, the "C" and "E" designations are indicators of the preset voltage level these devices are set to look for. A "C" trigger is set to activate at between 2.0 and 2.2 volts, whereas an "E" trigger is set for 2.4–2.6 volts. Make sure your solar cell can exceed the 1381 trigger point by about 0.5–1.0 volts; otherwise, it will simply sit there doing nothing but getting a suntan. Since *this* Solaroller will use a 5.5-volt solar cell, we know a 1381-S (4.8 V trigger) will be suitable, but to be safe, you might want to start with the lower voltage–triggering 1381-C or -E. Check the technical appendix for a full set of 1381 values.

❏   **1 ×** Storage capacitor. Minimum 4700µF, because it will need a fair bit of stored energy to get the whole thing moving.

❏   **1 ×** 0.47µF timer capacitor (labeled "474"). This is the capacitor that sets how long the Millerengine activates for. The bigger it is, the longer it stays on, dumping power from the power storage capacitor. Good values to try are between 0.47µF and 47µF.

❏   **1 ×** Signal diode (usually a 1N914). This is the most common type of diode you'll find in practically all electronic devices. Look for a small, glass cylinder with the black stripe.

❏   Duct tape, pop-rivets, chewing gum—any method of attaching two things together into one. Glue and epoxy are a bit odd, but they've been known to work.

Figure 8-3
Solaroller parts, ready for assembly

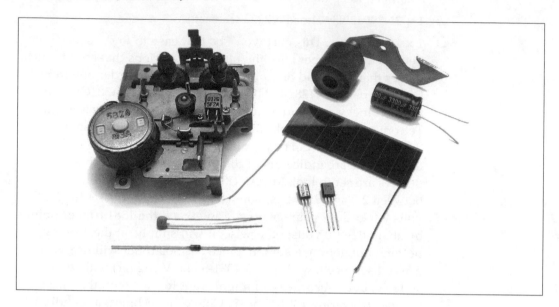

Just as with the Symet project, it's a good idea to actually breadboard the parts you'll use to *make sure* that everything is going to work. Nothing is more frustrating than to spend hours soldering something together just to find out that you were using a dead motor or bad capacitor. Spend ten minutes, breadboard the circuit, and shine a light on it. If you're not getting any action out of the motor, time to practice your troubleshooting skills.

Figure 8-4
Millerengine
on the testing
breadboard

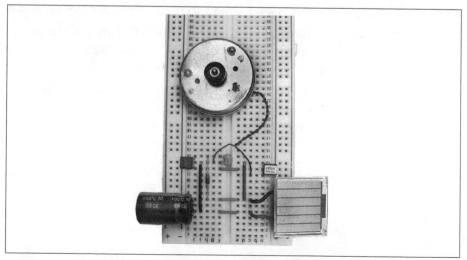

The Robot Geek Says

Troubleshooting Your Millerengine

✖ The Millerengine is one of the simplest, most robust solarengines around. There's not much to go wrong with it, so the first thing to do is to *recheck* your connections to make sure the components are correctly wired, and in the right way around.

✖ If you're not using a breadboard, check your solder connections! A simple reheat and a bit of solder fixes the vast majority of bad circuits we've seen! A good test is to go to each component, give it a firm but gentle wiggle, and watch the solder joint. If the leg moves or pulls out of the solder joint, it's the culprit!

✖ If your motor is going in very short bursts, the timer capacitor may be too small. Try different capacitor values between $0.47\mu F$ and $47\mu F$.

✖ Can your solar cell generate enough voltage? Are you *sure?* A 1381-C trigger makes the Millerengine activate at near 2.51 volts, so your solar cell *must* be able to reach this voltage. The best test is to check the unloaded voltage (*not* connected to any circuit) with a multimeter, and aim for 3 volts from your solar cell.

✖ Can your solar cell generate enough current? Use your multimeter's "current" function to measure how much current the solar cell can generate. Under pretty strong light, you should be getting *at least* 2 or 3 milliamperes (mA).

✖ If you're measuring the voltage on your power storage capacitor and you watch it go from trigger voltage (2.51 volts for a 1381-C trigger) to 0.6 volts and the motor does *nothing*, your transistor may be in backward. Or you are using a very inefficient motor, in which case you can try adding more power storage capacitors or go shopping for a new motor.

✖ To test your Millerengine *without* a motor, simply put an LED where you would put the motor. The LED leg nearest the flat spot on the collar goes to the transistor, and the other (longer) leg goes to the power storage capacitor positive (+). If the Millerengine was properly assembled, you'll see a blink when it activates.

✖ If your solar cell passes the above tests but you're not charging up your power storage capacitor above 1.2 volts, you may have the capacitor installed backward.

✖ Still not working? We'll say it again: Make *sure* your components are in the right way around, and that your solder connections are secure.

Building It!

Before we get too far into the actual electronic construction of your Solaroller, I'd like to remind you that *you don't have to use a Millerengine* to build your Solaroller. The Millerengine is pretty much the simplest, most effective solarengine design to date, but it does use the harder-to-get 1381 trigger. If you have trouble finding the 1381, you're more than welcome to use a flashing LED engine like the one you used on the Symet (hey, even totally borrow it from the Symet). If you're interested in tackling a different type of solarengine and have the necessary parts, continue on. If you're going to use a FLED solarengine, just skip ahead to step 8, the mechanical construction of the Solaroller.

First make note of what type of 1381 it is, and scratch it onto the bottom or backside of the 1381 itself, as we'll glue the 2N3904/PN2222 transistor to it face-to-face (Figure 8-5). When somebody comes up to you and asks what parts you used to build it, you can check the flavor of 1381 by checking for the scratch (Figure 8-6). You may have noticed that the 1381 (which is rated to send a signal between 2.0 and 2.2 volts) makes the Millerengine activate at 2.51 volts. It's the nature of the circuit to activate at whatever the 1381 trigger voltage is *plus* about 0.5 volts. Keep that in mind when selecting a 1381 for your Millerengine.

Glue the 1381 and transistor together, making a neat little bundle. Don't worry about figuring out which one is which later—see how the 1381 *looks* like a transistor but is actually bigger? That's how to tell them apart during construction. Don't mix them up!

Figure 8-5
The 1381 and the transistor, smoochy-faced together

Figure 8-6
The larger one with the *S* is a 1381-S trigger.

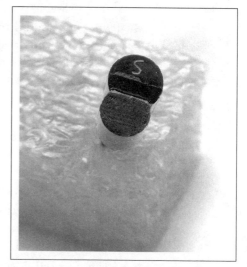

Although this method of solarengine assembly is fairly easy, it isn't that simple to describe, so we'll heavily depend on the photographs to illustrate the procedure, okay? Remember that the larger of the two is the 1381 trigger, and you'll do fine. In this step, we bend the right lead of the transistor out to the side, and we fold the right lead of the 1381 in toward the middle pin of the transistor, so that they can be soldered together. After soldering, trim that long middle leg of the transistor down to the solder joint.

Figure 8-7
Preparing to
solder the
transistor to
the 1381

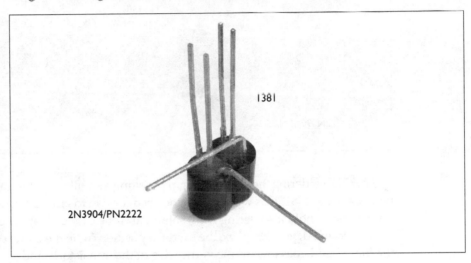

Solder together the legs you just folded near each other, and trim off the excess leads so you have a nice and tidy connection.

Figure 8-8
Soldering and
clipping off
the legs

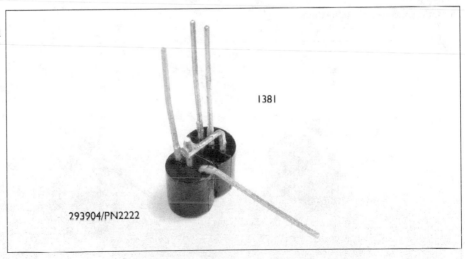

Next we'll get ready to solder on the diode by bending back the remaining two legs of the 1381 trigger.

Figure 8-9
Bending back
the 1381 leads

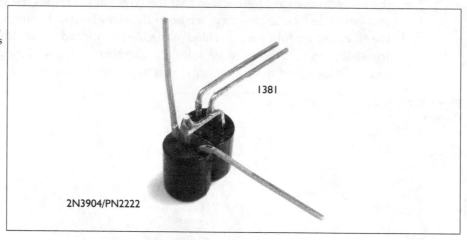

To make soldering the diode easier, try melting a small blob of solder to the far bent leg of the 1381. This will remove the need for you to grow a third arm out of your chest to hold a soldering iron, solder, and the diode all at once. Once the lead is blobified, you can place the diode in position (note the diode orientation: the black band goes toward the vertical leg of the transistor!), and simple remelt the blob to make the connection. Once that end is held in place, solder the black band (the "cathode") side of the diode to the far vertical leg of the transistor.

Figure 8-10
Preparing and soldering the diode

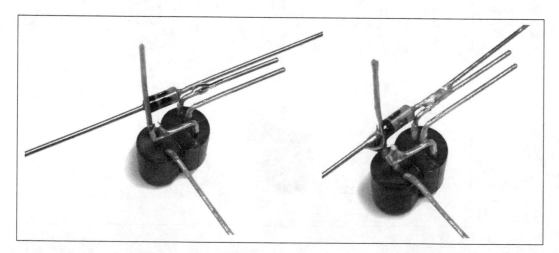

After soldering the diode in place, clean it up a bit by trimming down the leads. Snip off most of the diode leg from the black-band side, as well as the extra little bit from the 1381 on the other side.

Figure 8-11
Cleaning up the soldering of the diode with a few well-placed snips

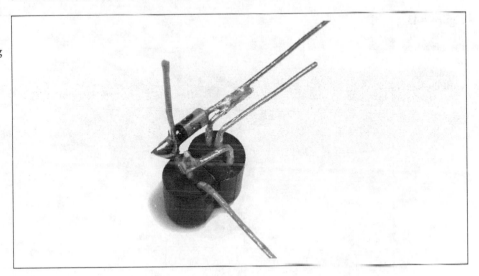

Now to solder on the final component of the core Millerengine circuit, in our case, the 6.8µF capacitor. When a capacitor gets larger than 1.0µF, it *may* have polarity, which means it has to go in the right way. We solder in our 6.8µF capacitor with the "+" mark soldered to the middle leg of the 1381 trigger.

Figure 8-12
Installing the discharge timer capacitor

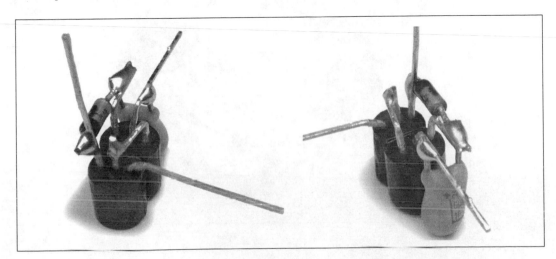

After you trim up the excess leg from the capacitor on the far solder joint with the 1381, you're ready to attach your Millerengine to a power storage capacitor and get to work on the main body of the Solaroller!

Figure 8-13
Cleaning up the capacitor solder connection with the snips

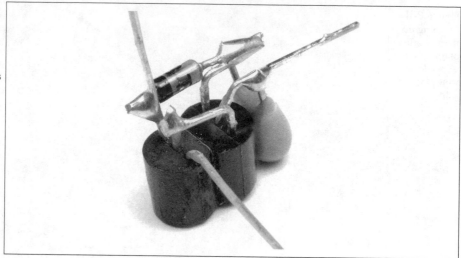

Before we solder a main power storage capacitor to the Solaroller, let's assemble the body so that we can find the best place to put the whole circuit. This particular Solaroller is built from the tape-transport roller from a VHS VCR, along with the motor and flywheel from a cassette deck.

Figure 8-14
The raw body components of our Solaroller

We're lucky with these components—we only need two halves to join up. The front roller is wide enough to keep the Solaroller from falling over, so we don't need a third "outrigger" wheel to keep it balanced. The trick is to figure out a way to connect them together. Our options include (but are not limited to) superglue, epoxy, solder, rivets, nuts and bolts, screws, hot glue, and chewing gum. I recommend avoiding the last two options, as they both tend to melt when exposed to the intense heat of halogen lamps during Solaroller competitions. It ain't a pretty sight watching a Solaroller slowly coming unglued and reglued to the track in the middle of a race, but it sure is funny if it isn't *your* Solaroller!

In this particular instance, we used solder. If your soldering iron can put out sufficient heat (like the big pistol-grip types), solder will most likely be the first method you should try. Remember to scuff/sand/file the gray surface of the metal so that you solder to the bright shiny stuff underneath. The gray stuff is the *oxide*, which is not very easy to solder to. Notice that since the motor drives the flywheel with a rubber belt, we're using the belt as a tire for traction too. Make sure that your Solaroller stands upright (that means *not* lying on its side like a dead fish) when you finish this step. The more stable it is now, the easier it will be to mount the rest of the stuff later.

Figure 8-15
Soldering the two halves of our Solaroller together

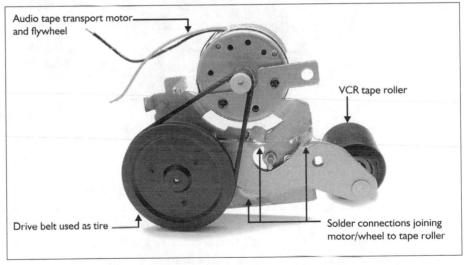

Audio tape transport motor and flywheel

VCR tape roller

Drive belt used as tire

Solder connections joining motor/wheel to tape roller

Get your power storage capacitor(s), as we're going to mount them to the Solaroller frame. Use glue, zip-ties, twist-ties, or whatever means handy to attach the capacitor in place, but if you have a metal framework (like with this project), you can solder it on and use the frame as both a mechanical *and* an electrical connection. For this Solaroller, we're going to use a 0.047F "Tokin" brand 5.5 V memory backup supercap we had on hand. A 0.047F capacitor is literally 47,000μF, the same as ten regular 4700μF capacitors, so this Solaroller will take a while to charge up, but it will shoot several inches instead of only the 1/4 to 1/2 inch it would do on a single 4700μF capacitor.

Solder the negative side of the capacitor (the side with the stripe, remember?) to the frame, using the scuff'n'solder technique we've used before. If your parts *aren't* metal, don't fret. You don't *have* to use the frame as part of the electrical connections—we did so mainly because it made for more secure mounting.

Figure 8-16
Mounting the power storage capacitor to the Solaroller frame

Power storage capacitator's "–" lead folded over and soldered to the frame

The Millerengine, being the compact little circuit that it is, gets mounted directly on top of the power storage capacitor. Don't worry too much about the extra leads poking out and about—we'll fix that in a second. Start by soldering the *middle* leg of the 1381 to the positive lead of the power storage capacitor, and then trim off the excess. Then solder the transistor leg with the diode to the power storage capacitor's "–" lead (or the frame—remember we already made the frame the same as the capacitor's "–" lead by soldering to it).

Figure 8-17
Soldering the solarengine circuit to the power storage capacitor

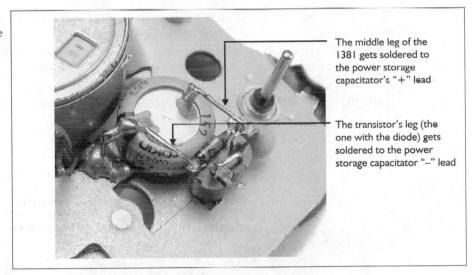

The middle leg of the 1381 gets soldered to the power storage capacitor's "+" lead

The transistor's leg (the one with the diode) gets soldered to the power storage capacitor "–" lead

Let's mount the solar cell. First prepare it by soldering on sufficiently long red (+) and black (–) wires to the pads on the back of the solar cell, then *glue them down*. As mentioned in the Symet chapter, these solar cell solder pads are fairly fragile, so we isolate them from any tugging by gluing the whole wire down across the backside. Next, we mount the solar cell on the motor with a bit of double-sided sticky tape, and we run the wires down the side of the Solaroller to near the solarengine circuit.

Figure 8-18
Mounting the solar cell

Take the solar cell positive (+) wire and solder it to the power storage ca-pacitor's positive (+) lead. Then (surprisingly enough) solder the solar cell negative (–) wire to the power storage capacitor's negative (–) lead. Remember that since we soldered the power storage capacitor to the metal frame, you could have soldered the negative wire to *anywhere* on the metal frame and made the same electrical connection as soldering it directly to the capacitor itself. Treat the big metal frame as one big wire.

Figure 8-19
Soldering the solar cell wires to the power storage capacitor

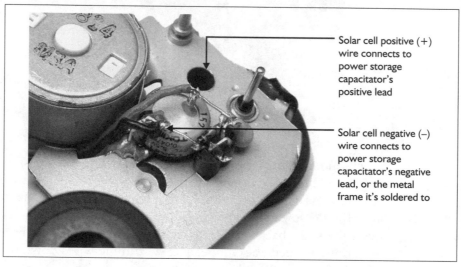

Solar cell positive (+) wire connects to power storage capacitor's positive lead

Solar cell negative (–) wire connects to power storage capacitator's negative lead, or the metal frame it's soldered to

You're almost finished—hold on! Next we're going to solder the wires from the motor to the solarengine circuit. Just as with the Symet, it really does-n't matter which wire gets soldered where, but it *will* affect the direction your Solaroller travels. If after you've put it together and it *seems* to be going in re-verse to you, simply swap the motor connection wires, and it will be going in the direction you consider forward.

Take one of the motor wires (assuming you have wires on your motor—if you don't, solder some on!), and solder it to the positive (+) leg of the power storage capacitor. The other motor wire gets connected to that last lonely leg poking out of your solarengine circuit, that being the *only* leg on the transistor that isn't attached to anything. After soldering, trim up any leads that may be poking out.

Figure 8-20
The final step:
Soldering on
the motor
wires

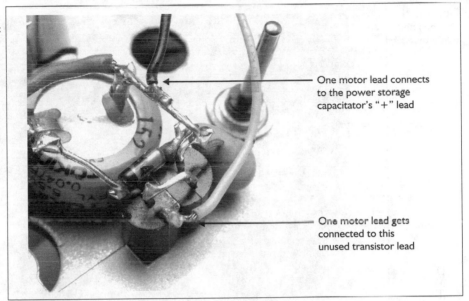

One motor lead connects
to the power storage
capacitator's "+" lead

One motor lead gets
connected to this
unused transistor lead

Hopefully, your circuitry went together well, and now your Solaroller is complete! If you put it into direct sunlight and you *don't* get any action out of it, it's time to revisit the troubleshooting section at the beginning of this chapter. If you breadboarded it first, you *know* your components are good, so there must be a bad connection somewhere.

Now that it's working, you may have to tune it a bit more. Solarollers must be able to travel a straight line, so if it's traveling in a curve, you have some wheel-bending to do. Another tuning tip is to watch how the light falls on the solar cell. You may want to have your solar cell mounted on some flexible wire so that you can better aim it at the light source. Another tuning tip is to watch the drive wheel when it pulses. If it's slipping, you're wasting power! Try moving the solarengine components around to put more weight on the drive wheel, or even try adding weight to see if you can get more traction. The increase in power passed from the wheel to the ground may make it worthwhile to put more weight on your Solaroller. Get out the stopwatch, and take some accurate time measurements to see what modifications work the best!

Figure 8-21
Finished and
ready to race!

Although we've built literally *dozens* of Solarollers out of scrap parts over the years, we thought we'd include this sample of another prototype we did for this book. Mechanically, this Solaroller uses a brass flywheel and motor from a microcassette mechanism, a length of 1/8" brass rod, a 1/8" retaining collar (an excellent part found at most hobby stores) a hose clamp, and a pair of salvaged pinch rollers. Electronically, it uses a Millerengine circuit with a 1381-G trigger and a 0.47μF timer capacitor on a 4700μF power storage capacitor, all powered by a Solarbotics SC2422 solar cell. Side-by-side, the project Solaroller out-classes this one mainly because of its 0.047F power storage capacitor, as motors use up the most power right when they start up. The fewer times it has to start up per run, the less energy wasted. This is another case of the long-charge tortoise kicking the quick-burst rabbit's butt every time.

Figure 8-22
Solaroller Beta 1

 The Robot Geek Says

Solarollers

✖ You don't *have* to use a Millerengine for your Solaroller. Use a FLED solarengine if you wish, or put a Millerengine into your Symet. Be creative!

✖ Make your Solaroller *light*. Less mass to move = *faster!* Use lightweight materials such as Balsa wood and plastic to build competition-grade Solarollers.

✖ Try to make it go in one long burst rather than many short bursts. Motors waste the most power the instant they start up, so you'll go farther with one start-up burst with a long run. Many short bursts mean many start-up bursts that waste power.

✖ Don't try to pile on too many capacitors in an attempt to get a good, long energy burst. More capacitors mean more weight, which can actually make your Solaroller perform *worse*. Experimentation will tell you what the best solution for your design is.

✖ Use nice, *smooth-running* wheels for your Solaroller. Flick a wheel with your finger—if it spins for quite a while, it has nice, energy-conserving bearings.

✖ Planning to compete with your Solaroller? Official Solaroller rules say it has to fit in a 6" cube, run from a single solar cell no larger than 1.25 square inches, and have shorting wires built-in so that it starts with *zero* stored energy. Check out the full rules at http://www.robotgames.com.

Care and Feeding of Your Solaroller

Being a device with a single intention in mind ("Go straight ahead, fast!"), a Solaroller isn't something you want to leave unattended. Deceleration trauma (informally know as "fall off shelf, go boom!") has killed more solarollers than all other causes combined. Either store it so it can't move, or put it in a well-shaded box. Better yet, stick it in a robot playpen with your Symet.

Solarollers will probably be your first experience with the effect of sunlight on rubber. Rubber wheels and belts will degrade much more rapidly than if they're left in the shade. Don't be surprised if you have to replace a split wheel or belt a year or two after you've finished your device, especially if you do what we do and keep our robots on display all year-round.

Surprisingly, low-power, efficient mechanics are easily gummed up by lubricants! Although of immense use in more powerful mechanical systems, most lubricating oils and greases are too *viscous* (stiff) to help a Solaroller run better. If you think you need to lubricate a bearing, use only a little light-grade sewing-machine oil or graphite powder. Dust sticks to oil, and can turn your finely tuned machine into a gummed-up slowpoke!

Chapter 9

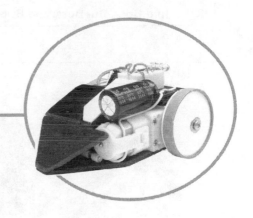

Project 3: The Herbie Photovore

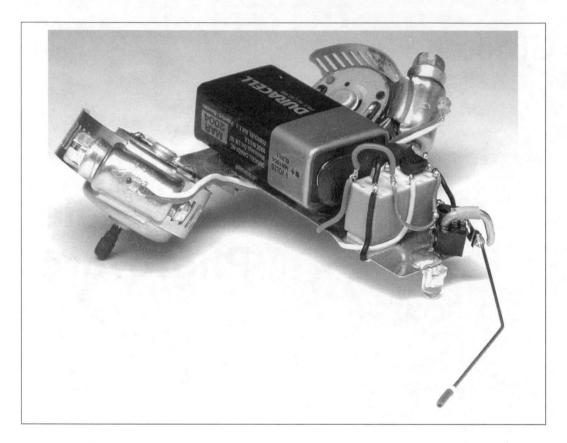

Parts List

- ❏ **2** × **Motors**
- ❏ **1** × LM386 audio operational amplifier
- ❏ **2** × Light sensors
- ❏ **1** × 9-volt battery and battery connector
- ❏ **1** × Power switch
- ❏ **2** × Hose clamps
- ❏ Herbie body material

Optional Parts for Backup Behavior

- ❏ **1** × Double-pole, double-throw relay

❑ **1** × Touch switch

❑ **1** × 2N3904 or PN2222 transistor

❑ **1** × 10kΩ resistor

❑ **1** × 10µF capacitor

The Herbie Light-Following Robot

Herbie isn't a robot we came up with—Randy Sargent is to credit for this little dude. Although he doesn't call it a BEAM robot, we think that the sheer genius of hacking a chip designed to power a speaker into a light-following robot easily qualifies it as an honorable BEAM robot of the first order. The original Herbie is a *very* simple robot that can only run forward and chase light. We'll be adding a second layer of ability to it by giving it the ability to back up if it bumps into something, which *greatly* increases how well it does in the real world. Think about it—how well could you do if you couldn't walk backward?

We call light-seeking robots "photovores" from the combination of the Greek word "photo" (light) and the Latin "vore" (to swallow up). It's a convenient term to describe a robot that "eats light." Light-seeking behavior isn't of too much importance to a battery-powered robot, but a solar-powered robot depends on this behavior to keep it alive. Light sensors are among the cheapest and most reliable parts available to the robotics community, and thus, light sensitivity is usually one of the first senses added to a robot. It's easy to demonstrate, it makes for some neat behavior, and until there is a good chocolate-detecting sensor on the market, light-chasing is as good as a behavior as any other to start with.

The idea behind the Herbie is this: Take a small, simple chip designed to amplify the signal from an answering machine, modem, or speakerphone and trick it into reading two light sensors and making a robot follow a line or a light. And with almost no extra parts. It's practically that simple. Randy originally built it as an entry to the "Line Follower" competition held at the Seattle Robotics Society Robothon in 1996 (http://www.seattlerobotics.org). Although it ended up in last place, it did impress all that saw it because of its bare-bones nature.

The simplicity and effectiveness of the Herbie has gained the admiration of quite a few roboticists, particularly those active in BEAM. A simple search on the Internet will show up a good many variations of the Herbie robot, with different added-on capabilities. Some designers have added solar power to it, converting the circuit to run a robot head, and others have added touch sensors so that it runs away from obstacles. Our version here is essentially like Randy's original, with the added option of a single "panic" touch sensor that makes it run away from light for a while.

Powering the Herbie

Unlike our previous two projects, *this* robot is battery powered, so there's no need to build a solar engine circuit. We'll be able to use a plain and simple 9-volt battery. Feed that to the chip and eye circuitry, hook up a pair of motors, and that's practically it! With a few extra parts, you can endow Herbie with a "run away" mode!

Herbie Behavior

The heart of Herbie is something called a "LM386 audio operational amplifier," which really means "a chip that's designed to compare two audio signals and amplify the difference between them." Being designed to power a speaker means the chip has quite a bit of power behind it—enough to drive a motor or two. Amplifying a difference is an excellent way of reading input from light sensors, as it doesn't matter if it's dark or very bright out. As long as there is a difference between the sensors, *that's* what counts. The Herbie circuit is pretty good at using almost any type of light sensor, like photodiodes, phototransistors, photoresistors, and even just plain old Infrared LEDs that *aren't designed* to sense light.

The circuit is pretty straightforward. We start by wiring two light sensors back-to-back, either by connecting both sensor's "-" leads together, or both sensor's "+" leads together—it doesn't matter which. The remaining lead from one sensor runs to the positive input of the LM386, and the remaining lead from the other sensor runs to the negative input of the LM386. The chip then compares these two inputs and tries to make them the same size. It does this by shifting the power output of the chip, which we use to steer the motors. When the motors aim the sensors so that they're both generating the same amount of signal, the LM386 puts out equal power to each motor, driving it in a straight line.

Figure 9-1
Randy
Sargent's
original
Herbie
circuit

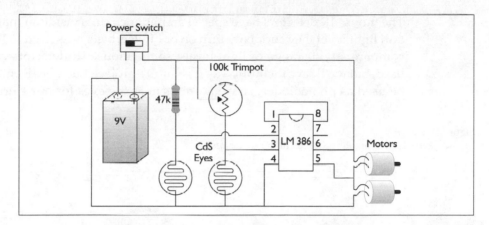

You'll notice the additional component called a "trimming potentiometer" (a "trimpot"). Because it's almost impossible to make two electronic devices *exactly* alike, you have to be able to tune out the minor differences in them. Even if our two light sensors were made one after the other out of the machine, out of the same batch of goop, and treated exactly alike all the way to your workbench, they would *still* have some tiny differences between them. The trimpot lets you balance out the differences so that your Herbie will have sensors that are equally sensitive. Of course, there's always the *easy* way out (we like easy)—simply tweak one eye a bit farther forward than the other to even out their inconsistencies.

The original Herbie used *photoresistors*, or *cadmium-sulfide (CdS)* cells to read light levels. These are commonly found in night lights and other automatic light dimmers and are available in stores like (can you guess?) Radio Shack and Future-Active. The Herbie we'll be building will use the infrared light (IR) emitters stripped from an old computer mouse. We searched a real mouse first, but ended up getting nasty little rodent-bites....

Every mouse with a ball uses four sets of IR emitters and detectors, one pair for each direction of movement (up, down, left, right). When you take your mouse apart, you'll see them mounted as a pair straddling the slotted wheel that gets turned by the ball. One member of the pair emits infrared light, and the other one detects it. When the slotted wheel passes between them, it generates pulses that are turned into the cursor-moving motion on your screen.

The mouse IR detectors have special amplifier circuits inside so that at a certain light level they suddenly turn on or off. Herbie's eyes need to be able to compare a wide range of light levels, so the mouse IR detectors cannot be used, but we'll save them anyway for a future project. Luckily, IR emitters can be used as photodiodes, so we'll use them as the eyes for our Herbie.

Figure 9-2
Mouse internals showing the infrared emitter/detectors

Once you get them out, you'll have to identify which are which—the light-givers or the light-receivers. If you have a video camera or Webcam, simply point it at the part while powering it from a button-cell battery or two 1.5-volt AA batteries (= 3 volts) through a 220 ohm to 1k resistor. (You *need* the resistor when using a AA battery; otherwise, you'll burn out the part!) If you see the part light up like a bright-white dot, you've found the IR emitter. Most kinds of video equipment that use a "CCD imager" (an electronic chip for digitizing light) are sensitive to infrared light, so the LED (IR emitter) shows up like a bright white light. Remember, we're using the mouse's IR emitters as light sensors for this project.

For the record, we've found that *photodiodes* like the Solarbotics IR1 (Siemens BPW-34) are superb as Herbie-eyes, with photoresistors and IR transmitters and receivers just behind. But since we're going to stick to our "junkyard robot" methodology, we're going to build this one with the IR emitters we've pulled out of a dead computer mouse.

Figure 9-3
Various
light-sensitive
sensors (from
left to right: mouse
IR phototransistor;
IR emitter LED;
CdS photoresistor;
IR photodiode; and
IR round-dome
photodiode)

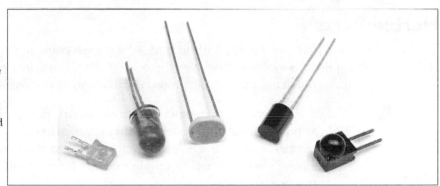

You can build your Herbie much the same way as Randy initially designed (but with our mouse eyes, see Figure 9-4), or you can expand on the design a bit by adding a switch, a relay, capacitor, a resistor, and a transistor. These components will swap around the motor connections and, when activated, make Herbie run away from light. Ideal behavior for getting a robot out of a sticky situation—run away and hide in the dark! It's your decision to build just a basic Herbie or to add in this extra behavior. We recommend scrounging up enough parts to build *both*—after all, the parts are practically free!

Figure 9-4
Herbie
schematic
("run away"
version)

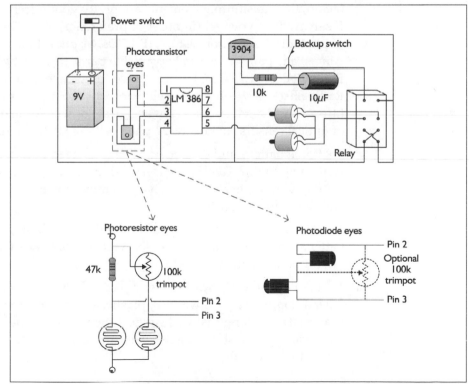

Herbie Parts

Herbie parts are not difficult to find. When push come to shove, practically everything is available from a well-stocked Radio Shack, but you'll find that it will be a much more satisfying project if you salvage your parts from junk.

❑ **2 ×** Motors. Again, something from battery-powered electronics would be ideal, but there are many inexpensive sources of suitable motors, such as the Solarbotics RM1. A gear motor will give slow, strong motion, whereas a plain ungeared motor will be very quick but not have any carpet-crossing ability.

❑ **1 ×** LM386 audio operational amplifier. This is most commonly found in any appliance with a small speaker, like an answering machine, dictation machine, or computer modem (what do you think makes that annoying "BLEEP-da-DING-KShhhhhh" sound so loud?). If you can't salvage it, you can find it at Future-Active (#LM386N-1, $3.49 for 4) or Radio Shack (#276-1731, $1.29/ea).

❑ **2 ×** Light sensors. You know you can get them from a computer mouse, but you also may want to check TV/VCR remote controls (again, the transmitting elements are pretty good receivers too). If salvage fails you, get (in order of preference) a matching pair of photodiodes, photoresistors, IR LEDs, or phototransistors. Almost any pair will work. For suitable parts, try Solarbotics (IR1 Photodiodes, $1.25/ea), Future-Active (they have a variety), or Radio Shack (#276-1657 CdS cell, 5 for $2.49). Surplus store like http://www.allelectronics.com are great sources for many types of optical sensors (their PRE-22 photocell are $0.75 each).

❑ **1 ×** 9-volt battery and connector. Well, you need power from something, right? The Herbie *will* work on voltages down to 3.6 volts, but higher voltages give you more power, speed, and light sensitivity.

❑ **1 ×** Power switch. Unless if you're comfortable in using the 9-volt battery connector as a means to kill your Herbie, look for a simple on/off power switch.

❑ **1 ×** Body framework. You can use a piece of scrap metal sheet from a dead floppy drive (as we did), plastic, a hunk of cardboard—practically anything that will support the weight of the parts. Dry pasta can work, just don't get it wet (turns Herbie into Herbichinni Alfredo).

❏ **2 ×** Motor mounts. If you don't have a better solution, try using appropriately sized hose clamps. These automotive accessories are good at clamping hoses, but they are *superb* at clamping motors down to frames. In a pinch, you can try using twist ties, zip-ties, or even copper wire twisted around and around.

Optional Components for Reverse Behavior

Going in reverse is hard when you don't have a transmission with an "R" setting. The following parts add little to Herbie's size, but vastly increase Herbie's ability:

❏ **1 ×** 5V DPDT relay. You will most likely find one on a computer modem, or in some VCRs. The DPDT means "*d*ouble *p*ole, *d*ouble *t*hrow," which translates to an electrically powered switch that can switch two separate circuits at the same time and has two positions. We found ours on a internal modem for a computer, where its purpose was to transfer the telephone connections from the telephone to the modem electronics

Figure 9-5
Relays found on a computer internal modem

5 volt double-pole/double-throw relays

❏ **1** × Touch switch. Almost any kind of sensitive switch that doesn't take much effort to activate. If you have a dead computer floppy drive, look for a tiny pin switch, or use a tape-insertion signal switch from a portable tape deck. Look around—you'll find something suitable somewhere.

❏ **1** × 2N3904 or PN2222 transistor. You should be an expert at finding these by now.

❏ **1** × Resistor, in the 1kΩ to 20kΩ range. The bigger it is, the longer the Herbie will be in "run away" mode.

❏ **1** × Capacitor, in the 10μ to 100μF range. Again, the bigger it is, the longer Herbie will be running away from light when the touch sensor activates.

Figure 9-6
Herbie parts, in all their glory!

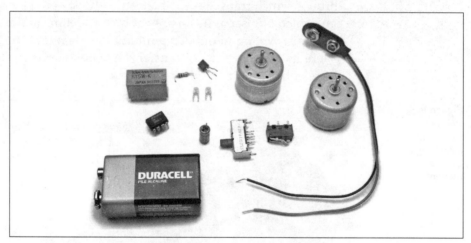

As per all of our past experiments, breadboarding up the circuit *first* is a good way to make sure all your parts will play nice with each other. Our experiments have shown that the most finicky parts have been the eyes, but even the worst of them have been good enough for our Herbie. Depending on the type of eye you've selected, pay attention to the way they're supposed to be hooked up. When you have them wired, you should be able to wave your hand over the sensors and see the motors twitch back and forth as the LM386 spins the motors in response to the changing light inputs. If you opted to build Herbie with the "run away" behavior, tapping the switch lines together should cause a "click" in the relay, which makes the motors reverse rotation for a few seconds, then "click" forward again.

Figure 9-7
Herbie on the breadboard, with and without the "run away" behavior

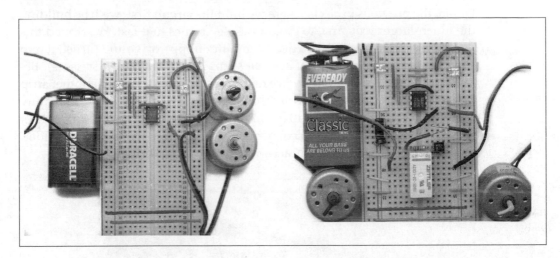

The Robot-Geek Says

Troubleshooting Your Breadboarded Herbie Circuit

✖ Only getting one motor to spin? The most likely cause is that you don't have enough power in the circuit. The Herbie circuit uses what's called a *split-power supply* to drive the motor. That means that a Herbie circuit given 9 volts will split it down the middle and try to give each motor 4.5 volts. If the voltage is too low, one motor will hog all the power, and only one motor will work. Keep the voltage to *at least* 3.6 volts (3 rechargeable batteries = 3.6 volts).

✖ Not getting very good reaction to the sensors? Generally, Herbie's eyes don't work too well in very low light levels, but anything at or above normal room lighting *should* be fine. Remember, there are several types of eye configurations to use, so you may want to experiment a bit with all the potential light sensors you have with different levels of light intensity.

✖ No action at all? QUICK—disconnect the battery! No action means one of two things: no power flowing, or *too much* (a short circuit—bad!). Double-check that your battery is good, the power switch connections are right, and you have the motors hooked up to the right pins on the chip. If these connections are right, you'll get *some sort* of motion, even if it's just one motor.

Building It!

Unlike the previous projects where we built the circuit first, we'll be building the much-larger *body* first, to mount the electronics to it last. We ripped this metal sheet from the back of a dead computer floppy drive and turned it into Herbie's body using a pair of *aviation shears* (big mama-sized scissors). Because the metal was a *bit* flimsy, we reinforced it by soldering on another strip underneath. Remember, this is *junk* robotics, and you're allowed to make any changes to your junk you want! If you can't cut your body from a single sheet as we did, cut two strips and connect them in a *T* arrangement with solder, glue, rivets, Bolivian snail extract—whatever works for you.

Figure 9-8
Cutting out the Herbie body

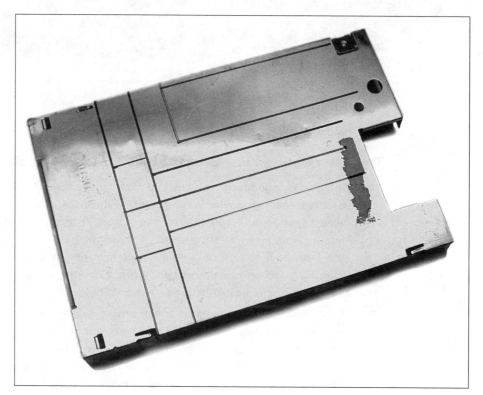

We have to bend the top part of the *T* down so that the motors (mounted with our friend, the hose clamp) can touch the surface. The idea is to arrange the motors so that the robot is touching the ground with *just* the tips of the motor shafts, and the bottom of the *T*. It's easy to mount the motors using hose clamps, which tighten down as you rotate the screw on the side.

Figure 9-9
Hose clamps make excellent motor mounts

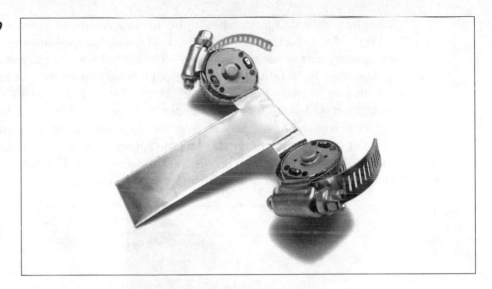

Next we'll attach the main power switch to the base. Usually we would do this later, but since the power switch we salvaged was a big one from a VCR, it is a good idea to do it now to make sure it fits on the robot. As the switch has a metal body, we solder it to the underside of the framework, between the motors. If your frame and switch aren't metal, pull out that Bolivian snail extract and glue it on.

Figure 9-10
Mounting the main power switch

A solidly mounted front wheel fights turning forces, so a caster wheel or skid is needed to let Herbie turn nimbly. Think about the last time you got a bum grocery cart at the supermarket—that's what we want to *avoid*. To the rescue comes the LED (light emitting diode)! Forget about using it to light up your life, we're using the hard plastic body of the LED as an inexpensive, low-friction skid-point for Herbie's nose. Simply desolder a nice, large LED from a piece of technoscrap, bend over the leads, and solder it to the nose of Herbie's body pointing down. If you can't solder it on because the body isn't metallic, snip the leads right off the LED and glue it on. The plastic used for LEDs glues particularly well with super glue or epoxy.

Figure 9-11
Herbie's nose;
a salvaged
LED

The battery is a pretty hefty component that should be installed next, so you can build the rest of Herbie around it. A *small* piece of double-sided sticky foam tape works very well, or you can get creative and build yourself a retaining clip so that you can easily remove the battery later for replacement/recharging. Try to mount the battery on top between the motors, as it will give the wheels the most traction and Herbie *great* maneuverability.

Figure 9-12
Mounting
the battery

We have a switch, and a battery—it seems natural to connect the two together! Let's grab the battery connector, snap it onto the battery, and solder the black wire to the metal body. This makes any electrical connection to the robot body the same as a wire to the battery's "−" terminal. If you're not building Herbie with a metal frame, leave the black wire hanging loose for now.

Connect the red wire to one of the end connections of the switch. We'll use the *middle* pin of the switch as the connection point for all the electronics needing a "+" (positive) connection. When we slide the switch to that position, it will connect the battery's "+" to the middle switch pin.

Figure 9-13
Adding the battery electrical connections

Time to play with Herbie's brains—the LM386. The first step is to wrap pins 1 and 8 across the top (or front) of the chip's body and solder them together. You remember how to identify the pins, right? With the chip "live bug" (pins down on the surface), start counting down from the top *left* corner, so the first pin is pin 1. When you get to the bottom of the row (pin 4), jump directly across to the *bottom* of the row on the right side (pin 5), and count upward to the top right corner (pin 8).

Connecting pins 1 and 8 together makes the chip ten times more sensitive to the input the eyes give them. This is a *good* thing. While we're at it, let's bend pin 7 over, as it isn't used at all in this circuit.

Figure 9-14
Connecting
the LM386
pins 1 and 8

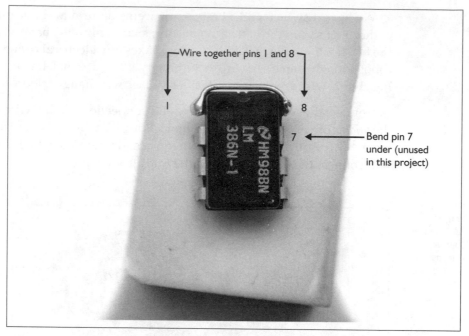

Before we do anything else, let's find a chunk of plastic or other nonmetallic material and glue it to the underside of the chip between the two rows of leads. We want to raise the chip off the surface of the metal body so that the other pins don't accidentally short out (not a problem if your Herbie body isn't metal).

Now that pins 1 and 8 are connected, let's mount Herbie's brains to the body. No need to call for Igor and stitch a tiny robot-skull closed, we'll simply use a bit o' solder and solder pin 4 to the robot body. Remember, we've already connected the battery's negative terminal to the body, so this connection is the same as connecting the pin to battery negative—useful to know if your robot body *isn't* metal. **Only** if your robot *doesn't* **have a metal body**, then glue that bad-boy LM386 down to the robot body and solder the dangling, black battery "–" wire to pin 4.

Figure 9-15
Attaching
the power
connections
to the
LM386's
pin 6

Please note that the steps with the relay and switch are necessary to perform only if you will be building a reversing Herbie.

The relay and the touch switch make up the bulk of the reverse circuit that makes Herbie "run away" when it bumps into something. The switch we are using has a definite "click" when activated, a metal lever we can solder a touch sensor extension to, and three connection posts. Most switches have the posts labeled with the letters "C," "N.O.," and "N.C." You'll find that the "C" terminal is a *common* terminal, which will pass a signal to the "N.O." (*normally open*) post when the switch closes. When the switch isn't being activated, it connects the common post to the "N.C." (*normally closed*) post. We want our switch to pass a signal only when it's activated, so if your switch doesn't have these markings, hook up your multimeter in resistance mode to the switch contact posts, and measure the resistance. Make note of the two posts that make the multimeter display go from "OL" (which means "nothing's connected" in multimeter-speak) to near "0" when you activate the switch. We'll need that information when we wire up the switch to the relay later.

This relay is like having two light switches side-by-side, with a bar connecting the switch levers. One flick, and you turn off (or on) two separate circuits at the same time. In our application, we're reversing the flow of power through the motors, so when the relay activates, it makes the Herbie kick into "run away" mode. We're using our familiar friend the 2N3904/PN2222 transistor as the finger that flicks that switch.

Some relays have a diagram printed right on them telling what each pin does. If you're unable to tell what pin does what, you'll have to get out your multimeter to do some pin testing. The first thing you want to find are the two pins that go to the little electromagnet on the inside of the relay that pulls the switches closed. The electromagnet coil is made from a long length of wire, so put your multimeter on the lowest "resistance" setting (the dial will probably be marked with something like "200") and check different combinations of pins, looking for the *highest* resistance. Our relay electromagnet coil reads about 120 ohms. When you find these pins, mark them as "relay coil."

Figure 9-16
Relay electromagnet coil identification

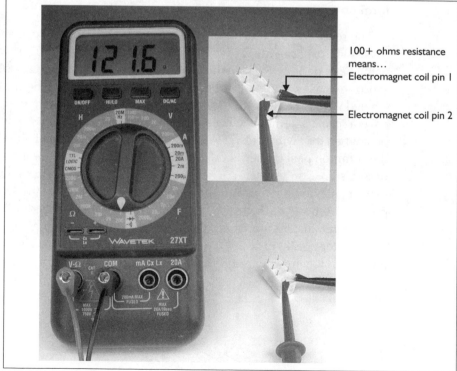

100+ ohms resistance means...
Electromagnet coil pin 1

Electromagnet coil pin 2

The remaining group of six pins is for the pair of two-position switches. Using the same resistance setting on your multimeter, you *should* find almost no resistance between the top pin of the group and one of the other two pins on each side. These middle pins of the group of six are your "N.C." pins (*normally closed*), which are the ones that receive the power from the top pins of the group of six when the relay electromagnet coil *isn't* powered. These contacts are normally closed and making electrical contact by default.

Figure 9-17
Relay "normally closed" pins identification

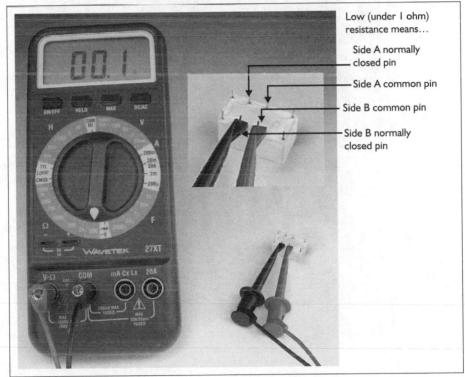

Low (under 1 ohm) resistance means...

Side A normally closed pin

Side A common pin

Side B common pin

Side B normally closed pin

The *other* outside pin on each side of the relay is the "N.O." pins (*normally open*, see Figure 9-18). The power from the "common" pin *will not* pass to this pin until the relay electromagnet coil is powered. As you check the resistance on these pins, your multimeter will read "OL," meaning it can't get a reading on it, as these relay contacts *aren't* making an electrical circuit (they're not touching—how could they?). The only way to make *absolutely sure* that these are the "N.O." pins is by measuring the resistance when you energize the relay electromagnet coil. While keeping the multimeter on the pins, put your

9-volt battery directly across the two relay electromagnet coil pins. You *should* here a "click," and the resistance reading should jump to near zero. Remove the battery from the pins, and the resistance should read "Infinite" again. When you're sure of each pin's function, mark it down on the relay (if you don't think you'll remember).

Figure 9-18
Relay "normally open" pins identification

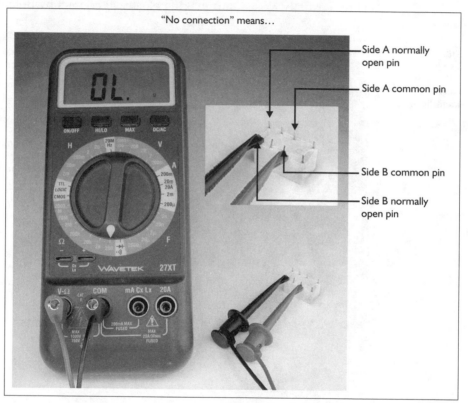

"No connection" means...

Side A normally open pin

Side A common pin

Side B common pin

Side B normally open pin

So now you're an expert at identifying the pins on an unmarked relay. Just in case you forgot to write it down, this is how *our* relay pins worked out. Remember, the relay electromagnet coil pulls the common connections on both side 1 and side 2 away from their normally closed ("N.C.") position to their normally open ("N.O.") partner—that's how we're rerouting the power to the motors to make them run backward.

Figure 9-19
Our
relay's pin
identification

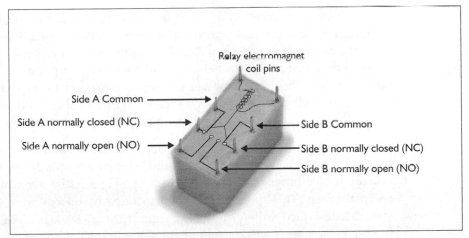

Let's mount switch and relay hardware to Herbie's nose. Mount your touch switch right on Herbie's nose, and glue or tape (with double-sided sticky-tape) the DPDT relay someplace near behind it. You'll see that we didn't arrange the switch so that it was directly flush with the front of Herbie, as this would mean that any attached sensor would cover only one side. By mounting it at an angle, we'll be able to make the sensor reach further forward and better sense the area in front of Herbie. Glue the switch down, and if you have a metal Herbie body, solder the switch's unused "N.C." (normally closed) pin to the frame for extra strength.

Figure 9-20
Mounting the
backup relay
and the
sensor switch

It's one thing to have "run away" behavior in your Herbie, but it's pretty important for it to *eventually* revert to its normal behavior of chasing light. We do this by using a capacitor and resistor combination. When activated, the touch sensor that causes the behavior quickly charges up the small timer capacitor, which then passes power through the resistor to the transistor and turns on the relay. When the power from the timer capacitor drains out, the transistor stops activating the relay, and Herbie goes back to normal.

Glue your relay down behind the sensor "dead-bug" (that's relay pins *up*, remember?) to the body of your Herbie and lay the transistor down on it so that you can solder its *right*-side pin to one of the pair of pins that are all alone at one end of the relay. These pins are the inputs to the relay coil that control the pair of switches described earlier. Applying a signal through these two pins will make the relay snap on; it will turn off again when that signal disappears.

The time Herbie stays in "run away" mode is set by the *both* the resistor and capacitor values. Aim to use a resistor in the 1kΩ to 20kΩ range with a capacitor in the 10μF to 100μF range. The 10kΩ resistor and 10μF capacitor we used gave us approximately a half-second of reverse-mode. The values we used were selected with a 9-volt battery in mind—lower-voltage batteries will mean you'll need a larger timer capacitor because not as much power gets shot to it when the touch sensor is activated.

Figure 9-21
Mounting the relay, and soldering on the 2N3904/ PN2222 transistor

Take your timer capacitor, and solder the "+" side of the capacitor to one of the two remaining pins of the switch. The negative side of the capacitor gets soldered either to the metal Herbie body or directly to the "−" of the battery connector.

Figure 9-22
Soldering
on the timer
capacitor

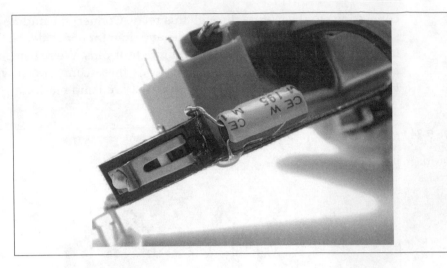

Take your 10kΩ resistor and solder it from the *middle* leg of the
2N3904/PN2222 transistor to someplace along the "+" leg of the timer capacitor you just soldered in. This will be the pathway for the power to flow from
the capacitor to the relay-activating transistor.

Figure 9-23
Installing the
resistor across
the capacitor
and transistor

The relay has to be wired to swap the motor power connections when it
activated. Each half of the relay (split between the group of six pins) is its ow
switch, with the top pin of each trio being connected to the middle pin *or* th
bottom pin. When the relay snaps on, it changes from the middle pin to th
bottom pin. With a little clever wiring, we're able to reroute the pow

connections to the motors through this relay. Connect the middle pin of one side to the bottom pin of the *other* side, and do it for both sides so that you're looking at an *X* of wires across the bottom four pins. We're using a red wire and a black wire for each leg of the *X*, as these connections will lead to Herbie's power lines (which are traditionally red and black).

Figure 9-24
Relay
cross-wiring

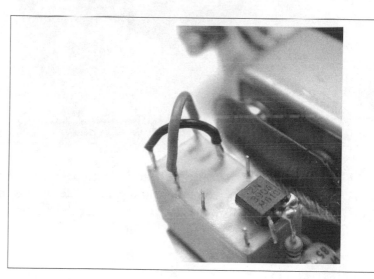

Let's continue wiring up the reversing relay. Run a wire (preferably red) continuing from one of the relay *X* connections to pin 6 of the LM386 *or* to the middle "+" connection on the switch coming from the battery—these are both the same connection, electrically. Solder the remaining leg of the relay *X* to Herbie's body or the battery "–" connection with a black wire if you can. By using red and black wires, you'll know exactly which connections are attached to "+" or "–".

While we're wiring up the power to the relay, let's finish off the connections to the switch and the transistor. This is where the red-wire color trick comes in handy: we need to run "+" power to the remaining pin on the touch sensor switch and the other relay electromagnet pin. Find one of those other red wires, and connect to one of the same points *they're* attached to.

Solder the *left* leg of the 2N3904/PN2222 transistor to a "–" connection, which would be Herbie's metal body or where one of the other black wire connections are.

Figure 9-25
Connecting
power to the
relay, switch,
and transistor

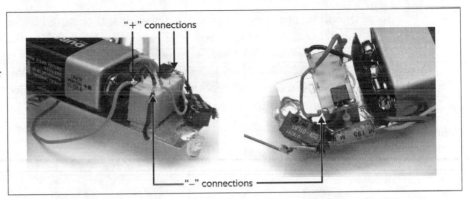

"+" connections

"–" connections

The Robot Geek Says

Building a *Non-Reversing* Herbie

If you are *not* building a reversing Herbie, do this step and then skip down to wiring up the motors to pin 5 of the LM386. If you *are* doing the reversing Herbie, skip this box entirely.

Run one wire from "+" to one connection of one motor, and another wire from "–" to the same polarity connection on *other* motor. For instance, run a wire from "+" to the "+" on motor A, and run a wire from "–" to the "+" on motor B.

If your motors don't have any polarity markings at all, make a wild guess—you'll be able to fix it later when we do troubleshooting.

To run power to the motors, a wire needs to be attached from each of the motors to one of the remaining pins next to the *X* we just soldered up. Do this for each motor, for a total of two new wires installed. Remember how we used red for "+" and black for "–"? With the motors, you can use a green-with-pink-polka-dots wire, but if you're lacking that color, use whatever wire you have handy…

Trying to decide which motor connection to use? There's a 50/50 chance of getting it right, as motors will spin either clockwise or counterclockwise depending on how power is flowed through them. As we're using salvaged motors, we're not sure until we hook them up to power, and your Herbie may scoot forward (good!) or backward (cute, but not so good). If your motors have any sort of polarity marking near the connection points (a "+" or red dot is common), make sure you solder the wires from the relay to *the same polarity connection* on each motor. We do this so that when Herbie is powered up, *both* motors will be spinning in opposite directions, thrusting Herbie forward or backward, but *not* in a spin. It sounds illogical, but remember, the relay sends "+" power down one line, and "−" power down the other. This will make the motors spin opposite to each other, which is what we want. Don't worry too much about the motor wiring at this point, as we'll be making final wiring adjustments when we do our testing and tuning later.

Figure 9-26
Motor relay wiring

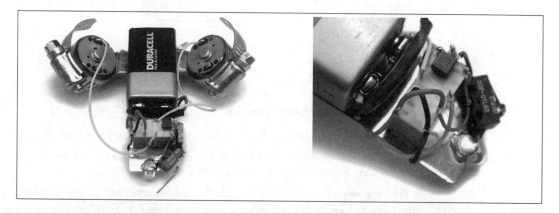

To finish up the electrical connections to the motors, we're going to take the remaining contact on each motor and solder them together to pin 5 on the LM386. You can solder a wire between the two remaining contacts on the motors, then run a second wire to the LM386 pin 5, or have a wire from each motor meet together at pin 5 (which is what we did). It doesn't matter electrically.

Figure 9-27
Connecting the motors to pin 5 on the LM386

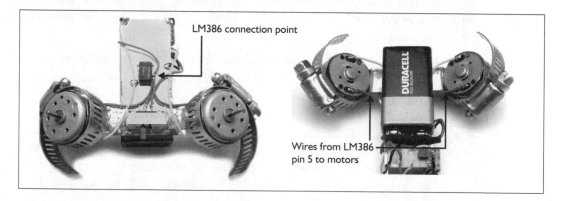

As mentioned in the troubleshooting section, the LM386 splits the power between the two motors, and by adjusting the output voltage at pin 5, where the motors are both connected, the chip can make one motor turn faster than the other. Let's assume we're using a 9-volt motor, and the eyes of the Herbie are perfectly equal. The output from pin 5 will be 4.5 volts, and each motor will turn at the same speed. If the input from the eyes becomes unbalanced, the LM386 amplifies this difference (for example) by raising the voltage at pin 5 to 6 volts. One motor will have 3 volts and the other will have 6 volts, which will make Herbie turn one way.

Figure 9-28
How Herbie's LM386 brain works

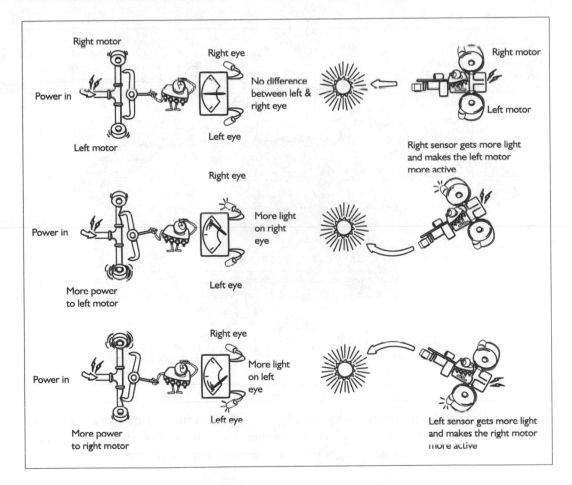

We've done the brains (the LM386) and the brawn (relay and motors), and now it's time for the *eyes*. This will take a bit more finicky wiring, as the eyes are generally pretty small parts. As a rule, you want to put your eyes as wide apart as you can, right near the edges of your robot, facing forward and *outward*. If your eyes are back-to-back at the front of the robot, the brains will try to just guide these two eyes toward the light. If the *whole body* is between the eyes, the brains will have a better chance to guide Herbie toward the light past the obstacles.

Figure 9-29
Eye location affects how Herbie runs around.

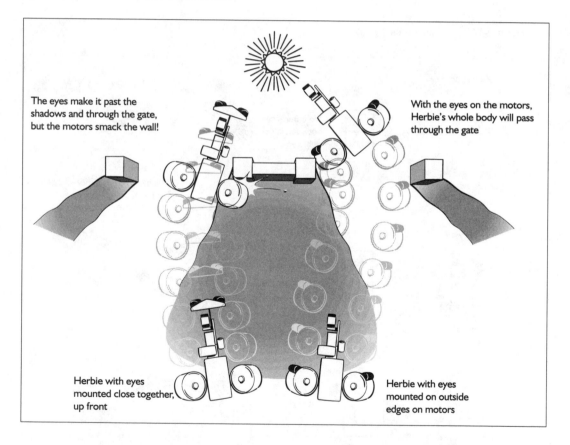

The IR receivers we salvaged from a dead computer mouse are polarity sensitive, meaning they have a way they prefer to be hooked up. If you examine one closely, you might see that one corner of the sensor is chamfered, or has a corner clipped off. The lead that is on the same side as this chamfer is called the cathode, or the negative lead, and the other side is called the anode, or the positive lead. We found that some of the optical sensors we found in mice *didn't* have any sort of marking to tell us which one was the cathode or the anode. There are two ways to figure out which lead is which (well, there are actually three ways, but we don't think you have access to a peanut butter–covered porcupine, so let's not go into that technique). The first way is to hook up your multimeter to the two leads, shine a strong light on the sensor, and measure the voltage being generated by the sensor. If you have the multimeter correctly connected and you read a voltage of around *positive* 0.6 volts, the red multimeter probe is connected to the anode (+), and the black probe is connected to the cathode (–). If the voltage reads *negative* 0.6 volts, your meter leads are reversed to the sensor pins.

The second technique is useful only if you have a *diode check* function on your multimeter. This function puts a signal into the part, and if it registers a voltage, the leads are connected correctly (red = anode, black = cathode). If the diode check function comes up "OL" (remember, that's multimeter-speak for "nothing's connected!"), reverse the connections to the part, and it should come up around 1 volt.

This may sound strange, wiring *what should be* the negative lead of the sensors to *positive* power, but this is a well-known technique called *reverse-biasing* the sensor. By trying to make power flow though it in reverse, we find we get better light sensitivity out of it. Trust us, it works!

Dig into your salvaged electronic goodies, and find some two-conductor wire (that's one length of wire with two separate strands, like speaker wire). Solder a nice, comfortable extension to each of your sensors, so you'll be able to easily position them later. We'll want to wire the sensor cathodes (the negative leads) to "+", being pin 6 of the LM386, or the middle leg of the switch.

With the other remaining wire of each sensor, solder one to pin 2 of the LM386, and the other to pin 3. These are the sensor inputs into the LM386, and since you have nice, long extensions on your sensors, it won't matter which input goes where. If it's wrong (that is, if Herbie runs away from light), simply make the eyes swap sides. Of course, you *can* change around the solder connections on pins 2 and 3 if Herbie is scared of light—whatever is the easiest solution for you.

Don't glue the eyes down to the Herbie's body permanently yet. Use some tape or hot glue to make a temporary eye mount until you're happy with

Herbie's performance, and then make the installation permanent. Eyes are fun to play with. You might even want to mount them on some stiff wires so that you can adjust their location and direction.

Figure 9-30
Wiring up the eye sensors

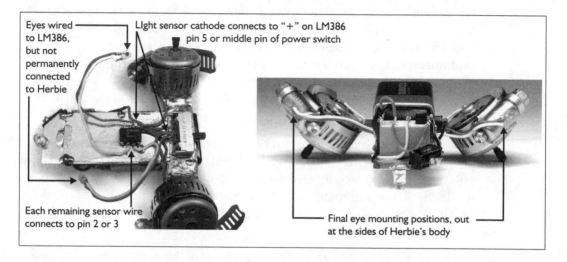

Let's test Herbie. Connect the battery to the switch, and turn it on, *but be ready to turn it off quickly.* If the motors don't *immediately* turn on, turn the switch off quickly. The reason for this is that if you've made a wiring mistake, you might have the battery shorted out, which can cause smoke, fire, burns, or any combination of the three! A sure sign of a short circuit is the battery getting *very* hot, *very* quickly, wisps of smoke coming from the circuitry, or the LM386 chip getting *very* hot. If *you are not* getting motor action, disconnect the battery and double-check your connections for anything wrong.

Most likely, you'll be successful and see the motors spinning. Cover up one sensor, then the other. Just as on your breadboarded version, the motors should change speed according to which sensor is covered. The next step is to put your Herbie down, and test it out! If you're in a room with a window, Herbie should make a beeline toward it, scooting around any shadows that may be in the way. If it heads for the shadows, it's time to swap the connections on pins 2 and 3, or physically swap the eye sensor positions.

Your switch may be mounted, and your Herbie may be accurately chasing light, but we'll bet it isn't doing much when Herbie hits the wall, right? We have to extend the switch so that it "feels" a much bigger area around the Herbie. Hopefully your switch has a metal tang that acts as the switch lever, which makes it a simple task to solder on a paper clip or something similar. The bump/"run away" behavior works best if your touch sensor is long and can be banged around without fear of it snapping. We've found that putting a little guard on the sensor nose keeps it from being bent too far outward, which could break it off. Ours simply press-fits into one of the holes in the switch.

Figure 9-31
Touch sensor extension and bend-back protection wire

The Robot Geek Says

How to Psychoanalyze a Demented Herbie

So you've powered up Herbie, and it's doing *something,* although you're not sure what to do to fix it. Well, pull up a comfy leather chair next to the sofa, and we'll delve into the causes and cures for any mental illnesses Herbie may have:

Herbie does...nothing! Disconnect the battery. Is the chip or battery warm to the touch? **Solution:** Search for a solder-blob or other short-circuit on the wiring. There should be no place where the "+" and "−" wiring come into direct contact. Measure the voltage on the battery. Is it below 6 volts? **Solution:** Dead battery (replace it!). Inspect the motor wiring and make sure both motors are connected to pin 5 of the LM386 chip, which is the power output of the chip. **Solution:** Fix them wires! Try running a temporary wire across the switch terminals. Does it activate Herbie? **Solution:** Bad switch/switch wiring.

Herbie spins clockwise on the spot. This indicates that the right motor is running forward and the left one is running backward. **Solution:** Reverse the motor connections on the left motor.

Herbie spins counterclockwise on the spot. Similar to the previous ailment. **Solution:** Reverse the motor connections on the right motor.

Herbie is running in reverse. This can arise from either of two problems, the first (and most likely) being that the connections on each motor are reversed. **Solution:** Swap the connections on each motor. The second problem could be that your relay is activating for some reason. If you disconnect power from the relay (via the "+" connection next to the transistor) and the problem disappears, you most likely have a false-triggering sensor switch. **Solution:** Fix the switch, which is probably wired normally closed rather than normally open.

Herbie doesn't reverse when the sensor is touched. Solder a temporary wire from "−" to the relay pin connected to the 2N3904/PN2222 right leg. Does Herbie now run in reverse? **Solution:** Wiring problem with the transistor/capacitor/resistor connections, or the touch switch is faulty. If the preceding test doesn't make a difference, the problem is with the relay wiring. **Solution:** Make sure the relay pin opposite the one the transistor is connected to is connected to "+". Some relays are polarity sensitive, so swapping the connections to the bottom two pins that control the relay electromagnetic coil may fix it. And remember, 5-volt and 9-volt relays will definitely work with a 9-volt battery. A 12-volt relay might not!

Herbie spins in clockwise circles around the right motor. This can be diagnosed by shining a strong light on Herbie. If you don't get *any* action from the right motor, there's a wiring problem. **Solution:** Search for a disconnected wire from/to the right motor, or a solder blob or broken wire on one of the light sensors. If you get a change in the spinning action (circles get bigger), you have a sensor tuning problem. **Solution:** Move the right sensor further outward.

Herbie spins in counterclockwise circles around the left motor. Similar to the previous problem. **Solution:** Check left motor wiring connections, and sensor wiring for shorts or breaks. If you get a change in the spinning action (circles get bigger), you have a sensor tuning problem. **Solution:** Move the right sensor further outward.

If your Herbie is more-or-less behaving properly, now you can fine-tune its operation. Start by using a desk lamp in a dark room to check to see how straight Herbie runs toward the light. If Herbie tends to wander right, that means the right-side sensor is aimed a bit too forward (or the left-side sensor is aimed too far out to the side). Reverse the logic if Herbie is wandering a bit to the left (right sensor is too sideways or left sensor is too forward). When you're happy with the tracking ability of Herbie, glue the eyes down securely.

The last thing we suggest you do with your Herbie is giving it bigger wheels. It doesn't look like a wheel, but the small spinning metal shaft that comes out of each motor is actually acting as a little wheel. And what's the best thing to put on wheels? Rubber tires! We like to use a few layers of electrical heat-shrink tubing to build up a nice rubber nub on the end of the shaft. If your motor has the power, you may be even lucky enough to be able to mount tiny rubber pinch-roller wheels from cassette decks on the shaft for better traction and higher speed.

Figure 9-32
Heat-shrink tires for Herbie

Here's a bare motor shaft: Not much grip with a steel shaft!

One layer of electrical heat-shrink tubing turns the steel shaft into a tiny rubber tire

A second layer makes the tire much stronger and improves traction

A third and final layer of heat-shrink tubing gives the steel shaft a small but durable tire

Care and Feeding of Your Herbie

Being a battery-powered device, Herbie has a relatively shorter lifetime than a solar-powered device. You should be able to get a good 1/2 hour of operation from your Herbie, depending on the size/power of your motors and the quality of your battery. If you're a performance freak, you *might* want to experiment with running a pair of batteries in series (Herbie "+" to "+" of battery 1; "–" of battery 1 to "+" of battery 2; "–" of battery 2 to Herbie "–"). A 12-volt Herbie is a *fast* robot, which just might break your touch sensor because it will be hitting objects with some force!

Herbies come in many sizes and shapes. Find a two-motor toy tank, and wire it up with Herbie brains.

Unlike the solar-powered robots, Herbie has power to spare. Don't be scared to decorate Herbie with a shell of some sort. We've even seen Herbies built into computer mouse shells.

Herbie was originally designed as a "line-follower" robot. Line-following is done by pointing the light sensors directly downward to the surface, where Herbie looks for a wide black line to follow (like black electrical tape) on a light surface. When one of Herbie's eyes would swing over the dark tape, it would try to move that eye away from it. As long as the tape stayed between the eyes, Herbie would try to keep straddling it as it scooted along.

To improve line-following performance, try wiring up a small flashlight bulb (of appropriate voltage rating) above the front of Herbie as a sort of miner's lamp. The more light Herbie has to illuminate the line, the better it will follow it.

If you need Herbie to line-follow a *white* line on a dark surface, swap the eyes around, or swap the light-sensor connections on pins 2 and 3. Even better, wire in a DPDT switch (wired similar to the reversing relay) to pins 2 and 3 so that you can easily swap Herbie's eyes from dark-line chasing mode to light-line chasing mode. Robot line-following contests are fairly common at robot competitions, so get your Herbie tuned up for race day!

Want to make further improvements to your Herbie? Wilf Rigter came up with these simple, clever hacks to the Herbie circuit (see Figure 9-33). Improve the overall dark-to-strong light sensitivity to any type of light sensor by adding an LED and a 1k resistor, which does double-duty as a "power on" indicator. Give Herbie left and right sensors by making use of pin 7, a pair of 10k resistors, two switches, and a 22–47µF capacitor.

Figure 9-33
Wilf Rigter's
clever Herbie
circuit hacks

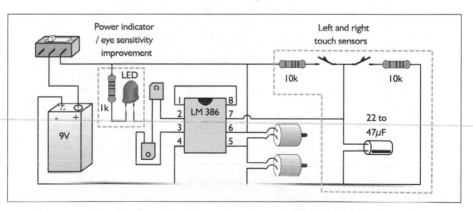

The Herbie circuit is like the old "Stone Soup" fable. Randy Sargent contributed a very simple, robust circuit to the robotics community, and with all the little bits contributed by other roboticists, Herbie has evolved into a startlingly capable little robot with many variations. Have fun with your Herbie, and perhaps you can come up with a new modification you can contribute too!

Chapter 10

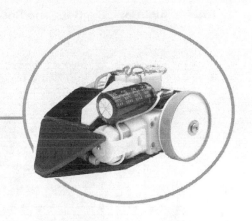

Project 4:
The Bicore Headbot

Parts List

❏ **1** × 74AC240 Inverting octal buffer chip

❏ **1** × Gear motor, or cassette deck motor with belt speed reducer

❏ **2** × Light sensors

❏ **1** × Set of batteries no more than 6 volts

❏ **2** × 0.47µF or smaller monolithic capacitors

❏ **1** × Power switch

❏ **3** × Paper clips for the base stand

The Bicore Headbot

A headbot is a robot that isn't mobile but turns its head in response to a stimulus. A stimulus is something in the environment that causes a response in some way, like how fresh-baked cookies are a stimulus that makes your mouth water. The headbot we'll be building will be light sensitive and will seek left and right trying to find the brightest source of light in its area.

Headbots come in a variety of complexities, with the one we're building being among the simplest. Other types of headbots will seek until they lock onto the brightest object, then shut down to conserve power. When the object moves, the headbot wakes up and starts tracking again. These "power smart heads" are a very popular series of robots circuits designed by Wilf Rigter, who regularly posts to the BEAM robotics Internet mailing list (archived at http://www.solarbotics.net). Other headbots that are solar-powered, like the ShokPhoto-Head (http://www.solarbotics.com/beam/circuits.asp), don't need a battery. If you want to make somebody paranoid, build one of these and stick it on the corner of his or her desk. Every few minutes, it will twitch just enough to make them wonder what the headbot is looking at.

Figure 10-1
A simple Bicore headbot and a complex up/down, left/right battery/solar operation headbot, both by Grant McKee

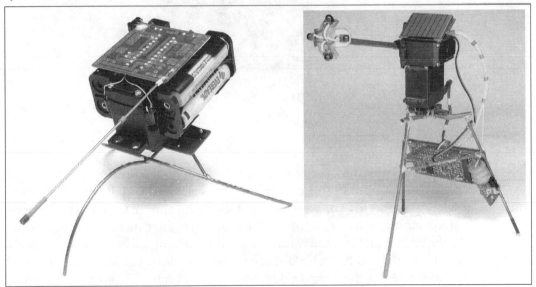

One of the largest BEAM headbots built to date includes this 24" tall, solar cell aiming, battery recharging, AC output monster built by Grant McKee. He constructed his headbot as his final Electrical Engineering project, complete with ball-bearing counterweights, slip-ring power transfer, and custom-made circuit boards. The two small solar cells on the edge of the head power the two motors that aim the head up/down and left/right, so the large 6"×6" solar cell array is optimally aimed to can charge the gel-cell battery in the base of the robot. When needed, the battery module can be removed and used to drive AC (house-style) appliances like laptops and small power tools.

Figure 10-2
Grant
McKee's
huge headbot

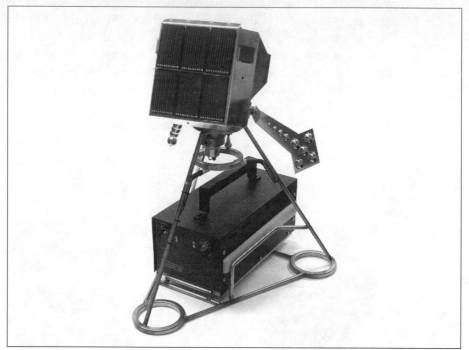

A headbot can be a very useful addition to a robot body. Imagine that your neck were in a brace, and you couldn't swivel your head. It would take considerable effort to twist your body left and right, and tilt up and down to look at something, wouldn't it? Most robots with eyes have them mounted directly to the body, so if the robot wants to look at something specific, the whole body has to turn. By adding a headbot on top of a mobile robot base, you can build what is called a "horse and rider" configuration robot, where the head looks around and steers the body much as a rider would steer a horse. The rider decides where to go, and the horse takes the rider there while doing all the smart "don't-step-in-the-hole" stuff horses do.

Solarbotics Ltd. has two kits that can be turned into a "horse and rider": the ScoutWalker 2 walker and the SunSeeker headbot ($339 combination special). By itself, the ScoutWalker 2 is a capable four-legged robot that can negotiate some complex terrain, but when the SunSeeker headbot is added, it has very good light-seeking ability.

Headbots are an addictive type of robot to build. Once you have a few finished, you have your own audience watching you while you build more and more robots! A simple search for "light-seeking head robot" on the Internet will return a great many Web sites with circuits, pictures, and videos. Start with our simple headbot, and start looking around! ("Looking around" "headbot"—get it? Hey, don't roll your eyes at us!)

The Bicore

Although there are a great many ways of building a light-seeking headbot (op-amps, microprocessors, comparators, transistors, the list goes on...), we'll be using the Bicore for ours. The Bicore is a very useful BEAM circuit that is used in many ways in many different types of robots. It's best described as a simple *oscillator*, or *clock*. Although there are many, many ways to build an electronic oscillator, the Bicore is handy because it's particularly easy to build, modify, and influence. We will build our Bicore circuit using the eight-channel 74AC240 chip.

Since the Bicore needs only two of the eight channels on the chip we build it on, we can use the extra channels to buffer (strengthen) the Bicore to directly run motors. There are even "Bicore Experimenter's PCBs" available from Solarbotics ($35 for the BEP printed circuit board) that simplify the wiring of the various Bicore circuits. If you're interested in other Bicore experiments, check out the free documentation at http://www.solarbotics.com/ under the "kits" section.

Figure 10-4
Bicore Experimenter's PCB and BEP headbot

Bicore Headbot Behavior

So how do we turn a clock circuit into a light-seeking head? Pretty easily! The Bicore is made up of two nodes (some call them "neurons," although this is a bit of a stretch in terminology) that pass a single signal back and forth between them, sort of like two people tossing a softball back and forth. The Bicore sets how long the nodes hold the signal with a single resistor, but we'll be adding optical sensors to the resistor connection to vary how long one side is on versus the other.

Using the ball-tossing analogy, each person (node) tells the motor to turn one way for the amount of time that the person holds the ball. The time it takes between throws is easily shortened or lengthened by the light sensor attached to that node. The longer that node has the signal, the longer it tells the motor to turn in one direction.

Figure 10-5
Bicores, ball-tossers, and headbots explained

The Bicore "eye" receiving more light powers the motor in one direction for less time before passing the process back to its partner

The Bicore we're using is called a "suspended Bicore" because it uses a single resistor (where our back-to-back eye sensors act as the resistor) suspended between the two nodes to provide a "virtual ground." This means that as the nodes trade the signal, the way the circuit discharges swaps back and forth too.

A Bicore is constructed from a pair of *inverter* gates. Each gate has an input and an output, where the output voltage is always the reverse of what the input voltage is. So if the input is +5 volts (what the chip considers a logic "1"), the output will be 0 volts (logic "0"). If the input is then swapped to 0 volts (logic "0") the output flips up to 5 volts. It's this flipping behavior with the resistor and capacitors that allows the Bicore to function, flipping the signal back and forth between them.

The 74AC240 chip has eight inverter gates, so it can make up to four individual Bicores, or (like what we will use) a single Bicore that sends its output signal to two teams of three gates each to "buffer" the signal and make it stronger. This buffering is like adding extra strands to a rope to make it stronger, and in this case, it allows us to easily drive a motor. We'll be using the top gate on each side of the chip to lay out our Bicore oscillator, and then we'll pass the output signaling down to the gates below them.

The chip uses 16 pins just for the gates (eight inputs and eight outputs), plus power and ground pins (the "+" and "−" connections) and two *enable* lines for a total of 20 pins. These enable lines turn on the left and right teams of gates, so at any moment in time you can turn off half or all of the chip by connecting the appropriate enable line to "+". For this circuit, we'll connect both enable lines together and feed them a connection to ground ("−"), which turns them on. We won't make any further use of the enable lines in this design, but it's worth knowing about for future reference.

Figure 10-6
74AC240 pin layout

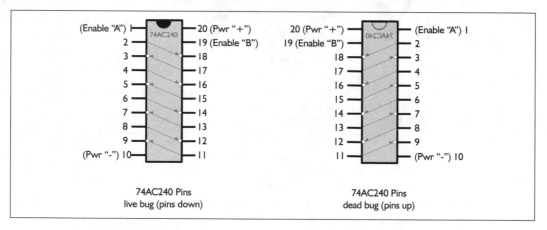

74AC240 Pins
live bug (pins down)

74AC240 Pins
dead bug (pins up)

We'll be using two optical sensors in series (hooked directly to each other) *instead* of the resistor.

When more light falls on one sensor than the other, it makes it easier for power to flow in one direction than the other, making one node "pass the ball" back quicker than it usually would. This difference in how long the nodes stay on makes the whole head rotate further in one direction than the other, until the light falling on the eyes is equal. This particular circuit will always keep seeking, making for an active, interesting head.

Figure 10-7
The Bicore
headbot
schematic

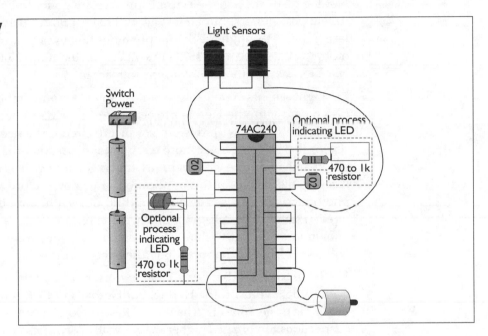

Headbot Parts

Headbot parts are a bit more difficult to find, as you require a fairly decent motor, a matched set of eyes, and the proper type of IC chip. Carefully select your parts, and you'll be rewarded with a very effective robot.

❏ **1** × 74AC240 Octal buffer inverter chip. The '240 style chip is a popular chip to build Bicores out of. We're using the "AC" flavor, as we'll be using battery power and driving a pretty good-sized motor. If you're lucky enough to have an efficient (under 30 mA current draw) motor, you may be able to use an HC- or HCT-style '240. If in doubt, find a 74**AC**240—you can't go wrong with it.

❏ **1** × Gear motor, or cassette deck motor with belt speed reducer. Not too many salvaged electronic devices are going to have decent gear motors, but almost all will have a motor driving a larger wheel through a belt. Simply mounting eyes to a regular motor's output shaft most likely will fail, as the motor will spin *much* too fast for the Bicore brains to react to.

❏ **2** × Light sensors. You can use almost any electronic light sensor (as you did with the Herbie project), *except* for CdS photoresistors, which don't work with this type of Bicore circuit. We need a sensor that passes power more easily in one direction than the other, and a photoresistor is pretty much equal in which way it resists (not good for this application). Keep on the prowl for phototransistors, IR sensors, IR-emitting LEDs, photodiodes, or even small solar cells. In a pinch, some red LEDs have been known to work, but with reduced sensitivity. Not sure what will work? That's what breadboarding the circuit is for!

❏ **1** × Set of batteries, between 3 and 6 volts, but no higher! We've been using 9 volts on the Herbie, but Herbie's LM386 is designed to handle up to 18 volts. The 74AC240 will blow out internal connections at voltages higher than 6 volts. A cordless telephone handset usually has a 3.6-volt rechargeable battery ideal for this application. The lighter the batteries are, the greater the chance of success that your headbot work properly.

❏ **2** × 0.47μF or smaller ceramic or monolithic capacitors. The faster the Bicore runs, the less energy it wastes seeking left and right, but the slower it runs, the wider it looks left and right. If you want a very direct light-seeking headbot, use small-value capacitors. If you want a more dynamic left/right-swinging headbot, use 0.22 or 0.47μF capacitors. Keep an eye peeled for a pair of capacitors labeled "102," "222," "472," "103," "104," "224," or "474."

Figure 10-8
Finding a
0.001μF "102"
(aka 1000pF)
capacitor in
technoscrap

❏ **1** × Power switch. Nothing magical, just something that will connect and disconnect power from the battery to the rest of the circuit.

❏ **1** × Framing material. Much as with Herbie, we'll make do with what you can find. Some paper clips are good for the Headbot's leg stands, and possibly some cardboard for shielding the eye sensors.

Figure 10-9
Headbot
parts, ready
for assembly

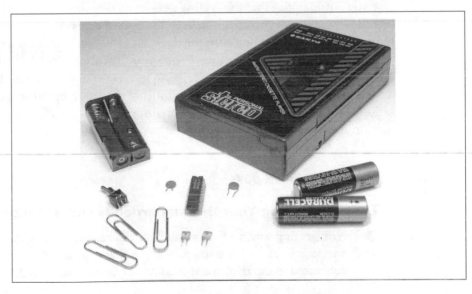

Again, now that you have got all your parts together, hook them up on the breadboard *first* so that you're absolutely sure that your selected components all play nice together. When powered up, the motor should start cycling left/right/left/right, and when you cover up one eye sensor, it will start favoring one side over the other.

Figure 10-10
Headbot circuit on breadboard

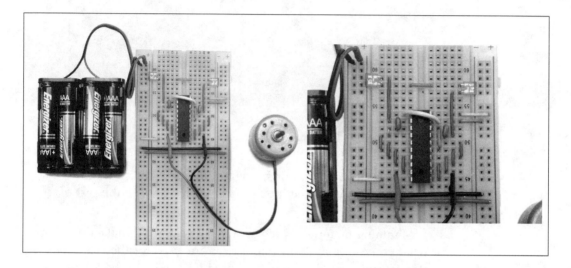

You should notice that the cycling gets faster when you shine more light on it, and slower when you cover up both the eyes. This is because the eyes have more resistance when they're in the dark, and it takes longer for each node to pass the signal back to its partner. When your headbot is finished, this behavior will show up as great, wide sweeping left/right motions in darkness, as if it's looking hard into the darkness (but only if your Bicore capacitors are around 0.1µF). In bright light, it may be running so fast that the light-tracking motion looks very smooth.

 The Robot Geek Says

Troubleshooting Your Breadboarded Headbot Circuit

✖ **Not getting any motion at all.** Did you remember to connect *both* enable lines to "–"? Are the power ("+") and ground ("–") connections connected to the chip, and is main power on *and* between 2.4 and 6 volts?

Your Bicore may be working, but you might not have enough power for your motor. Check this by running an LED instead. Disconnect the motors and connect an LED from pin 3 to ground, with the long leg of the LED (the "anode") connected to pin 3 and another LED from pin 18 (anode) to ground. If nothing's blinking, your Bicore isn't running. Double-check that you have the connections correct, and then try replacing the two optical sensors with a 1 megohm or higher resistor. If the replacement resistor fixes the "no blinky light" problem, you may have a bad sensor. Try reinstalling both sensors and swapping the resistor in for each sensor, one at a time, to find the bad sensor.

- **You have an oscillating (blinking) Bicore, but not enough power to move your motor.** Are you connecting the extra buffers on the '240 together? The top two inverter gates feed their outputs to the six gates below them, and that's where you should be tapping the power for your motor.
- **Your motor moves, but not with much power.** You can try doubling-up the power output by literally stacking another (identical!) 74AC240 on top of the first. Just push the enable wire so that it goes around the front of your chip, and simply slide another chip right on top of the first, aligned pin for pin. The legs should provide a nice friction-fit that will let you treat both chips as one thick chip. If this works in getting your motor to move with more authority, you can stack chips when you solder.
- **Your motor moves, but in only one direction.** Your eyes are probably not hooked in correctly, and the Bicore isn't able to "pass" the signal over to the other side. Make sure the eyes are hooked together anode-to-anode *or* cathode-to-cathode.

Building It!

Let's *leave* your components on the breadboard for now and construct the headbot body first. That way, we can hook up the Bicore to the headbot body and make sure the components selected will make the headbot run in a suitable manner.

First thing we need is a suitable donor. *"Igor! Go to the village and find me a suitable candidate! Nobody named Abby!"*

Bad Frankenstein movies aside, we'll be sacrificing a well-loved but worn out Sanyo portable cassette player. Remember, we want something with a gear motor, or a belt-reduction system. We'll be moving a fair amount of weight, so power is much more important than speed.

Figure 10-11
Our sacrifice to the robot gods: A Sanyo portable cassette player

We're on the hunt for the main motor, which will *most likely* be driving a larger flywheel disk. In a cassette mechanism, a heavy flywheel disk is spun to smoothen out the speed of the motor and bring it down to the proper speed to move the cassette tape across the electronic tape pickup head. Find the motor and flywheel assembly, and get it out by unscrewing, snipping, and cutting anything holding it in. Get nasty if you need to—this is a dead piece of electronic equipment, so you don't need to feel bad if you have to take a pickaxe to it. Just don't damage that motor and wheel assembly! (And you *are* still wearing your safety glasses, aren't you? Thought so.)

Figure 10-12
Salvaging the motor and flywheel assembly

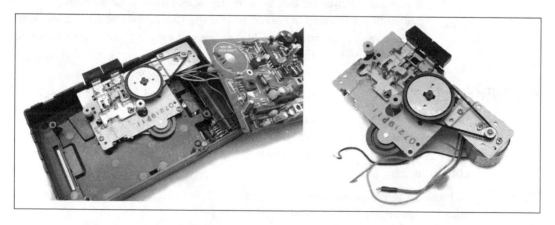

Now that the mechanism is stripped out, we're going to attach a stand to it. In this case, we used a pair of paper clips soldered to the metal flywheel disk. To be able to solder to the steel wheel embedded in the hub, we used sandpaper to scrub it down to the nice, shiny, solderable metal just below the surface. If you wish, you're encouraged to glue a base to this disk instead. Use some epoxy or hot glue to make a nice, gap-filling joint between the flywheel and something really solid, like a wooden block, a plastic container lid, or your friend's forehead (ask permission first).

Figure 10-13
Attaching a
stand to the
flywheel disk

Your base has to be wide and strong enough to support the weight of the headbot *and* the rotation forces it will be exposed to. Remember, the whole headbot mechanics, electronics, and batteries will be sitting on your base. After attaching the base to the flywheel, flip it over and make sure the whole assembly is stable, not tippy.

Figure 10-14
The headbot
body sitting
stable on
its feet

The next thing to attach is the battery pack, as it is the next heaviest thing we have. Try to find a convenient place near the middle of the headbot to put the batteries, as the more central they are, the easier it will be for the motor to twist the head.

Although you can use glue or screws, we used double-sided sticky foam tape to mount our battery pack where the cassette would usually be placed in the mechanism. Make sure that the connector wires to the battery pack are still easily accessed, and that the headbot still balances—you may need to adjust your base if it easily tips over

The Safety Geek Says

Batteries

We don't recommend you attach your battery pack to the headbot body with the batteries installed. As a rule, that's a *bad* idea, as shorting out the battery pack's connectors on the metal frame is a good way to cause a meltdown. We have batteries in our photographs because we were continually testing the device as we went through each assembly stage. But we're professionals (that means we asked our Moms, and they said it was okay).

Figure 10-15
Mounting the batteries to the headbot body

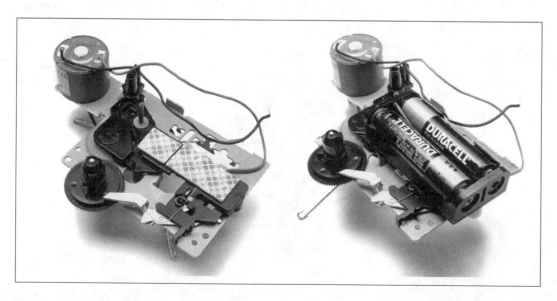

The body is about done, so now we start on headbot-brains! We're going to free-form the Bicore circuit much as we did for the Herbie, by soldering the necessary components directly to each other. We're going to take our 74AC240, flip it over "dead bug" (pins up) with the front end away from us (the end with the 1/2 moon cut out of the body).

If your breadboard experiments show that you need to stack *two* 74AC240s to get enough power to your motor, you should start by stacking the two chips together now. Then solder each pair of pins carefully together, avoiding solder-blobs, which could cause serious problems later. The rest of the steps remain the same.

Start by folding in the two "enable" pins (1 and 19) diagonally at the top of the chip so that they touch, as this will be the easiest way for you to identify the front end of the chip. Splay out the six pins shown (5, 7, 9 and 12, 14, 16) and fold in the other seven pins shown (6, 8, 10, and 11, 13, 15, 18). Remember, when counting pins, you start *live bug* (pins down) on the top-left corner and work down, across, and back up again. When the chip is *dead bug* (like now, pins up), you start on the top-*right* corner, work down, across, and back up.

The pair of adjacent pins 3 and 4 on the right side have to be folded over so that they touch. Don't do any soldering yet—just make your 74AC240 look like the one in Figure 10-16.

Figure 10-16
Folding the 74A240's legs

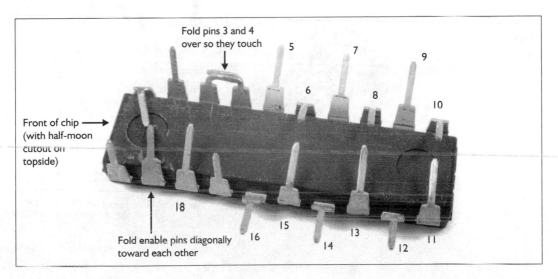

Now that the legs are folded, we have to trim down the three pairs of leads that are folded in at the bottom of the chip (6, 8, 10, and 11, 13, 15). Snip off *most* of the thin portion of the lead, so that each lead doesn't touch the one opposite to it. Do the same to the single folded-in pin 18.

Figure 10-17
Trimming down the bottom six leads of the 74AC240

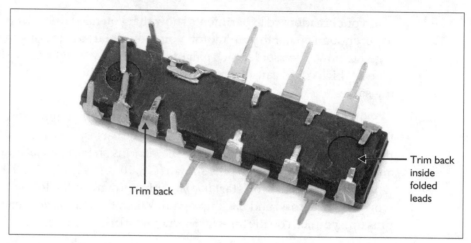

Okay, *now* you can fire up your soldering iron again and get to more soldering. Find two resistor clippings, and solder one across each of the sets of splayed-out legs. Then solder the diagonal enable pins (1 and 19) together, and the two adjacent pins (3 and 4).

Figure 10-18
Start of the 74AC240 pin soldering

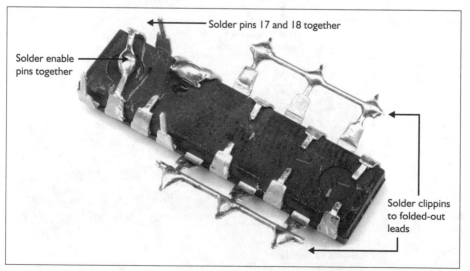

Find your Bicore timing capacitors (we're using 0.001µF "102"-labeled capacitors) and solder them to the forward sets of adjacent pins (pins 2 and 3, and 17 and 18), as shown in Figure 10-19. Remember, these capacitors *aren't* polarity sensitive and don't care which way around they're installed.

Figure 10-19
Installing the Bicore timing capacitors

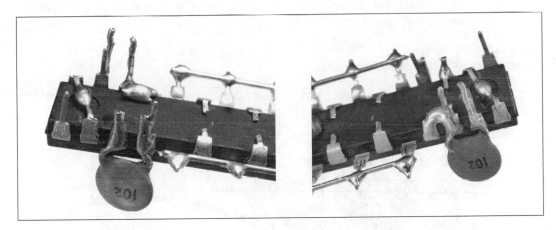

The inner sets of folded-in leads are next to solder together. Find another two resistor clippings and solder one across pins 3–4 (they're already joined, remember?), 6, 8, and 10. The other clipping gets soldered across pins 11, 13, 15, and 18. Follow Figure 10-20, and you'll be fine.

Figure 10-20
Connecting the folded-in pins

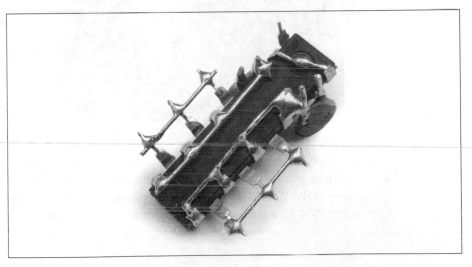

The Bicore is essentially done, so let's mount it to the headbot body. When dealing with motors, it's always a good idea to put the motor driver chip as near the motor as possible, to avoid something called "line loss." Line loss is power that gets used up pushing the power down the resistance load of the lines to the motor. By keeping the wires to the motor as short as possible, you get the most power.

We super-glued our Bicore assembly down between the power connections to the motor.

Figure 10-21
Mounting the Bicore to the motor of the headbot

The next step is pretty obvious—let's connect the Bicore to the motor using short wires, one from each motor connection to one of the outside rails of the Bicore assembly. It doesn't matter at this point which Bicore output attaches to which motor terminal, as we'll sort it out when we install the eyes.

Figure 10-22
Wiring the motor to the Bicore assembly

Let's install and wire the power switch. We're simply going to be interrupting the power from the battery "+" side to where it powers up the Bicore circuit. The switch we're using is a "single-pole, double-throw" switch, meaning that it can take power in and run it to one of two possible outputs. If you find a switch with only two poles, it's all the simpler to wire up!

After you find a convenient place to solder or glue your switch to the headbot, run a wire (red is a good choice, being the standard color for positive) from the battery holder "+" connection to one of the end poles of the switch and solder it on. Solder another red wire from the middle pole of the switch to pin 20 (top-left corner pin, dead bug) of the 74AC240.

Figure 10-23
Wiring the battery "+" to the switch and Bicore chip

Run another wire (black, the standard for negative, is another *excellent* choice) from the battery holder "–" connection directly to pin 10 of the 74AC240 (bottom-right corner pin, dead bug). Run another wire from pin 10 to the two diagonally connected "enable" pins up near the top of the chip.

Figure 10-24
Wiring the battery "–" to the Bicore chip and enable pins

The next step is adding the eyes (light sensors) to the headbot. As they're a pretty important aspect of the robot, let's see what the Robot Geek has to say about it.

The Robot Geek Says

Headbot Eyes

The optical sensors can be mounted practically wherever you want them to go. On the side of the motor, underneath, up on a long neck—the ultimate choice is up to you, as long as you follow these basic rules of placement:

✖ The eyes should be shielded from each other. That is, when light is falling on the front of one sensor, that light shouldn't be seen by the *backside* of the other sensor. Most optical sensors are still sensitive on the backside, and if they are not shielded, you can expect to get some funky behavior.

✖ Don't aim the eyes both straight forward in the same direction. If you look down two parallel soda straws, your eyes see much the same target. By aiming the eyes outward from 15 degrees all the way to 180 degrees (back-to-back), you give your sensors much better "peripheral vision." The more parallel the eyes are aimed, the more "locked on" the headbot will be when it finds a suitable light target.

✖ Think about whether you want your sensors out in the open or underneath in the shade. When they are in the open, strong sources of light (like the sun) will overwhelm most sensors, making it the only thing that they can see. If your eyes are shaded, they're more likely to detect the more subtle shadowing in the environment and look around a bit more creatively. Either approach is totally acceptable.

Our headbot has its eyes mounted one on each side of the battery pack, giving it the ability to see almost all the full way around it without moving. This will make our headbot very curious, making it "easily distracted" when in operation.

Figure 10-25
Gluing the light sensors to the battery pack

Wiring up the sensors is really no mystery this time. As long as they're wired up in series (one after the other) in reverse polarities, they'll give your headbot eyes that directional light sensitivity behavior we discussed earlier. So what does that exactly mean? Pick a leg on the sensor (left, for example), and wire it to the same (left) leg on the other sensor. Or wire the right one to the right one of the other sensor. It doesn't make a difference in this circuit. If you're using new eye sensors, you'll notice that one lead is longer than the other. Simply wire either the short leads *or* the long leads together for the same effect.

After you've wired the two sensors together, there's only one pin left on each sensor. Solder some long wire to each one of these pins as we're going to run back to the Bicore sensor inputs (pins 2 and 17). Remember, these sensors are acting as the resistor in the "back and forth" signal tossing in the Bicore. The lower the light level, the higher the resistance, and the slower the oscillations become.

Figure 10-26
Light sensor wiring

In the arrangement we're using, the sensors are fully responsible for the resistance. If you wish, you have the option of installing a resistor *in series* (directly in line) with the sensors, which will set the upper end of the speed at which the headbot will operate. Instead of having the headbot just stare at a bright light source, a 47kΩ "dazzle-limiting" resistor will keep it swinging a bit, left and right. But nothing comes for free, and making this resistor *too* big will reduce the sensitivity of your eyes.

On the other end of the behavior scale is the dark-performance. To keep the head from swinging too violently left and right, you can put a "dark-response" resistor *in parallel* (connecting to the same Bicore input pins as the sensors) to the light sensors. This low-light swinging becomes a problem only if your Bicore timer capacitors are in the 0.1μF range or larger, in which case a 470kΩ resistor will get you in the ballpark of acceptable behavior. As with the "dazzle" resistor, using the "dark-response" resistor decreases the eye's sensitivity.

Figure 10-27
Optional
"dark" and
"dazzle"
limiting
resistors for
the light
sensors

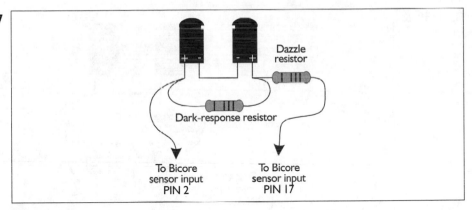

Well, we're about ready to throw the switch to see if our creation comes to life. Is a late-night thunderstorm booming outside, and lightning striking the rods on the top of your castle? Is your assistant giggling insanely, and bad sci-fi monster music playing in the background? Cool. Every good roboticist needs a lab like that.

Just as with the battery-powered Herbie, if nothing happens right away when you throw the switch, *turn it off, pronto!* You don't want to accidentally burn something up. Go ahead and turn it on—I'll wait here.

So it moved? Excellent! Did it look toward a light source, or did it stare at the darkest thing it could find? Here's where you roll the dice: depending on how you wired the motor to the Bicore outputs *and* how you wired the eyes to the Bicore inputs, your Headbot might be *photophobic* or scared of light. Not necessarily a bad thing, depending on what you want your headbot to look at. If you're in a well-lit room most of the time, a person with a dark shirt will be of particular interest to your headbot.

If you want to correct this, it's a simple matter of swapping the motor connections *or* the eye sensor inputs to the Bicore. If you wish to make it easily changeable, you can wire in a line-swapping switch between the eyes and the sensor inputs with a common "double-pole, double-throw" switch. This is a similar hack you can also perform on the Herbie project we did to make it light-seeking or light-avoiding.

Figure 10-28
Optional
eye-swapping
DPDT switch
hack

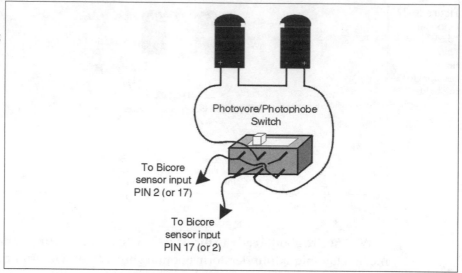

If your headbot failed to move, or moved strangely, and you're sure it's not for the reasons covered in the breadboard troubleshooting, it's time to consult the Robot Geek.

The Robot Geek Says

Bicore Headbot Troubleshooting

✖ **Is the head too heavy?** Lift the headbot up, and hold it by the head. Does the base spin? **Solution:** Add more batteries (not exceeding 6 V) or stack another 74AC240 to the Bicore to increase current output to the motor. If that fails, you may need to investigate a way to gear the motor down even slower to get more torque out of the motor so that it will turn.

✖ **Is nothing still happening?** Are you sure the battery connections were made to the *right* corners of the chip? Remember, we wired it "dead bug," which can get confusing. If you did wire it backward to power, the 74AC240 is most likely "dead chip." **Solution:** Build a new Bicore brain. Sorry for the bad news, but that's all you can do when you force power through the chip backward!

✖ **Are you sure the Bicore is oscillating?** Try soldering on an LED from pin 3 to "–" (ground), with the LED cathode (short leg nearest the flat spot on the LED) going to ground. If you wish, connect another LED to pin 18, cathode going to ground. Although this is not completely necessary, you'll get better behavior out of the circuit if you solder a 470 ohm to 1k resistor in series with each LED. Are these LEDs not blinking? **Solution:** Double-check your free-form wiring. That'll be the most likely place for an error. Only one place should have a solder blob crossing two pins side-by-side (pins 3 and 4)—nowhere else!

✖ Use a meter to measure the voltage across pins 10 and 20 (opposite corners). If you're not getting the full voltage output of your batteries, you may have a faulty switch. **Solution:** Run a temporary jumper wire from the battery "+" connection straight to pin 20 of the 74AC240, bypassing the switch. If it works, your switch is at fault.

✖ Another place to look at is the enable lines. Those diagonally connecting pins *must* be connected to "−" to activate the chip!

✖ **Is your headbot spinning like crazy in one direction? Solution:** Your eyes may be aimed too far apart. Try aiming them more toward the front. Also double-check that you wired the optical sensors *opposite* to each other, as in Figure 10-27. If they're in series and in phase, they'll be sensitive to light in only one direction. Like any siblings, they're only happy when they're fighting against each other!

✖ **Is your headbot looking *almost* in the right direction? Solution:** You could add a trimming potentiometer (trimpot) to balance the eyes, but it's much easier just to adjust one eye until the "face" of the headbot is looking straight ahead.

Figure 10-29
Headbot spinning out of control: Needs more trouble-shooting!

Care and Feeding of Your Headbot

Your headbot being a battery-powered device, you can expect to change batteries after a few hours of operation. *Or* you can use rechargeable batteries, add a solar cell to the top of your headbot, and hook them together so that when the headbot is off, it's being trickle-charged.

It's a pretty straightforward hook-up: Simply wire the solar cell's "–" to the rechargeable battery terminal's "–" and wire the solar cell "+" to the battery "+" terminal, but *through* a diode. This means that you want to run the connection from the solar cell "+" to a diode's anode (the end of the diode *opposite* the stripe) and then to run a wire from the diode's cathode (near the stripe) to the battery "+". The purpose of this diode is to keep the battery from discharging through the solar cell when it's dark. Make sure the solar cell you use can generate a voltage at least 1 volt higher than your batteries. So if you're using a 2.4-volt set of nicad batteries, you want a *minimum* of a 3.4-volt solar cell to charge them.

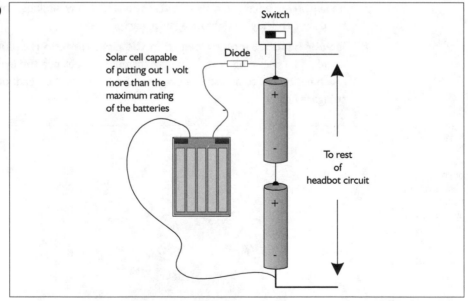

Figure I0-30 Wiring diagram for using a solar cell to trickle-charge your headbot's nicad batteries

We earlier made mention of how you can use a headbot to control a robot body "horse and rider" style. If you want to try adding your headbot to another robot, you will have to come up with a method by which the head can tell the body which way to go. If your robot body already has the ability to turn left and right, your head simply has to tap into the same control lines to steer the body. The trick to this is in the *neck*.

One of the first successful BEAM robots to use a neck is *Strider*, built back in 1998. Strider uses a Bicore head similar to the one you've built here, on top of a four-motor, radially symmetric (like a starfish) walking body. The way the head controls the body is via the neck connection, which is nothing more complex than a flexible metal stalk sitting in the center of four pins arranged like the corners of a box. When the head rotates enough, the center stalk moves to one side and touches two of the four pins, closing a switch that passes a signal to the body circuit to control the leg motors to turn the body in the direction the head was looking. It's that simple!

Figure 10-31
Strider, one of the first BEAM robots with head/body neck mechanics, showing back-of-neck switch detail

Now that you have the basic understanding of how the Bicore head works, think about adding a head and neck to a wheeled robot, or get creative and add one to the dashboard of your car. Imagine activating a sentry guard headbot that starts scanning when you take the keys out of the ignition—I'm sure it would give any would-be criminals a reason to reconsider!

Chapter 11

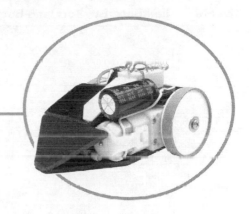

Project 5: The BEAM Magbot Pendulum

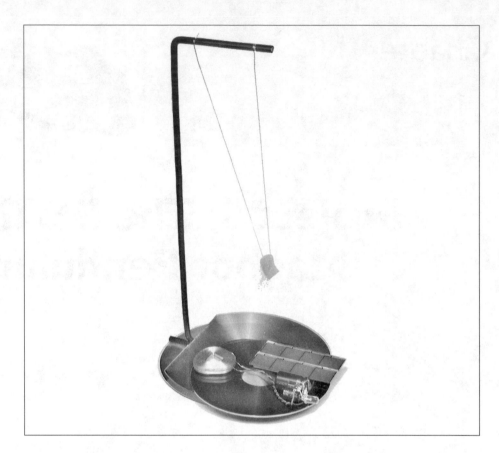

Parts List

- ❑ **1** × Solar cell
- ❑ **2** × Coils
- ❑ **1** × Supermagnet
- ❑ **1** × 4700µF capacitor
- ❑ **1** × 1000µF capacitor
- ❑ **1** × 2N3904/PN2222 transistor
- ❑ **1** × 2N3906/PN2907 transistor
- ❑ **2** × 100K resistors
- ❑ **1** × Diode
- ❑ **1** × Base material

Optional

❏ 1 × LED

❏ 1 × Battery with 4.7k resistor, and connector

The BEAM Magbot Pendulum

Magbot technology is about using a nontraditional technique to get motion that can be used in robotics. Traditional electric motors are excellent in most robot applications, but there is occasionally the need for something a bit different. Magbots create motion with components that can be separated and mounted on different parts of the device. This project is one such example of using nontraditional ways of making motion.

Although a magbot doesn't use a motor, it uses the same operating principles of a motor. We'll be creating our magbot in much the same way we'd build an electric motor. Here's a ten-second lesson in how to build an electric motor: A motor is nothing simpler than a current flowing through a coil of wire suspended in a magnetic field. There—you're all experts on building electric motors. Well, *simple* electric motors, anyway. A magbot uses the principle of electromagnetic induction, which means that electrons flowing through a conductor (a coil of wire) produce a magnetic field that can attract or repel other electromagnetic fields (in this case, from a permanent magnet).

Our project is going to use a deceptively simple application of magbot technology in a self-starting, solar-powered (battery optional) pendulum. A pendulum is simply a swinging mass on the end of an arm. Our pendulum's mass will be a magnet pushed by the invisible magnetic field of the magbot coil.

Most BEAM magbots to date have been built around the core components of a coil of wire and a high-strength magnet. By pulsing power through the coil, we get the magnet to either push away or pull toward the coil. This general layout has been used to make self-mobile butterflies (like the Solarbotics' SunDancer), sliding wheel-less solarollers, and flapping wing mechanisms.

Figure 11-1
The Solarbotics' SunDancer magbot, an experimental magbot Solaroller, and a miniature flapping wing mechanism by Mark Tilden

The ability to totally separate the power system from the parts that actually move make magbot technology ideal for building underwater swimmers, or for very robust flapping wing mechanisms. With an aquatic robot, water is your worst enemy. By sealing the coil in the body and placing the magnet on a fin just outside the body, you can easily make a swimming robot with no leaky seals to worry about. Very small and fast flapping mechanisms have been built with magbot techniques that don't have fragile wires or mechanics to wear out.

Usually, these devices are hooked up to a solarengine or similar circuit that periodically pulses power through the coil and makes the magnet jump in response. Grant McKee came up with a "magbot force-coil" circuit that is a simple arrangement of parts that waits until the coil comes near, then pulses power to the coil to give the swinging magnet a bit of a pull. As the magnet swings past, it stops pulling, letting the magnet swing a bit higher each time, just like when you were being pushed on a swing as a kid. This circuit will make it easy for you to build a pendulum as tall or short as you wish, with minimal circuit tuning.

Figure 11-2
Magbot pendulum schematic

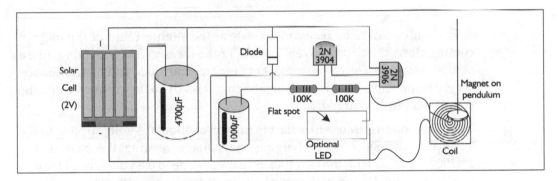

The circuit operation sounds a bit like a solarengine circuit, where we've got a power-storage capacitor and a pair of transistors designed to latch on and stay on. The difference lies in how the circuit is triggered, because timing here is more important than how much power is stored. Even gentle shoves can get a huge adult swinging on a swing if you time it right, and that's the principle we want to exploit with our circuit—well-timed gentle tugs on the magnet to get it swinging higher and higher.

The trick to the circuit is building a sensitive trigger that can detect the magnet approaching the coil, then turning the coil on to accelerate the coil faster. The interesting thing about magnets swinging over coils is that they generate a *positive* voltage on their approach to the center of the coil and then generate a *negative* voltage on their way out (or vice versa, depending on which pole of the magnet is facing the coil). The force-coil circuit takes advantage of this principle by turning off when the magnet passes dead-center over the coil, letting the magnet coast on its way out.

Figure II-3
Voltage curve
of a magnet
swinging past
our coil

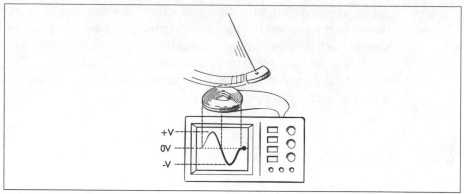

For our circuit to be ready to activate at the slightest hint of the magnet coming close, the circuit hovers just under the threshold of activating, like a skittish race-horse ready to leap out of the gate. The diode and trigger capacitor are responsible for this, keeping the circuit ready to trigger even when the circuit isn't fully charged.

By their nature, transistors start to turn on at about 0.4 volts applied to the base pin, and since we're halving the voltage feeding the base of the 2N3904/PN2222 with the two 100k resistors, we need 0.8 volts stored for it to start activating. On top of that, we have the 0.4 volts consumed by the diode, so in fact we need a total of 1.2 volts stored up before our 2N3904/PN2222 transistor can turn on. This transistor then turns on the 2N3906/PN2907 transistor, which dumps power through the coil *and* tries to keep the 2N3904/PN2222 transistor on as well. And as you noticed, that very 2N3904/PN2222 transistor is the one that turned it on in the first place, so for a short instant, they feed upon each other's energy while shooting power through the coil.

So what's exactly responsible for synchronizing the actual triggering of the circuit when the magnet is in just the right position? The coil. When the magnet zooms past the coil, it can generate up to 0.4 volts in the coil, which isn't much, but it's more than enough to push up the voltage needed to turn on the base of the 2N3904/PN2222. That extra 0.4 volts shoves the hovering 1.2 volts at the trigger level up to a solid 1.6 volts, turning this transistor on with extra kick and passing power to the coil, causing the desired effect of accelerating the magnet faster toward the coil. After the magnet passes the center of the coil, the induced voltage in the coil spikes downward –0.4 volts and firmly shuts the circuit off, letting the magnet coast away.

When the magnet is arranged to sit stationary just off to one side of the coil, it will start quivering. This is because the longer the circuit is left to charge up, the more twitchy and sensitive it becomes. Any minor signal "noise" picked up by the coil is causing short-lived activation cycles that cause pulses of power to shoot back through the coil. If the magnet is close enough (but *not* directly overhead, as it won't have much effect), the magnet responds to these minor "tremors" of electromagnetic energy and starts moving. The slightest movement of the magnet near the coil in turn causes a much stronger input signal than the surrounding "noise" and will start making the force-coil circuit activate in response. If all goes well, there is *just* enough movement to cause the back-and-forth motion of the pendulum to start. And if there isn't enough movement, a simple breeze caused by a person walking by may be just the thing to cause the pendulum to start swaying enough to get the force-coil circuit rolling along.

Magbot Pendulum Parts

The magbot project requires a fairly low number of simple parts. It's one of the most elegant BEAM projects of late because of its simple yet very effective design.

- ❏ 1 × Solar cell. We need one that produces a minimum of 2 volts, with 2 or 3 milliamperes of current. A tiny calculator cell won't quite be large enough by itself, but three or four cells wired in parallel ("+" to "+", "–" to "–") may do the trick. We're using a pair of 59×17 mm solar cells wired in parallel to get enough power. At this low voltage, you might even consider buying a four-pack of silicon crystalline solar cells found at Radio Shack and some science stores, or even a quad of the tiny SCPD solar cells from Solarbotics (truly cool). Wire them up in series to add their voltages together (4×0.5 volts per cell = 2 volts!), and you'll have a very strong source of power for your magbot pendulum.

- ❏ 2 × Coils. Ideally, we want coils with the finest wire and maximum number of windings (number of wraps) possible. A Solarbotics "Major Henry" coil ($2 each) is designed for the maximum kick out of a magbot, but we got sufficient performance out of a pair of stacked coils salvaged from an old 5 1/4" floppy drive. Flat pancake coils are also available in some 3 1/2" floppy drives but aren't as common. If you want, try winding your own around a nonmagnetic base, with as fine a wire as you can find, with as many turns as you can fit on. Radio Shack even sells "magnet wire" (part #278-1345, for about $4.00, for a variety pack of different-sized wire), which is ideal for winding your own coils. If you have the skill, you might want to salvage one from a hard drive's swing arm that is suspended between the supermagnets. It's difficult to do but may be worth trying if you can't find a coil anywhere else.

Figure 11-4
Coils from a 5 1/4" floppy drive, ready to liberate

❑ **1 × Supermagnet.** Technically called "neodymium" magnets, these magnets are made of materials that give them extraordinary magnetic strength. They've become fairly inexpensive due to their extensive use in the computer industry, where they're used in practically every modern hard drive on the market. Although a regular magnet *might* work, we suggest you hunt around for a dead or obsolete hard drive, or contact your local surplus-goods dealer or hobby shop for one. Solarbotics Ltd. sells a large 3/4" version for $2.50, but given how easy it should be to find one, we strongly recommend getting it from a dead hard drive. Ask around—somebody you know is bound to have one. When taking the drive apart, look closely at the fat backside of the arm that swings over the platters. You'll see a coil mounted in the arm, and nice, strong supermagnets just above and below it. It may seem contrary to common sense to have such powerful magnets in a sensitive device like a hard drive, but they are specially mounted and shielded so that they don't delete the saved data.

It's interesting how hard-drive swing arms move using the same principle we'll be using for our magbot pendulum! One word of caution: these magnets attract each other so strongly that they can seriously pinch your fingers if they get caught between the two magnets. The only way to separate two supermagnets stuck together is to slide them apart.

Figure 11-5
Supermagnets, found sandwiched between two spacer plates in a dead hard drive

- ❏ 1 × 4700µF power storage capacitor. This capacitor will act much like any other power storage capacitor we use in a solar-powered device. A 4700µF part worked fine in ours, but tests show anything 1000µF or greater at practically any voltage rating is acceptable. As the circuit will automatically be triggering at near 1.2 volts, the maximum voltage rating won't be a concern.

- ❏ 1 × 1000µF trigger capacitor. This capacitor helps keep the circuit always near the trigger voltage, so it's ready to fire as soon as the magnet swings near the coil. If you can't find a 1000µF capacitor, choose something between 470µF and 4700µF. Again, the maximum voltage rating isn't a concern with this circuit.

- ❏ 1 × 2N3904 transistor. Find one of these transistors, or its stronger brother, the PN2222. Either will work fine.

❏ **1** × 2N3906 transistor. Or find the stronger PN2907, which works equally as well.

❏ **2** × 100k resistors. We're using these resistors to set up the triggering voltage for our circuit. A pair of equal-value resistors in the 10k to 100k range work well.

❏ **1** × Diode. Any small signal diode (usually glass-encased) will suffice. The diode works with the 1000μF capacitor to keep the circuit near the activation point.

❏ **1** × LED. Although it isn't absolutely necessary for the proper operation of the circuit, we *strongly* suggest that you don't ignore adding the LED to the circuit. We'll be using it with the coil as a diagnostic tool and BLIFNAR. Never heard of a BLIFNAR? It's a highly technical term meaning "Blinky LIght For No Apparent Reason." Besides, it'll be powered by the otherwise wasted energy from the coil. It's like getting sprinkles on your ice cream for free!

❏ **1** × Base or suspension point. Use whatever nonmagnetic material you like to build a suspension point for your magnet to swing from. Drinking straws, wood, aluminum, brass, dog biscuits—we don't care, as long as it's nonmagnetic! A magnetic base will *definitely* make your magnet stick to the base instead of swinging freely. We've used discarded recordable CD-ROMs for one base, heavy-gauge copper wire, and the disk platters from the hard drive we harvested the magnets from. The platters aren't magnetic (in any sense that will affect our magbot), but they are conductive, so any electronics mounted on them should be kept from directly touching the surface.

Don't forget to make the base heavy and sturdy. The back-and-forth swinging of the magnet will make a weak base sway and possibly fail after a few thousand swings.

Figure 11-6
Magbot parts,
ready for
assembly

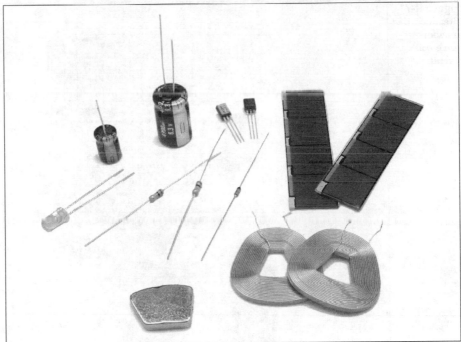

Optional

❏ **1** × Battery, with resistor and connector. If you simply can't find
suitable solar cells, you can build a substitute with a pair of
1.5-volt batteries or a 9-volt battery running through a 4.7k to
10k resistor. A weak 9-volt carbon battery gave us about a week
of continuous operation with our prototype pendulum.

As with our previous projects, let's breadboard the parts to make sure they
are compatible right from the beginning. Even if you're not going to use the
LED in your final design, add it to your breadboarded circuit for diagnostic
purposes. You should tape down the coil to keep it from moving while you're
testing the circuit.

Figure II-7
Breadboarded
magbot
force-coil
circuit

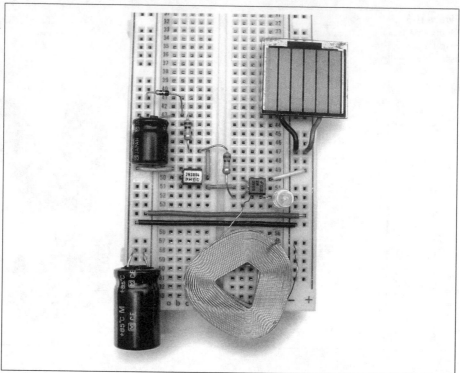

After the circuit is left by itself for a few seconds with adequate light on the solar cell, you should notice the LED starting to flicker dimly. This is an indication that the circuit is near activation and is taking any stray signal from the coil as an indication to activate. The LED draws its power from the stored energy in the coil, but it only gets it when the coil is de-energized. This "flyback effect" or "back-electromagnetic field" that is a characteristic of coils (formally know as "inductors") would otherwise be wasted as heat in the circuit, so why not use it to power an LED?

Take a 10 cm (4") piece of stiff wire and wrap it around the magnet you plan to use for your pendulum. Hold the other end of the wire so that the magnet just hovers above (within 5 mm or 1/4") the coil, with the flattest face of the magnet facing the coil. As you move the magnet off to one side of the coil so that it's just above the coil's wire windings, you should start to see the magnet vibrate. Pay attention to which way the magnet tries to pulse—is it going *toward* the middle of the coil or *away* from the coil? You want your magnet to be attracted to the coil, although both techniques will initially work equally well.

If you build your pendulum so that the magnet pushes against the coil, the magnet will eventually degauss, or lose its magnetic field from all the pushing. When it's arranged to pull to the middle of the coil, you're actually reinforcing the magnet's strength. If your magnet is pushing away from the coil, bend the wire so that the other side of the magnet is facing the coil, or reverse the connections from the circuit to the coil itself.

While you're hovering your magnet over the coil, pay attention to the LED. With the magnet just slightly off to one side of the coil, the LED will give a solid blink every time the magnet comes closer. Remember, the actual motion of the magnet's approach to the coil causes a tiny voltage to be generated, which is then amplified by our circuit to cause a much bigger dump of energy to pass through the coil, making the magnet move more.

The Robot Geek Says

Troubleshooting Your Breadboarded Magbot Circuit

* **LED not flickering.** There's definitely a power problem or circuit hookup problem. **Solution:** First check to see if your solar cell is *definitely* putting out around 2 volts. When the solar cell is plugged into the circuit, the voltage in the power storage capacitor will rise only to about 1.3 volts when the pendulum isn't present, and only to about 1.16 volts with the pendulum swinging. If the voltage is higher, there's something wrong with the circuit setup. Recheck your wiring! Especially the coil, as it must be connected from pin 3 (collector) of the 2N3906/PN2907 to ground ("–").

* **LED flickering very dimly.** If it's in backward, you're effectively stealing the power from your coil and limiting how much power can be transferred to the coil. **Solution:** Turn the LED around—when it's in correctly, it's also *much* brighter when it blinks.

* **Only a slight shivering motion from the suspended magnet.** You're close to working! The magnet shivering (especially noticeable when suspended from a string) means the circuit is trying to make the magnet move but just doesn't have enough magnetic field to do the job. **Solution:** Move the magnet closer to the coil. If that isn't possible, check your junk for more parts to augment the magnet field strength. The dead hard drive should have at least two magnets, and there are at least five or six coils in a floppy drive. Stack the magnets up, or wire up

two coils in series. With the coils, make sure the direction the wire is wound up is the same when you stack the coils. Check wind direction by pulling on one of the wires and checking which way it starts to come unthreaded from the coil. If it's clockwise, you want to wire and sandwich up the second coil so that it's *also* oriented with a similar clockwise unthreading. If you don't do this, the two coils will fight each other and have a net effect of zero!

✖ **Light is flickering, but you're getting absolutely no motion.** The coil connections or wires may be damaged. The coils are constructed from *very* fine wire that is coated in a thin lacquer insulator. Any excess bending of this fine wire can very easily cause it to break. Disconnect the coil from the circuit, and test it with your multimeter's resistance setting. It should measure between 5 and 20 ohms. If it comes up "OL," that means there's a break in the wire and the meter can't get a reading from it. Look carefully at any fatigue points where you may have been flexing the wire, and see if it's still intact. **Solution:** If you find the break, scrape off a bit of the lacquer coating with a knife and solder it back together. Otherwise, go back to the junk pile and pry loose another set of coils!

Note that this circuit cannot be run directly from a battery. Battery operation requires a 4.7k to 10k resistor in series with the battery to limit the current. Otherwise, the coil will always be energized and will not let the magnet "coast away" from it.

Figure 11-8
Wiring up two coils in series: Pay attention to the direction the windings circle around! The wires on both coils must unwind both clockwise or counter-clockwise when you glue them together.

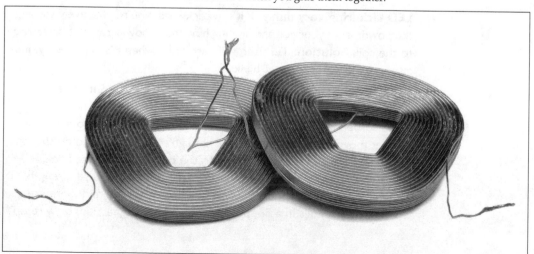

Building Your Magbot Pendulum

You might be tempted to just permanently glue your breadboarded circuit to the windowsill and suction-cup a magnet on a string to the window, but it ain't very pretty. Let's take the time and build a magbot power module—it won't take very long, we promise!

Before we start getting all the complicated folding and soldering started, let's do a quick review of the transistors and their pin designations. The common pinout for transistors of the TO-92 shape we'll be using (and for a large majority of transistors used in North America) is (read left to right; pins down; flat face with writing toward you) emitter, base, and collector. If you have any problems with this, refer to Figure 11-9.

Figure 11-9
Pin designations for most standard TO-92-packaged transistors

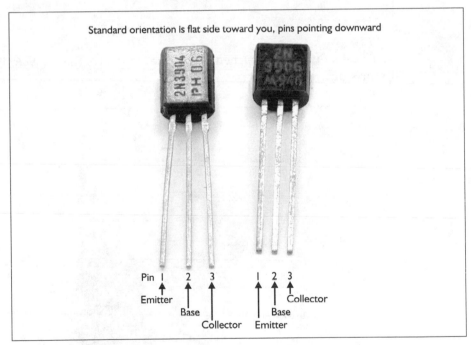

Start by taking your 2N3904/PN2222 and 2N3906/PN2907 and scratching a 4 and a 6 (or a 2 and a 7 as the case may be) on the top flat surface of each transistor. We'll be gluing these two transistors face-to-face where their lettering is, and you'll want to be able to identify which is which afterward.

Glue the two transistors together smoochy-faced, with the transistor pins all pointing the same way.

Figure II-I0
Gluing the
transistors
together,
face-to-face

To get it out of the way, bend pin 1 (the emitter) of the 2N3906/PN2907 90°
to the side.

Figure II-II
Bending the
2N3906/
PN2907
emitter out
to the side

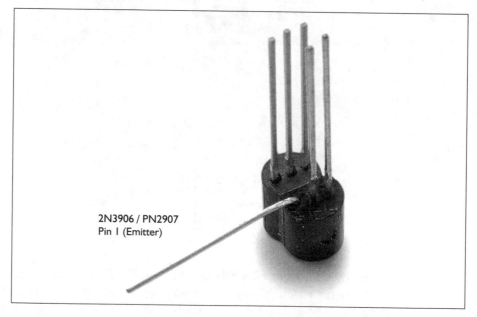

2N3906 / PN2907
Pin I (Emitter)

When that's done, bend pin 3 (the collector) of the 2N3904/PN2222 over to meet pin 2 (the base) of the 2N3906/PN2907. Carefully solder the two pins together, and clip off the excess lead from each.

Note that some people find it easier to cut the leads first, then solder them together. Use whatever method suits you best.

Figure 11-12
Folding over the 2N3904/PN2222 collector pin to the 2N3906/PN2907 base pin

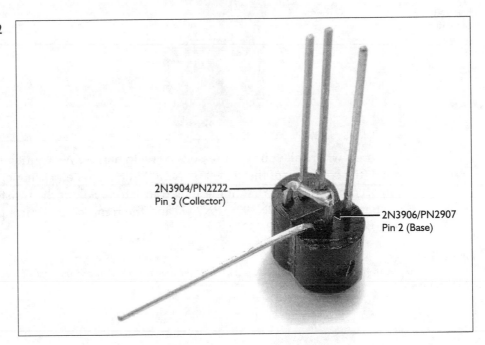

Glue the transistor assembly to the side of your trigger capacitor, so that the negative lead of the capacitor (the one nearest the stripe on the capacitor body) is close to the pin 1 (the emitter) of the 2N3904/PN2222. Bend this transistor lead over so that it touches the trigger capacitor's negative lead, and solder them together. After soldering, trim off any excess leads from this solder joint.

Figure II-I3
Gluing the transistors to the trigger capacitor and soldering the 2N3904/PN2222 emitter lead to the capacitor's negative ("–") lead

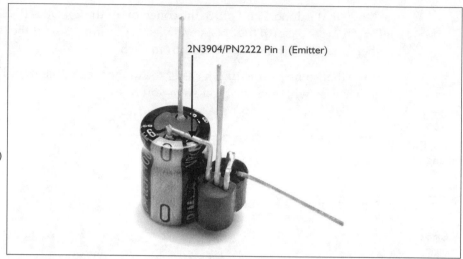

2N3904/PN2222 Pin I (Emitter)

Here's where all your yoga lessons come in handy. We want you to bend pin 3 (the collector) of the 2N3906/PN2907 into a twisted *U* shape, so that it can accommodate the first of the 100k transistors. Solder the resistor across the bent pin 3 of the 2N3906/PN2907 and the remaining vertical pin 2 (the base) of the 2N3904/PN2222.

Figure II-I4
Twisting the collector of the 2N3906/PN2907 to attach the first 100k resistor to it and the base of the 2N3904/PN2222

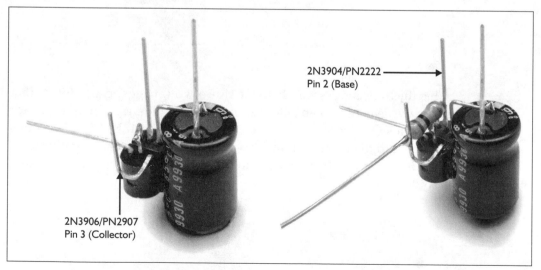

2N3904/PN2222
Pin 2 (Base)

2N3906/PN2907
Pin 3 (Collector)

Find your diode, and identify its cathode (that's the end near the stripe). Solder the diode's cathode to the trigger capacitor's positive lead (that's the one *not* near the stripe on the capacitor body).

Remember that very first transistor lead we bent off to the side to get out of the way? We need to solder the diode's anode to that pin 1 (the emitter) of the 2N3906/PN2907 now. When done, neaten up the solder joint by trimming off any excess lead from the diode.

Figure 11-15
Soldering the diode between the 2N3906/PN2907 emitter and the trigger capacitor's positive lead

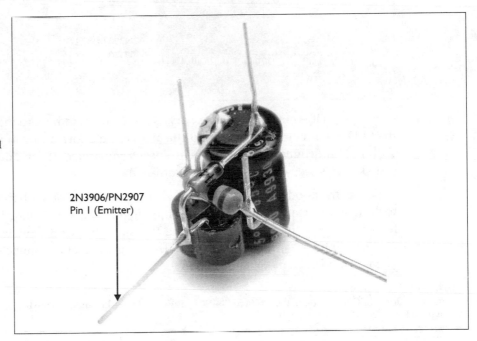

2N3906/PN2907
Pin 1 (Emitter)

Let's add the second 100k resistor in between the positive lead of the trigger capacitor and pin 2 (the base) of the 2N3904/PN2222. Again, after soldering, trim the resistor leads down to keep the solder joint nice and compact. Too many stray wires are a recipe for shorting out the circuit! A wire touching something it shouldn't be will most likely cause the circuit to fail.

Figure II-I6
Adding the second 100k resistor to the trigger capacitor's positive lead and the base of the 2N3904/PN2222

2N3904/PN2222
Pin 2 (Base)

Although it is not entirely necessary, we *really* do recommend that you add the LED to your circuit. It's only a little bit of extra effort, and you get (essentially) a blinky light for no extra cost in energy consumed. If you don't want it, just skip this step—no harm in not adding it.

Solder the anode of the LED (the lead *opposite* to the side with the flat spot) to the negative lead (near the stripe) of the trigger capacitor. Connect the other leg of the LED (the cathode, near the flat spot) to pin 3 (collector) of the 2N3906/PN2907—this was the first lead we bent and connected to the yoga-shaped *U*, remember?

Figure II-I7
Wiring the optional LED's cathode to the 2N3906/PN2907 emitter and the LED anode to the trigger capacitor's negative lead

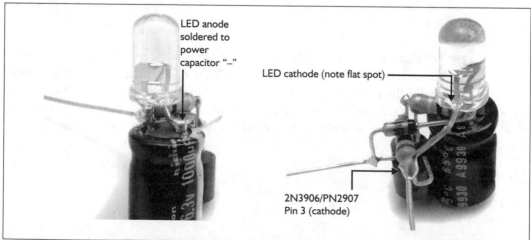

LED anode soldered to power capacitor "–"

LED cathode (note flat spot)

2N3906/PN2907
Pin 3 (cathode)

Attaching the power storage capacitor is our next task. Again, you can make the assembly process easier by gluing what you've assembled so far to the big power storage capacitor and bending the leads over to make the final connections.

Solder the 4700µF power storage capacitor's negative ("–") lead (nearest the stripe) to the negative lead of the smaller trigger capacitor. The other (positive) lead of the power storage capacitor will be soldered to pin 1 (the emitter) of the 2N3906/PN2907.

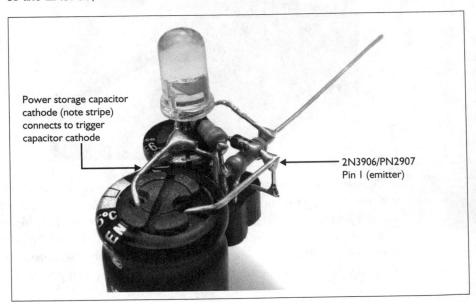

Figure 11-18
Soldering the main power storage to the trigger capacitor and 2N3906/PN2907 emitter

Power storage capacitor cathode (note stripe) connects to trigger capacitor cathode

2N3906/PN2907 Pin 1 (emitter)

We'll need a source of power for our magbot, and we'll concentrate on using solar cells for our assembly process (battery instructions come later). Solar cells in some solar-powered calculators will work quite well for this magbot application, but the calculator industry has some sneaky tricks up their sleeves that are going to make *using* these solar cells a bit more complicated. As most solar-powered calculators need very little power to run, the solar cells are installed using a conductive tape as the wires to pass power to the circuits. You will have most likely ripped this tape when you uninstalled the solar cells, and even if you were lucky enough to salvage them with the tape intact, you *cannot* solder to the tape, and the electrical contact pads on the solar cell are most likely not solder-friendly! Fortunately, there's a way around this, and all it requires is a little 3 mm ×6 mm (1/8"×1/4") hunk of thin sheet brass. Fold it into a *C* shape, slide it onto the solar cell so that the metal *C* is pinching the power connection pad, and then solder a wire to the *C* instead o

the pad. Use your multimeter to check for voltage, and if you're successful, super-glue that C down in place. You're good to go!

Figure II-19
Salvaging solar cells that don't have a place to solder to: The brass sheet metal C to the rescue!

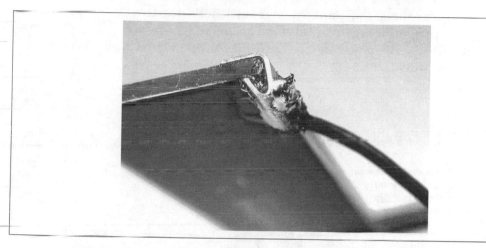

Another perfectly acceptable (but more expensive) solution is to use *silver conductive epoxy* to glue your wire to the electrical connection pads of the solar cells. If you really want to spend $20 on 14 ml (1/2 oz) of glue, *and* you can find it, *and* the hazardous chemical warnings don't put you off, be our guest. Just be careful, and you'll have a fully functional solar cell. Sometimes it's the only way to salvage a badly damaged solar cell connection pad.

Figure II-20
Sometimes conductive epoxy is the only way to save a solar cell and turn it into a glue and double-sided sticky tape–reinforced twinpack of solar cell lovin'!

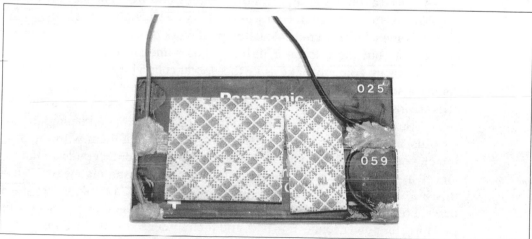

To complete your "force-coil" magbot circuit, all you need to do is wire up a solar cell across the leads of the main storage capacitor ("+" to "+", "−" to "−"), and add the coil to a ground ("−") connection (like the "−" of the main storage capacitor) and pin 3 (collector) of the 2N3906/PN2907. You may want to wait until your pendulum base is finished, or do the final wiring now and repeat the same tests you did with the breadboarded version.

Figure 11-21
Final wiring of the magbot circuit by soldering the solar cell and coil connections

Coil connections to power storage capacitor"−" and pin 3 (collector) of the 2N3906/PN2907

Solar cell connections to power storage capacitor "−" and "+"

The magbot circuit is practically finished, but let's not forget about the star of the show—the magnet! We still have to find a way to hang the magnet so that we can suspend it securely. The chrome/nickel plating on most supermagnets *is* solderable, so if you are up to the task, solder a wire hook to it. But be warned—it isn't easy to solder to such a high-strength magnet, as it will keep trying to jump and stick to your soldering iron.

An alternative procedure you may find easier is to take a chunk of PCB from a dead Walkman and use that as a base to glue the magnet to. Start by examining the PCBs until you find a spot with a nice large metal pad under the masking (the film protecting the metal traces). Isolate an area about the size of your magnet, and mark it out for cutting.

Figure 11-22
Find a chunk
of PCB with a
nice, large
pad that is
easily cut out.

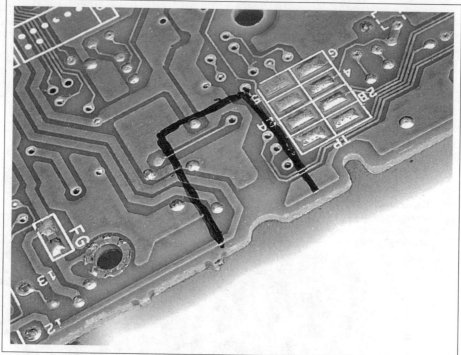

Using a pair of heavy scissors or a saw, remove the section of the PCB you
marked out. The (usually green) protective masking film on the surface of the
PCB is not difficult to scrap off, so use a knife or other suitably sharp scraper to
remove a 6 mm (1/4") square patch. Underneath, you'll find a nice, bright
copper surface that you can solder to.

Figure 11-23
Scrape off the masking to reveal the bare copper underneath.

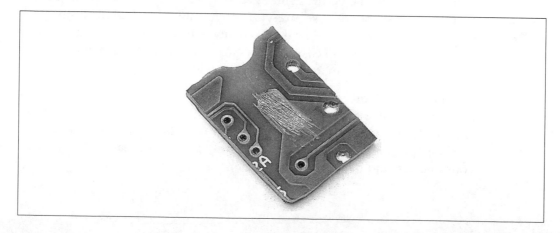

Take a long resistor or capacitor clipping, and solder it to this bare copper surface. Try to mount it right in the middle of the board, which is the best hanging point for the whole magnet assembly.

Figure 11-24
Solder a long metal clipping securely to the bare pad

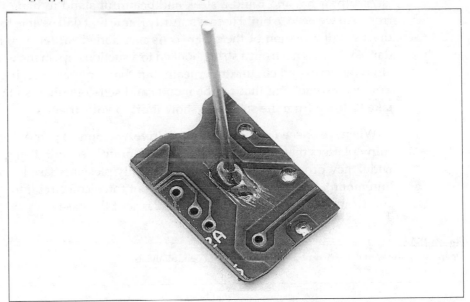

Fold the free end of the clipping around into a nice round shape that you can hook onto the suspension wire, and glue or double-sticky tape the magnet to the bottom of the holder.

Figure 11-25
The finished magnet assembly, ready to hang over the coil!

Building the Pendulum Base

With the geeky electronics stuff out of the way, you can put on your art-ist/sculptor hat and build a sleek and beautiful stand to hang the magnet from. All we need to build here is a sturdy frame that will be able to withstand the swinging motion of the magnet. As mentioned earlier, you *can* simply dangle the magnet from a string hooked to a suction cup on the window, and align the force-coil circuit underneath, but that'll be easy pickings for a cat. You need something that can be mobile and self-contained so that you can take it down from the shelf and show it off to your friends.

When we opened up our dead hard drive, we found a pair of very nice and shiny platters that we *simply* had to have for our base unit. Being heavy and wide, they proved to be an ideal, aesthetically pleasing base for our pendu-lum mount. We mounted our entire magbot force-coil circuit to this platter, and then we went to work building the rest of the base.

Figure II-26
Opening up the hard drive revealed our future magbot pendulum base

Sticking with the simple but elegant idea, we started with a 30 cm (12") length of solid 10-gauge household copper wire, available from almost any building supply store. It comes in a variety of colors, but we chose black (you can never go wrong with black).

Figure 11-27
Ten-gauge
house-wiring
electrical wire
is not just
for routing
electricity
anymore.

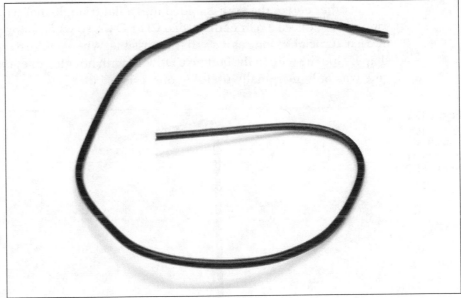

We bent our wire into a simple upside-down *L* shape and cut two small grooves in the electrical insulation to have an easy place to tie our fishing line to.

Figure 11-28
Cutting a pair
of grooves in
the insulation
where we'll
tie our
magnet-
hanging line

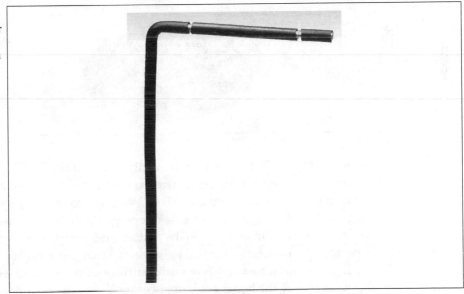

The other end of the wire is folded into a flat triangle that we're going to sandwich between a pair of discarded CD-ROMs, so what shape you bend it into isn't crucial, as long as it's as flat as possible. When you're happy with the shape, glue the wire to the bottom CD-ROM with hot glue or epoxy, as super glue was only marginally useful in our tests.

Figure II-29
Wire support arm glued down to the first CD-ROM

Our second CD-ROM disk won't fit exactly on top of the first because of the upright portion of our wire support arm, so we cut a chunk off the CD-ROM so that it fit better. Again, glue this CD-ROM down to the wire support and the first CD-ROM using more hot glue or epoxy. With this finished, you can put your magbot circuit and coil on the platter, and hang your magnet from a V-shaped length of fishing line tied between the two grooves. Try to arrange the magnet so that it just skims over the surface of the coil—the closer it is (without touching), the better performance you'll get out of your pendulum.

Figure 11-30
Glue down the second CD-ROM, position the magbot circuit, and hang the magnet.

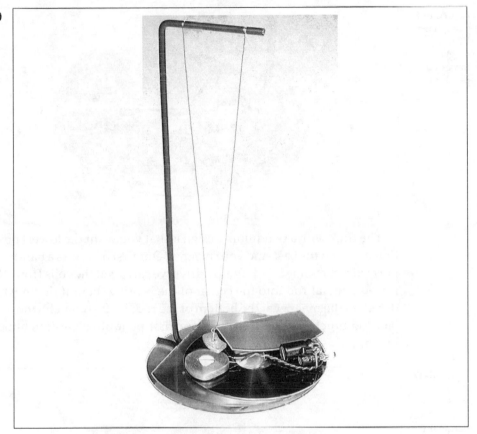

As soon as you pull your fingers away from the magnet, it should start moving almost immediately. We had to resort to using a cut piece of CD-ROM to cover the solar cells so that we could keep the magnet still long enough to take some of these pictures. Without the solar cell cover, the magnet really starts to zoom!

When you're happy with the location of parts and the action of the magnet swing, glue down the coil and circuit (see Figure 11-31—don't mind the chunk of CD covering the solar cell that kept the pendulum still for the picture). Or not. If you leave the magbot circuitry loose, you have a portable pendulum-generator. Just take the magnet off its swing, hook it up to a different pendulum, and bring the magbot circuitry module over to the new location. It opens up a whole new avenue of experimentation when you can play with new geometries of pendulums and locations!

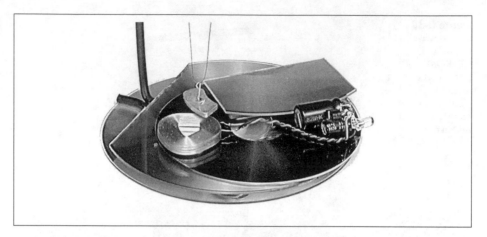

The trick with a pendulum design is that you want the lowest possible friction between the base and your magnet. Our first base was a ball-bearing support from the same 5 1/4" floppy drive we salvaged the coils from. We simply forced a metal rod into the center of the bearing, bent it down 90°, and soldered on the magnet at the bottom of the rod. Unfortunately, the bearing still had too much friction in it, and our first pendulum design, although cool looking, was only marginally successful.

Figure II-32
Magbot
Pendulum
beta 0.1: Only
marginally
successful,
it uses a
floppy-drive
bearing as
the rotation
point.

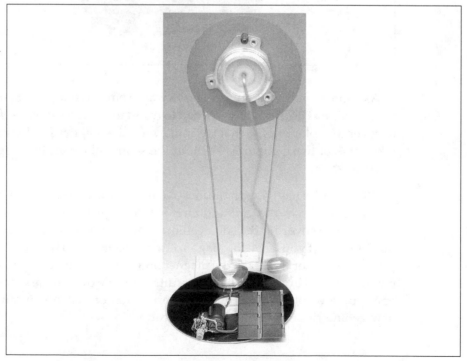

Giving up on a mechanical rotation point, we found that the obvious answer was to suspend the magnet by a string or thin wire. The spool of fine 4-pound-test monofilament line (fishing line) we found in the junk drawer proved to be an excellent solution, and being almost transparent, it adds to the "cool" effect of the whole project.

Figure 11-33
Our solution to low-friction pendulum motion!

We experimented with other pendulum bases, trying to find what materials worked best. The one we build out of discarded CD-ROMs proved a trickier task than expected, as the plastic wouldn't take glue very well, and the thinness of it made for a very flexible, bobbing base (bad). A little more engineering with some stiffening members solved that problem, but it was proving to be more work than it was worth.

Figure 11-34
Discarded CD-ROMs as construction material? Not one of our best ideas...

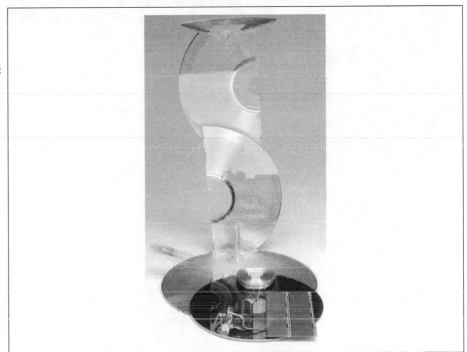

Another base we built used another pair of hard-drive platters as the top and bottom elements, held apart by a thick Sintra spacer. We mounted the magbot force-coil circuit and a quad of crystalline solar cells on the top platter, and we ran extension wires to the bottom platter, where we mounted the coil. Double-sided sticky tape was an excellent choice for mounting these components to the base, as it electrically insulated the parts from the conductive surface of the platter and allowed for slight repositioning of the parts for ideal placement. We cut a slot in the top platter with a jeweler's hand saw and secured the magnet line in place with a knot and some tape.

Figure II-35
Dual hard-drive platters with a Sintra upright make for a suitably high-tech base for our magbot pendulum.

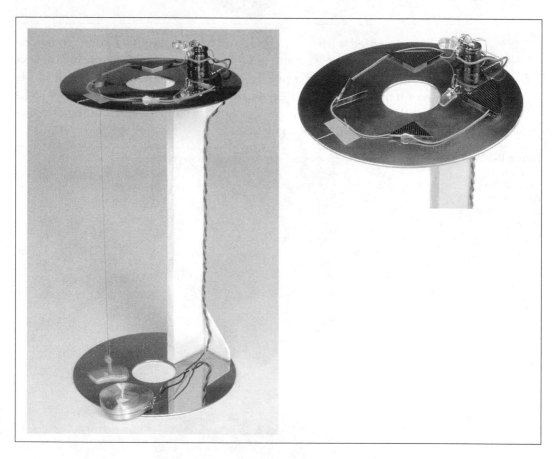

The Robot Geek Says

Troubleshooting Your Magbot

Anything that essentially that could have gone wrong should have been caught with the breadboarded version of the circuit. A problem in transferring the circuit from breadboard to the operational version means that there is most likely an error in the freeform wiring.

Care and Feeding of Your Magbot Pendulum

Now that you've got your magbot force-coil pendulum working, you can experiment with the mathematics of it all. Yup, mathematics (whoohoo!), specifically from the field of Physics. The neat thing about pendulums is that it doesn't matter what the mass of the weight on the end of the string is; as long as the length of string is the same, it *always* takes the same amount of time to swing back and forth.

The simple version of the formula to figure how many seconds to swing back and forth once is:

$$T = 6.28 \times \sqrt{(L/981)} \text{ (in metric cm)}$$

or

$$T = 6.28 \times \sqrt{(L/386)} \text{ (in imperial inches)}$$

One of our pendulums has a string length of 15.7 cm, and the calculation came to 0.79 seconds. Measuring the time for ten full swings and then dividing by 10 yielded 0.81 seconds per swing—close enough, given our not-so-accurate timing ability!

You can bend the equation around to calculate what length of line you need to get a specific period (time for one full back-and-forth swing) in seconds:

$$L = 981 \times (T/6.28)^2 \text{ (in metric cm)}$$
$$L = 386 \times (T/6.28)^2 \text{ (in imperial inches)}$$

Imagine a very slow pendulum needing a period of two seconds per swing. That would need a string 99 cm long (39")! A full window-sized magbot pendulum would indeed be an interesting sight to see.

Battery operation isn't that hard to implement, as we just substitute, for the solar cell, a 3- to 9-volt battery running through a 4.7k to 10k resistor. You'll need a power switch, unless you can come up with a "turn-on" circuit that activates the magbot when somebody turns on the lights, but we'll leave that little project up to you to figure out.

Figure II-36
Replacing the solar cell with a battery

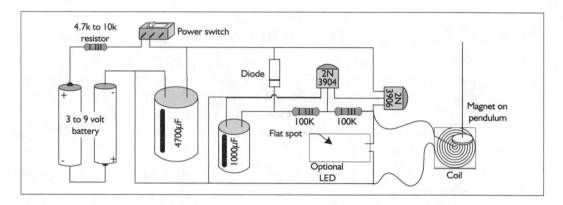

Besides being an interesting mathematical diversion, the magbot pendulum leaves you other things to watch out for. Other pieces of metal, for instance. Our experience with the pendulum has taught us to keep any magnetic material well out of the swinging arc path of the magnet, as we've seen the magnet glom onto other robots on the same shelf that we *thought* were well out of the way.

Another concern about having a free-swinging magbot pendulum is that it may not always swing exactly left-to-right all the time. There's nothing keeping it from deviating from its course slightly, occasionally making it crash into part of the base structure. This may be of interest to some of you who may want to combine your magbot with chime technology, but we find it to be a bit of a pain to hear "CLUNK" every few minutes from the windowsill.

There are three solutions to this problem. The first we've already explored and told you about: using, instead of fishing line, a bearing as a swing mount holding a rod. Bearing friction eats lots of the power, but you very well could find a better-quality bearing than the one we have.

The second solution was to build a second magbot force-coil circuit and locate it next to the first so the swinging magnet passes directly over both. The two circuits work well in concert, accelerating and pulling the swinging magnet in an arc directly above the two coils. It's a simple circuit, so why not just build another? If you have an ample power supply, you very well could power both circuits from the same supply lines.

The third solution is to use a *V* loop of line that suspends the magnet from two points, as a swing is. This is the easiest of solutions, and it is the one we chose for our project. It uses up twice as much line, but we think it's worth the extra $0.0042....

One final experiment you may want to try with your pendulum is to put a second bar under the first magnet wire support bar. With a little creativity, you can get your pendulum to move in ways like Olympic gymnasts!

Figure 11-37
The dual-bar pendulum stand, for a bit more creative swing motion

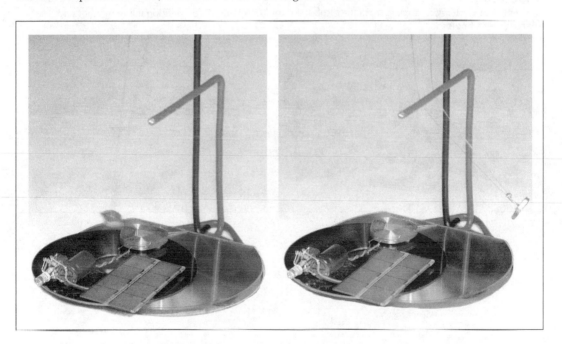

Magbots don't have to follow the traditional restrictions of wheeled or legged devices. If you can find an application for simple motion, there's a good chance a magbot can be adapted to it. One of the more innovative devices built around this idea we've seen is the "Hand of God," an entry in the "Robot Art and Innovation" competition at the BEAM/WCRG Millennium Robot Games. Coming all the way from City Montessori School in Chowk, India, the team of Yousuf Fauzan, Devvrat Shukla, Vaibhav Pankaj, Diwakar Shukla, and Chetan Mehrotra entered many of the competitions, but they showed particular creativity in this heavily modified hard-drive mechanism driven by two independent solarengines. One solarengine drove a small gear motor that slowly rotated a paper disk mounted on the hard-drive spindle, and the other solarengine fired pulses to the swing-arm mechanism modified to hold a pen. By using nothing more than the energy in the immediate environment, this solar-powered data recorder created spectacularly colorful images. As for their device's name, their instructor, Swami Amar Bedi, called this device "a true inspiration from God; as if God's own hand determines the final outcome of each paper disk."

Figure II-38
The "Hand of God": A creative entry in the "Robot Art and Innovation" competition using magbot and solarengine technology

Chapter 12

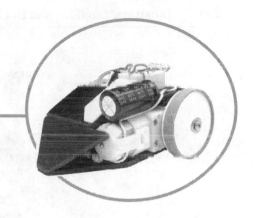

Project 6: The BEAM Mini–Sumo Wrestling Edgebot

Parts List

- ❏ **2** × Light emitting diodes (LEDs)
- ❏ **2** × DPDT relays
- ❏ **1** × 4700μF capacitor
- ❏ **1** × Power switch
- ❏ **1** × 9V battery and connector
- ❏ **2** × Motors/wheels
- ❏ **1** × Bump sensor switch
- ❏ **1** × Body material

Optional Parts for Five-Second Delay Timer

- ❏ **1** × Push-button switch
- ❏ **1** × 1000μF capacitor
- ❏ **1** × 1kΩ to 47kΩ resistor
- ❏ **1** × 2N3904/PN2222 transistor
- ❏ **1** × LED

The BEAM Mini–Sumo Wrestling Edgebot

Up until now, we've been working on robot designs for their own sake—building robots strictly for the fun of it. With this project, you can enter robot competitions and battle your robot against others in an event called *robot mini–sumo wrestling*. Just as in real Japanese sumo wrestling, the basic idea is to push your opponent out of a ring without falling out yourself!

Mini–sumo wresting is an offshoot of (can you guess?) *robot sumo wrestling,* where the robots are larger, are heavier, and compete on a bigger platform. Although lots of fun, these bigger robots are substantially more expensive, as they use bigger stronger motors and batteries. Bill Harrison (http://www.sinerobotics.com) saw a need for a scaled-down version, where the robots would be smaller, lighter, and (most importantly) cheaper. A competitive mini–sumo wrestling robot could be built for under $50 (less, if you use your super-scrounging skills), so almost anybody who wanted to could compete. Harrison took it upon himself to take the original "Japanese" standard robot sumo rules originally written by Fujisoft ABC, Inc., and convert them to a standard that is now used by over ten different robot competitions worldwide.

The basic rules for mini-sumo are

- ❏ The robot must fit in a square tube measuring 10 cm × 10 cm × any height. (10 cm = 2.54").
- ❏ The robot must weight under 500 grams (17.6 oz).
- ❏ The match is run on a 2.5 cm (1") thick, 77 cm (30.3") diameter black competition ring, with a 2.5 cm (1") wide white line marking the edge.
- ❏ The robot must wait five seconds (or more) after being turned on before moving.
- ❏ Robots are not allowed to jam opponent's sensors, be destructive, or be harmful in any way. The match is wholly intended to be along the lines of a pushing/shoving match and nothing else. (Want Battlebots? Look up "Antweight Battlebots" on the Internet. Mini-sumo isn't violent!)
- ❏ The first robot to touch outside of the ring loses the round.
- ❏ There are three rounds to a match, best two out of three wins.

Technically, there are two types of mini–sumo wrestlers, being *autonomous* and *remote control (r/c).* The difference between them is pretty obvious: autonomous ones do not need any assistance from you after you turn them on. Once activated, they (should) have all the brains they need to do some sumo wrestling without interference from humans. The remote control versions aren't much different from a toy car that you steer remotely. Although r/c sumobots are fun, it's much more satisfying to build your own true mini-sumo robot to do battle, and cheer it on from the sidelines!

Figure 12-1
Mini-sumo
at the 2002
Western
Canadian
Robot Games,
with Roger
Korus
and Beau
Johansen

The basic strategy of competition is to make the other guy fall out before you. The way you go about that is where the fun comes in, as there's countless ways of getting this done. Whatever way you decide to ultimately follow, the first behavior your robot should have is to *back away from the edge*. A robot that blindly charges off the edge of the ring won't do very well, so making your robot scared of the edge is an excellent first-level behavior, and this is the sole behavior we'll build into your BEAM mini-sumo. After that, you can develop seeking strategies with optical or touch sensors that scan for your opponent, chase it down, and shove it out.

The edge-scared behavior we're going to build is something we like to call an *edgebot* circuit. An edgebot performs the same behavior every time it senses an edge, which is to

1. Reverse away from the edge
2. Spin one direction
3. Go forward

This edge-detection routine doesn't care if the front left or front right of your robot is over the edge, even if you have a sensor on each front corner—it will do the same procedure regardless of which sensor triggers it. A true edge-detection procedure is smarter in that it knows which of the robot's corners is nearer the edge, and it chooses the best direction to turn. It would operate something like this:

If LEFT corner is over edge, back up, turn RIGHT, then go forward again.

If RIGHT corner is over edge, back up, turn LEFT, then go forward again.

This sort of behavior isn't impossible using BEAM circuitry, but it is more complicated and uses more parts than the very simple edgebot solution we've come up with. Start by building an edgebot-type mini-sumo, then start thinking about how you can further improve it. Besides, building more than one mini-sumo is a great way to train—you need at least two to fight!

Figure 12-2
MiniCAB:
An opponent-
seeking,
copper-shelled,
microprocessor/
BEAM hybrid
mini-sumo
robot wrestler

Figure 12-3
Edgebot
mini-sumo
schematic

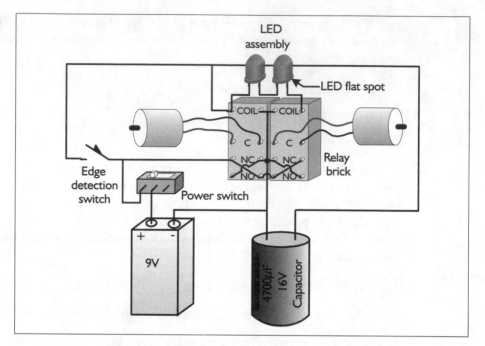

The "brains" of our edgebot mini-sumo are a pair of double-pole, double-throw (DPDT) relays, which control the forward/backward motion of each wheel. You should be getting good at spotting and using these relays—they're the same type as the one we used on the Herbie project backup sensor circuit. We're using a switch on the nose of our mini-sumo to detect the edge of the platform, so that when it closes, it quickly snap-charges the backup capacitor. When this capacitor has a charge, it bleeds its energy through both relays, making both motors run in reverse. Since we have a pair of LEDs between the first and second relay signal inputs, one relay turns off before the other, making it spin; then, finally, both relays turn off, making the mini-sumo go forward again.

LEDs consume power, just like anything else in a circuit, so when we put these in the same circuit as the relay activation electromagnet coil, it doesn't get as much power as the other relay, which *doesn't* have any LEDs connected to it. Our handicapped relay still has enough power to turn on, but it will turn off sooner due to the power eaten by the LEDs.

Edgebot Mini-Sumo Parts

The mini-sumo parts list consists of fairly common parts, but you should spend extra effort on the motors and wheels. Without pushing power and traction, a mini-sumo robot is an easy target!

❑ **2 × LEDs.** These set the time difference between the two relays. Color won't matter too much, although red makes for a quick turn. Green and yellow are slightly longer, and blue or white LEDs are longest. Different colors consume different amounts of energy, so depending on the LED color, your reverse time will be different.

Figure 12-4
This VCR front control panel has *lots* of LEDs to pick from.

❑ **2 × Double-pole, double-throw (DPDT) relays.** These will be routing power to the motors and need to be rated at 5, 6, or 9 volts. You can use a 12-volt relay *only* if you are using a 12-volt or greater battery to power your mini-sumo. A 5-volt relay is preferable.

❏ **1** × 4700µF, 16-volt capacitor. This capacitor sets the time your mini-sumo is in "reverse and turn" mode. A smaller value may be needed if your motors are particularly speedy.

❏ **1** × Power switch. Nothing special here, just something to pass power from the battery to the rest of the mini-sumo circuit. Ideally, a single-pole, double-throw (SPDT, has three pins) switch would be ideal.

Figure 12-5

External modem innards: Here's our power switch and an SPDT relay for our optional five-second delay circuit.

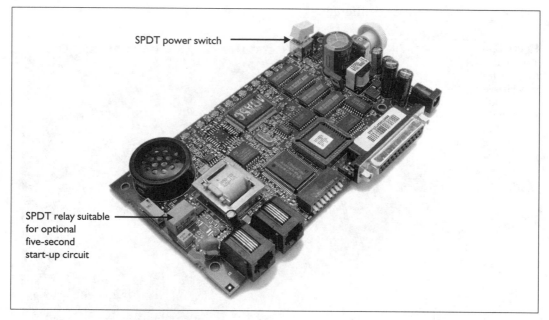

SPDT power switch

SPDT relay suitable for optional five-second start-up circuit

❏ **1** × 9V battery and connector. A single alkaline or rechargeable 9-volt battery does well, although you can use more voltage if your motors can handle it and your "reverse and turn" capacitor has a high enough voltage rating. 18 volts from a pair of 9-volt batteries wired in series makes for impressive performance but short motor life!

❏ **2** × Motors. The most critical part of a mini-sumo is the power train. It's no good to have a super-speedy robot if you don't have the power to shove your opponent's robot out of the ring when you catch him. We need motors with *torque*, which gives our bot the ability to shove, and which usually means using some sort of motor with gear reduction to slow it down but increase its ability to turn. Try to avoid speedy toy race cars, and concentrate on getting the motors out of slow toy tanks or walking robot toys like the WowWee "B.I.O.-Bug" insect robot (as we did, but we killed two identical bugs to get a matched set of motors). It's worth noting that these very gear motors are also available from Solarbotics with wheels for $11.50 a pair. Another popular technique is to use standard hobby servos, strip out their electronic brains, trim off the rotation-stop nub, and turn them into simple gear motors. Most servos can be modified pretty easily, so in a pinch, visit a hobby shop and expect to spend $15 each.

Figure 12-6
B.I.O.-Bug motors: Off with the legs, on with the wheels!

❏ **2 × Wheels.** It's no good having the power but no traction. That's why drag racers have big, fat rubber tires—for maximum grip. The wider wheel you can get, the better, but to keep things simple, we're using pill bottle/film canister lids for wheels and rubber bands for tires. Don't be afraid to rip whole hubs off toy cars, especially the "pull back and release" type, as they have pretty good rubber on the rim. You'll also need epoxy glue if you will be custom-mounting your wheels to the motors.

Figure 12-7
Wheels can be made from plastic bottle and film canister lids, or get them from a toy.

❏ **1** × Edge sensor switch. This switch won't be detecting bumps as much as it will be detecting the edge of the ring. It can be made from a paper clip and some thin wire, or it can even salvaged from a dead mouse (mmmm…love them dead mice!). We used a bit of 10-gauge solid copper wire and some fine guitar-string wire.

Figure 12-8
Mouse switches are very suitable for edge detection.

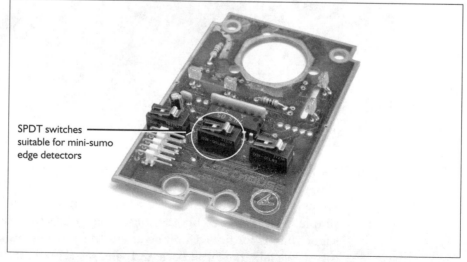

SPDT switches suitable for mini-sumo edge detectors

❏ **1** × Body material. Every robot needs a body, and the mini-sumo needs something tough and easy to form. We're using a material called *Sintra,* which was salvaged from a sign maker's shop.

Alternatively, a nice, flat, stiff piece of plastic from the shell of a piece of electroscrap would do nicely.

Optional Parts for Five-Second Delay Timer

If you want your robot to be fully competition-legal, you'll have to add an additional circuit to control when your mini-sumo activates. These parts will make your mini-sumo start approximately five seconds after the "reset" button is pushed.

❏ **1** × Push button reset switch. You'll need this to prepare your mini-sumo for each round. Nothing very complicated is required, just a push button of some sort with two (or more) contacts

Figure 12-9
Reset switches are easily salvaged from the front panel of a dead VCR.

❏ **1** × 5-, 6-, or 9-volt relay. It won't matter if it's single-pole, single-throw (SPST); single-pole, double-throw (SPDT); or one of our friends, the DPDT relay. We're simply going to use it to connect the battery to the rest of the mini-sumo circuit, and that takes just the simplest of relays to do.

❏ **1 × 1000μF capacitor.** This capacitor sets the start-up delay time—the bigger it is, the longer before activation occurs. As the voltage on this capacitor won't rise very high (about 3 volts), practically any voltage rating over 6 volts will be sufficient.

❏ **1 × Resistor.** This resistor powers the relay activation transistor. Any value between 1kΩ and 47kΩ can be used. You may want to use a 50k trimpot (adjustable resistor) instead, so that you can use it to tune how long the bot stays in reverse and turn modes.

❏ **1 × 2N3904/PN2222 transistor.** This transistor activates the main power relay when the start-up delay capacitor has charged high enough to turn it on.

❏ **1 × LED.** Because the LED consumes some of the power passing through it, we're using one to delay when the main power relay activates. Without it, we would need a much larger start-up delay capacitor. You won't see it light up unless you're looking very closely, or if you have a really efficient LED. For our circuit, we're using a salvaged green LED, although most any other color will work (but may throw off the time value a bit).

Figure 12-10
Mini-sumo parts, ready to go!

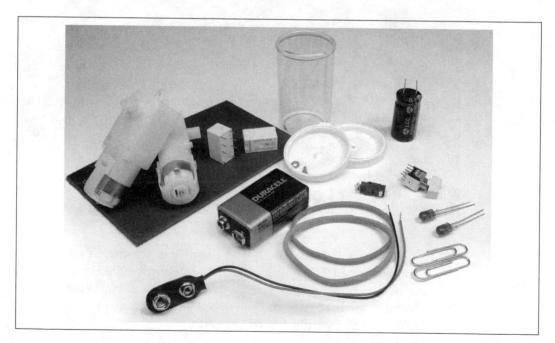

Again, breadboarding your parts to make sure they are compatible is a very good idea. When everything is functioning properly, you'll have two motors spinning until you momentarily tap the sensor switch, then the two LEDs light up and both motors go in reverse. After an instant, one motor should kick back into forward motion again, followed shortly by the other motor.

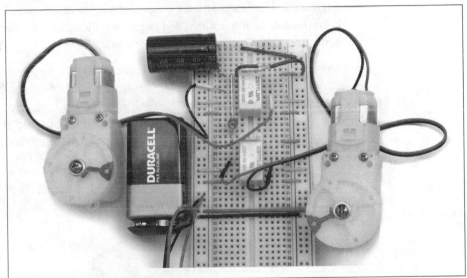

Figure 12-11
Mini-sumo
breadboarded
for testing

The Robot Geek Says

Troubleshooting Your Breadboarded Mini-Sumo Circuit

The circuit is very straightforward, so any possible error will most likely come from wiring up the relays. You already have experience using relays from the Herbie project, and the same rules apply here.

✖ **The motors aren't turning.** First check your motors by connecting them each to the battery. They should turn nice and strong. If not, your batteries are too weak, or your motors are too power-hungry or possibly even dead. Try using a fresh alkaline 9-volt battery, such as an Energizer or Duracell.

✖ **Motors work but don't when you connect them to the relay.** This surely indicates a pin identification problem. Just as when we identified the mystery pins on the relay we used on the Herbie project, you want to find the pairs of pins with practically no resistance. You want your motor connections wired one each to a single pin of each pair.

✖ **Motors work, but they don't reverse direction when the edge
sensor is activated.** Make sure your edge sensor is passing a positive
("+") signal to the relay, not a negative ("−") signal. Perhaps your relays
are polarity sensitive. Try swapping around the "+" and "−" connections
to the relay activation electromagnet pins.

✖ **Only one motor kicks into reverse when the edge sensor is
activated.** That's a pretty sure sign that you have the relay LEDs
in backward, or the positive and negative connections to the relay
activation electromagnet pins are reversed.

The best place to start is to take your motors, wheels, battery, and 4700μF
"reverse and turn" capacitor and play around with how they fit together.
Measure and mark out a 10×10 cm (2.54"×2.54") box on a piece of paper, and
play with orientations until you're happy with the layout and it doesn't go
outside the 10 cm box. Our B.I.O.-Bug motors fit well side-by-side with the
servo wedge between them, and the capacitor just ahead. Trace the layout
onto your base material and trim it out.

Figure 12-12
Basic
mini-sumo
parts physical
layout sitting
within
10×10 cm
maximum-
size boundary

If your gear motors don't have easily attached wheels, we'll start by attaching those to the motors first. We used the lids from large pill bottles as our
wheels, as they had a dimple in the middle so that we could easily locate the
wheel's exact center. A self-threading #2 screw punctured this dimple and
threaded into the hole in the middle of our gear motor shaft.

Figure 12-13
Mounting wheels to motors with screws and washers

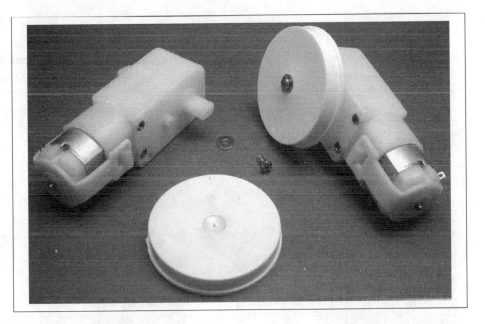

If this was all we did to mount the wheels, we'd be in big trouble in our first mini-sumo match, as the screw by itself isn't strong enough to transfer the power of the motor to the wheel itself. Our answer is to tip the motor on its side so that the cap is flat on the table and fill the cap's cavity with epoxy gluer. This hardens into a tough resin that stiffens the wheel and locks the motor's shaft to the wheel.

Figure 12-14
Filling the wheel cavities with epoxy

While the motors are gluing to the wheels, let's cut out the base of our robot mini-sumo. We've taken the sketch of our outline and cut it out, using it as a pattern to make the base out of some sheet Sintra plastic. Sintra glues very well, comes in nice bright colors, and can be very cheap. But if you have the plastic bottom to an old external modem, use that instead. We're not picky.

Figure 12-15
Cutting out the mini-sumo base and support strip

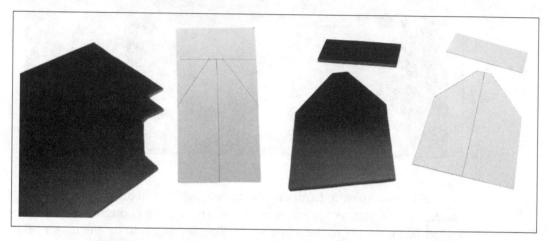

Glue dry on the wheels yet? No? Well, best leave it cure overnight, so it'll be nice and strong. Let's work on the mini-sumo brains in the meantime. Start by sitting your two DPDT relays side-by-side, and glue them together into a nice relay brick (a drop of superglue works great here—just don't pick your nose at the same time). We're going to make this dual-relay brick the heart of your mini-sumo.

Figure 12-16
Gluing the relays together

We'll be wiring these relays together in a tidy bundle, but this will work correctly only if your relays follow the pinout diagram shown in Figure 12-17 (which *most* should). You should double-check your relays against the figure and make sure they match ours; otherwise, you'll have to make wiring changes according to the original schematic in Figure 12-3.

Figure 12-17
Our relay pinout diagram: Make sure yours matches this before getting started!

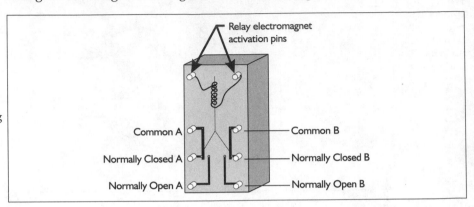

We'll consider the "top" of the relay brick the part with the two pairs of pins sitting all by themselves. Start by pinching over the top middle pair and bottom middle two pairs of leads and soldering them together. We're looking for a nice, tidy solder job here, so take your time and do it well. You don't want a bad solder joint to make your mini-sumo die in the middle of battle! Don't solder the second pins down from the top together—these are left individual for soldering to the motors.

Figure 12-18
Soldering most of the middle row of relay pins

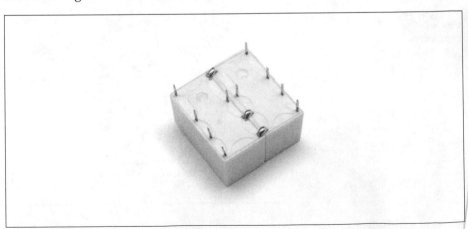

Find a resistor clipping (there should be a good several dozen on your workbench by now) and bend it from the bottom-left corner to the second pin

up in the middle row, and back down to the bottom-right corner of the relay assembly. This prepares the relay brick to swap half of the power connections (the "−" connections) to the motors.

Figure 12-19
Wiring the corners of the relay to the second pin up in the middle row

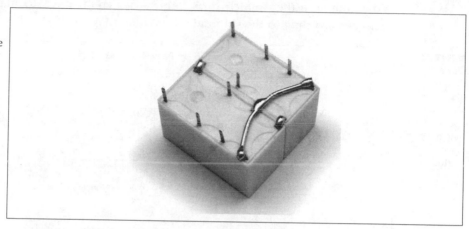

Next we'll wire relay connections to the "+" side of the power supply, so guess what color of wire we need? No, not pink or chartreuse—*red*. You don't *need* red, but it sure helps identify what power is going where later. Connect the two pins that are second up from the bottom on each side to the one at the bottom middle. When done, this makes the relay brick ready to swap the other half of the power connections (the "+" connections) to the motors.

Figure 12-20
Wiring up the relay's "+" connections

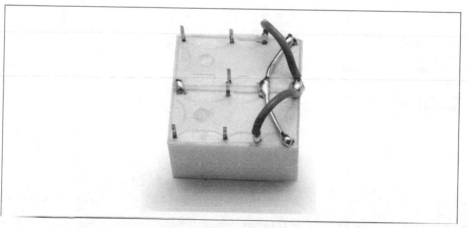

While we're wiring up power connections, let's take a black wire (for "−") and solder it from the first connection we made (second pin up from bottom middle) to the top-middle connection.

Figure 12-21
Wiring up the
relay's "−"
connections

This next bit is a two-stage process. Solder your two LEDs together in series, so that they're connected cathode-to-anode (long lead to short lead). Make this a nice and tidy job of soldering, as a compact set of LEDs is easier to install than a pair with long, dangly legs.

Solder the LED set to the outside two leads of your relay brick. It really doesn't matter which way it goes around (unless your relay is a higher-voltage type with a reverse blocking diode), but it will decide which way your mini-sumo will always turn when it detects an edge. If your relay does have a blocking diode on the activation inputs, then make sure you orient your LED set so that the lead nearest the flat side (the cathode) goes to the "−" input pin. Discover this using the same troubleshooting technique used in the Herbie project chapter.

Whichever way you install the LED set, you will be able to swap motor connections to the relays if you want your mini-sumo to turn in the opposite direction. Decisions, decisions!

Figure 12-22
Preparing and installing the LEDs

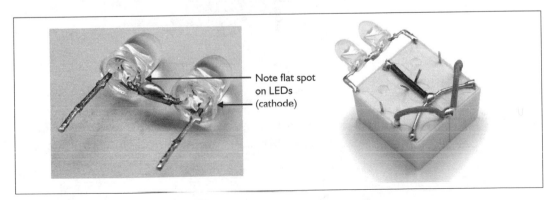

Note flat spot
on LEDs
(cathode)

Now that your relay brick is assembled, we can mount it onto your mini-sumo body. Well, we suppose it would be a good idea to *finish* the body first, so let's go check our wheels and motors to see how well they've glued together. Epoxy glue usually takes a good 24 hours to properly set, even if it's labeled the "5-minute" or "12-minute" type, so if you haven't given it enough time to dry, leave the project here and come back to it tomorrow. We'll wait here for you, okay? We'll just play some cards and talk about your funny-smelling socks...

Back already? Good—we were running out of smelly-sock comments. Now that you're *sure* your wheels are securely mounted to the motors, let's glue them down to the mini-sumo body you cut out earlier. We used super glue, but you may find it more suitable to use epoxy, hose clamps, zip-ties, half-chewed gummy bears, or even just twisted wire to hold the motors to the frame. Use whatever technique you're happiest with (but gummy bears really don't work that well—trust us).

Our layout of parts also required that we add some spacers to the top of the motors so that we could easily slide the 9-volt battery between the motors and still be able to mount more stuff on top.

Figure 12-23
Motors and spacers glued to the mini-sumo base

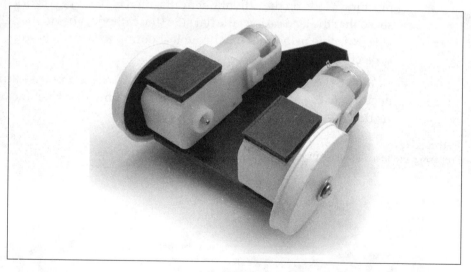

We next glue our bridge piece across the top of the spacers and test-fit our battery, backup capacitor, relay brick, and power switch. Things look good!

Figure 12-24
Gluing the
bridge
piece and
test-fitting the
components

We'll position the switch so that it's easily accessed but in far enough that it won't get accidentally bumped during a competition. We don't want to give our opponent a nice, easy target that would kill our robot, right?

Generally, you don't want to use super glue near a switch, for fear of gumming up the works and destroying the switch. Our switch has a metal body that solders nicely to a chunk of brass scrap we found, and we simply glue the whole works to the mini-sumo body.

Figure 12-25
Soldering
the switch
to a holding
plate and
gluing the
plate to the
mini-sumo
body

Position your relay brick on your mini-sumo in a nice, compact location where you can still access all the relay pins. We're placing ours next to the power switch, right above where the battery is, so our wiring will be easy to do and tidy. When you're happy with its location, glue it down.

Figure 12-26
Gluing the relay brick to the mini-sumo body

We're almost ready to finish up the wiring, but we're still missing a critical element—the edge-detection switch! This is possibly the most important component of the whole robot, because without it, your mini-sumo is doomed, doomed, DOOMED! Being doomed isn't a good thing, so let's install that switch and finish up our mini-sumo.

You can build your edge-detection switch by modifying a regular switch, or you can build one from scratch as we did. A regular switch may be a bit easier to install, but a custom-built switch will be easier to tweak and tune. Our switch is constructed out of a heavy piece of solid 10-gauge household electrical wire and a piece of metal guitar string wire. You'll get similar results from using a paper clip and a piece of fine spring wire (look for any fine springs in your technoscrap, and straighten out a bit of one).

Figure 12-27
Edge detector
sensor parts

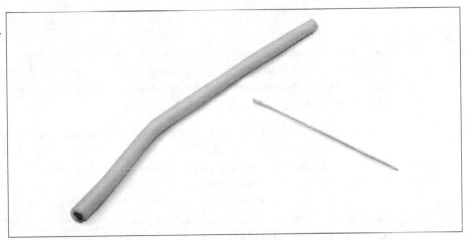

Our edge sensor is made up of three parts: the sensor anchor, the sensor pin, and the sensor itself. The thin sensor wire gets soldered to the sensor anchor and bent over the sensor pin; it then passes through a hole on the mini-sumo base. When the sensor falls down (by slipping over the edge of the sumo ring), it contacts the sensor pin, closing the circuit that makes the mini-sumo kick into reverse and turn mode. Start by cutting two small lengths of the thick wire and stripping off the insulation as shown in Figure 12-28. A razor blade may come in handy for separating the insulation off the middle portions. Glue doesn't stick to copper wire particularly well, and if you have a metal mini-sumo body, you don't want to cause strange electrical short-circuits, so by exposing bare metal only where we need it, we get better electrical isolation and less chance of a short-circuit.

Figure 12-28
Cutting and
stripping the
sensor mount
wires

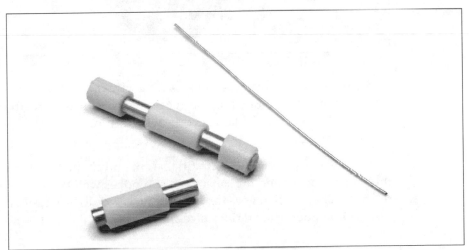

You want your sensor as close to the front-middle of your robot as possible. Ideally, you'll want to wire *two* sets of sensors, one for each front corner of your mini-sumo, but we'll keep the project simpler by using just the one. If you do wish to mount two sensors, simply wire them up to the same connection points on the relay brick, and either sensor will trigger the reverse and turn behavior.

Drill a small hole in the front of your mini-sumo where you want the sensor wire to poke through. If possible, make it a slot about 1×4 mm long (1/16"×1/4"), so that we can shape a nice loop on the end of the sensor later. Just behind this slot, glue the sensor pin. The fine sensor wire will hover just above this pin, until the sensor wire falls down (over the edge of the sumo ring) and touches it. The second, longer pin is where we'll solder on the fine sensor wire, so locate it about 12 mm (1/2") behind the sensor pin.

Figure 12-29
Drilling the slot and gluing down the two large sensor wires

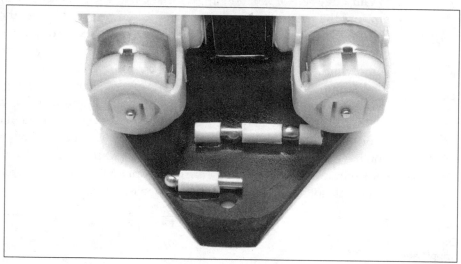

Before we do anything else, let's solder a wire each to the sensor pin and the sensor anchor. Green or white is a good color for sensor wires, but again, use what you have on hand. Make sure the wires are long enough to get back near the relay brick.

The fine sensor wire needs to first be cut and shaped so that it lies across the sensor anchor and the sensor pin and pokes well through the bottom of the hole. The part that goes through the hole should be wrapped back into a little "O" shape so that it rides nice and smooth on the competition ring surface and isn't simply a sharp wire poking straight down. A poky wire tends to dig in and will get caught on the edge of the ring when the mini-sumo tries to back up.

When you're happy with the shape of your sensor, solder it down *just* to the anchor, so that the other end is poking through the hole. When you hold your mini-sumo in the air, this fine sensor wire should be pressing down against the sensor pin. When you put it down on the table, the part of the fine wire poking through the hole should bend the wire upward, separating it from the sensor pin.

Figure 12-30
Fine sensor wire installation and tweaking

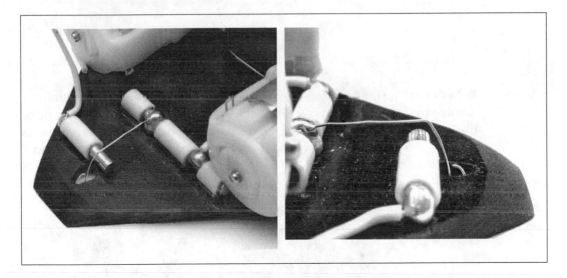

If you wish to use a salvaged switch, this is how you may want to use it. Most of these types of switches have three poles, and much like relays, they have a common terminal ("C"), a normally open terminal ("N.O."), and a normally closed terminal ("N.C."). Since you want your switch to pass a signal only when the lever falls off the edge, you'll want to hook your wires up to the "C" and "N.C." terminals. The switch is activated by the pressure of the sumo competition platform, so *most* of the time it makes the normally closed terminal *open*. When the mini-sumo detects the edge, the switch goes back to its normal state, being *closed*, which sends the activation signal to the reverse and turn circuit.

Figure 12-31
Alternate
sensor
installation
example

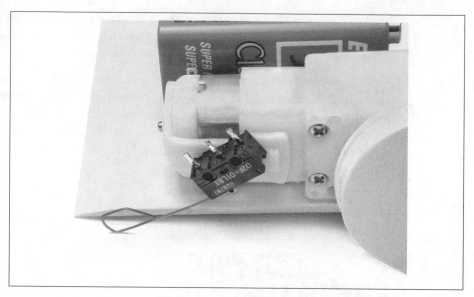

Let's wire up the battery connectors next by taking the red wire and soldering it to one of the switch pins. The black battery wire gets soldered to one of
the bottom corner connections of the relay brick, which is one of connections
that share the black wiring we did during relay brick construction. See how
handy that color coding is?

Figure 12-32
Red to switch,
black to relay
brick

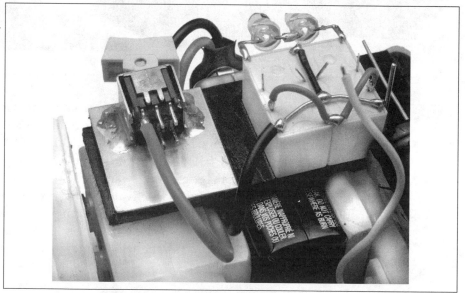

The reverse and turn capacitor is next to be installed. We're going to place it on top of one of the motors, so that the cathode ("–", the striped side) connection of the capacitor is close to the relay brick corner, where we solder it on. Again, that black-wire identification makes it easy to identify where to solder the capacitor's "–" connection to a ground wire.

We'll take one of the wires from our sensor (doesn't matter which) and solder it to the anode ("+") of the capacitor. When the switch closes, this is the path the power will take to snap-charge the capacitor for the reverse and turn process. We won't attach the second sensor wire until after we power up the motors and make sure they're going the right way first.

Figure 12-33
Soldering on the reverse and turn capacitor

Solder a pair of wires to each motor and run them back up to the relay brick. If you use a different color of wire for each motor, it will make the wiring process go easier. You'll get strange results if the motor wires get mixed up with each other.

Run each pair of motor wires up to the relay brick, leaving enough wire to allow for some resoldering and repositioning.

Figure 12-34
Running the motor connection wires up to the relay brick

The process of wiring up the motors to the relays will determine the initial direction of rotation of each motor (which matters), and which way your mini-sumo will turn when the reverse and turn behavior is activated (doesn't matter). Pick a relay and a set of motor wires and solder them to the pins shown in Figure 12-35 (repeat for each motor). The only thing we currently don't have hooked up is the edge sensor, so when we power the mini-sumo on, it will run in its default "run around the sumo platform" mode. So turn it on, put it down, and see what happens!

Figure 12-35
Initial wiring of gear motors to relays: Prepare to swap a few connections!

If your mini-sumo is running forward, congratulations—you've lucked out and managed to wire up both motors correctly!

If the mini-sumo is spinning *clockwise,* swap the connections on the right-side motor (right side when viewed from the back, with the mini-sumo nose pointing away from you).

If the mini-sumo is spinning *counter-clockwise,* swap the connections on the (guess what?) left-side motor.

A mini-sumo that is running fully in reverse shows great defensive capabilities ("Run away!") but will ultimately not be an effective competitor. Reverse all the motor connections, and all will be fine again.

You might have noticed that with plastic wheels, your mini-sumo doesn't move very well, especially when turning. There's a reason why your car tires are made of rubber and not plastic—rubber grips the surface *much* better than plastic. Running a hard plastic wheel on your mini-sumo will leave you at great disadvantage against rubber-clad opponents. The simple solution is to take a rubber band, stretch it over the lip of the wheel, then super-glue it in place. We've found that the rubber bands used to hold vegetable produce (like broccoli) together are quite good, as are the claw-bands used to keep shellfish from pinching other seafood. You will most likely find nice, fat #64 rubber bands holding your mail in a bundle, but their being too large in diameter means cutting them down to size. It isn't that hard to slowly wrap a cut rubber band around the edge of a wheel, gluing it while you go. If you cut it a bit shorter than the circumference of the wheel, you can pull the trailing edge of the rubber up to meet where you started gluing, making a nearly perfect rubber wheel. Experiment with your tires; add another layer or two of rubber to make the tire thicker. Think about smearing silicone caulking around the lip of the wheel to get a nice, sticky grip. Tires are an important part of your mini-sumo, so keep experimenting with different ideas to get the best traction possible.

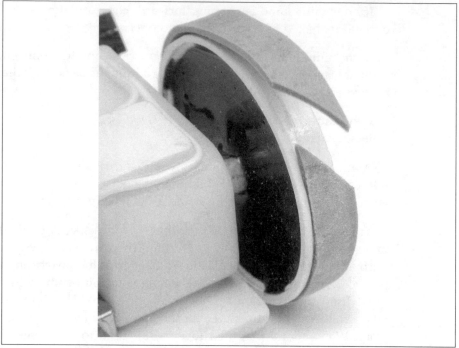

With your motors running in the right direction, it's time to finish wiring up the edge sensor. Start by adding another wire (white if you can; let's keep signal wire colors consistent) from the anode ("+", the side opposite the stripe) of the capacitor to the relay block. You want to connect this wire to the top pin of the relay block that is *also* wired to the LED assembly anode (the side opposite the flat spot on the LED). If it isn't wired to the LED assembly anode, your mini-sumo will simply reverse one motor, then go forward again.

Take the other remaining sensor wire that we left dangling earlier, and solder it to the bottom middle pin of the relay brick. This should be connecting to the same points as a few red wires, which means we're actually connecting this sensor wire to "+" (color-coded wires really make assembly easier...). For convenience, we followed the red wire back to the switch's middle pin, which was easier for us to access.

Figure 12-37
Soldering the remaining sensor wires in place

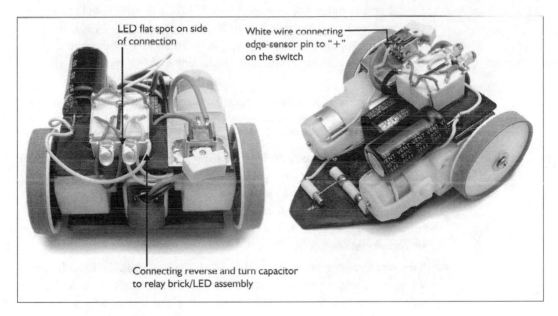

Your mini-sumo is technically finished. You should be able to put it down on a smooth circular platform, and it should happily scoot away from the edges for as long as it has battery power.

The Robot Geek Says

Troubleshooting Your Mini-Sumo Robot

Any possible problems you have should be pretty easy to solve, as this circuit is quite straightforward. Start by reviewing the breadboarded-circuit troubleshooting section.

✖ **Your mini-sumo does everything it should, but doesn't have much pushing power.** Friction is your friend and your foe all at the same time. You want as much friction as possible between your drive wheels and the surface, but as little friction as possible anywhere else. That means the nose of your mini-sumo should slide easily, where the wheels should grip as much as possible. If your mini-sumo can't spin in place very well, add a hard-plastic nub to the nose. **Solution:** If your drive wheels are slipping and spinning, you need to add a rubber band or other traction-assisting compound to the wheels until they don't slip anymore.

You can also assist wheel traction by placing as much weight over the drive wheels as possible. The more weight above the wheels, the more traction they'll have.

✱ **Your mini-sumo starts running strong but quickly slows down and stops.** You *must* use a strong battery to power your mini-sumo. Most carbon-cell-type batteries can't provide enough power to drive motors continuously under load. A carbon-cell battery may do fine on the breadboard, but not in actual operation. **Solution:** Use a strong alkaline or rechargable battery.

✱ **The edge sensor snags the edge of the sumo ring.** This is a hazard when using a touch-sensor instead of an optical sensor that looks for the edge's white line. **Solution:** Make the part of the sensor that pokes through only as long as it has to be. A sensor that is too long will definitely snag the edge more than a short sensor. Be sure that you form a round loop to the tip to the wire, so that it slides off and back onto the edge of the ring easily.

Are you running out of shelf space for all the competition trophies your mini-sumo is winning? Well, trophies can be good source material for new robots....

To make your mini-sumo contest-ready, you *need* a five-second start-up timer circuit. Wire up the following circuit, and patch it in between the "+" power of the switch and the rest of the mini-sumo circuit. You will also need to find a convenient place to stick the reset button. Simply turning your mini-sumo off and on again *won't* reset the timer fully—you will need to press the reset button. When you lift your finger off the reset, you can be assured that you'll be getting the whole five-second start-up delay.

Note that as your battery wears down, the start-up delay will increase with this circuit. Tune it with a new, fresh battery so that you won't "jump the gun"!

Figure 12-38
Optional five-second start-up delay schematic and sample soldered-up module

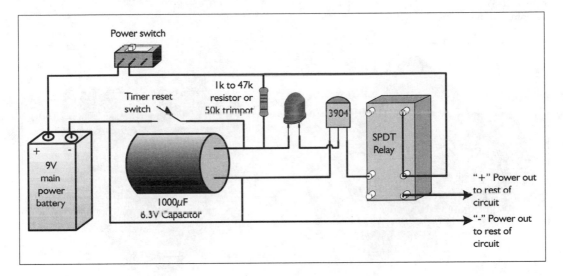

If you find that your mini-sumo isn't turning around enough per reverse and turn cycle, you might want to try adding a third LED in series with your LED assembly. If it's already turning too much, short out one of the LEDs by soldering a jumper wire around it. Your robot should be turning between 90 and 180 degrees each time, but, then again, you may have a perfectly good strategy to make it turn more or less.

You'll see with our mini-sumo robot that all of our wires have been trimmed back and glued down/together so that they aren't poking out all over the place. It goes back to the "A" for aesthetics in BEAM. Make your wiring clean and compact, and you will be sure that your mini-sumo won't lose due to a wire pulling loose.

Figure 12-39
Cleaning up the wiring

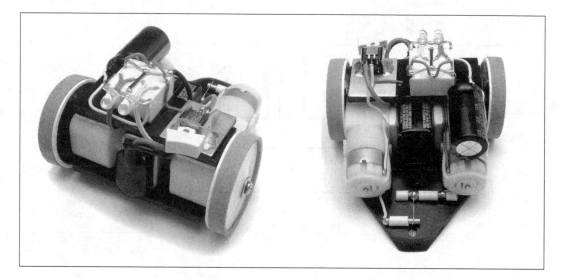

Another reason for preparing our wiring carefully is that, like any good warrior, our mini-sumo needs *armor*. With our edge-detection sensor at the very nose of our robot, any smart opponent would simply try to keep hitting it to force our mini-sumo into its reverse and turn behavior. If we shield the sensor, our robot will do its best to blindly shove whatever is in its way off the edge of the ring, until its edge sensor tells it to back away and turn.

Our mini-sumo has a pointed nose (which we later found to be not a great idea) that we built up out of more Sintra plastic. You can use cardboard and tape, or even hammered metal, to build your armor—whichever technique you're most comfortable with. Besides being protective, an armored shell gives your robot personality, as you can color and decorate it any way you wish. Be silly or serious—a pink, flower-covered robot has just as good a chance of winning as a robot named "Black DeathBat 2000."

Figure 12-40
The finished BEAM junkbot mini-sumo, ready to do battle!

Any style of sumo wrestling boils down to three points of strategy:

1. Power

2. Agility

3. Strategy

Your mini-sumo has reasonable power, minimal agility, and almost no strategy. What can you do to correct this? Power can be increased by adding an additional battery in series to the first, adding their voltages together. This assumes that your motor will be able to handle the extra power, so be careful when doing this! If your mini-sumo spins its tires when pushing a load, work on increasing the tire traction. All that spinning is a sign that the weak link lies in getting that motor power transferred into a pushing force.

Agility is how quickly your robot can react. Speed is only a part of that. Your mini-sumo has pretty simple brains and will only turn one way when it detects the edge. A more agile mini-sumo would take the closest direction to getting away from the edge. Investigate some of the other mini-sumo projects on the Internet—they may be more complicated, but agility comes at that cost.

Our junkbot mini-sumo has practically no strategic ability. It stumbles blindly about, hoping to bump into something it can push out of the ring. You can add strategy by adding additional side sensor arms that fall down and sweep around, feeling for your opponent. Another strategic technique is to add another front sensor that kicks your mini-sumo into "high gear" when it's pushing against the other robot. This can be done by adding another relay that temporarily wires another battery in series with the first, giving the motors a quick high-energy burst.

Figure 12-41
Mini-sumo wrestlers with strategy: Don Papp's "Double Your Pleasure" at the Western Canadian Robot Games searches for his opponents with fold-down arms.

To add side sensors, you need to mount a single-pole, double-throw (SPDT) switch on the side of your robot with an arm extension on it. Route one of the wires from the motor on the *same* side of the robot as this switch, then back again. By routing the power of one motor through this switch's "common" and "normally closed" poles, you cause your mini-sumo to turn toward anything touching this switch. Note that you still have to fit within a 10 cm box when competition starts. Either make your sensors short or have them fold down at the start of the match. Also note that activating this sensor turns off a motor. If you install two sensors and have them poke too far forward and they both activate, your mini-sumo may actually *turn off* and be a sitting duck! Start by using just one sensor and see how that goes in your sumo wrestling tests. Our sensor is a long spring that presses against a thick copper wire. It takes only a bit of movement to make it separate the spring from the wire, making the mini-sumo turn.

Figure 12-42
Mini-sumo side-arm sensor schematic and installed flexible arm

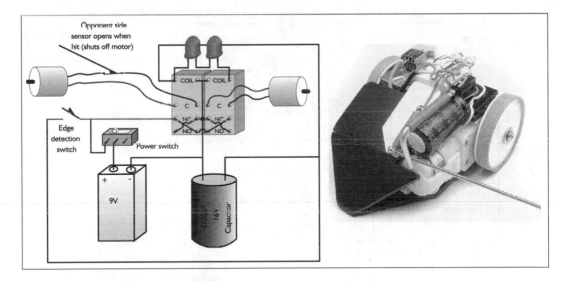

Do you remember any episodes of *Star Trek* where they *didn't* push their phasers, engines, or tractor beam to over 100 percent of the limit? You can abuse and get extra performance from a good number of systems for short periods of time, and electric motors are one of these systems. The following modification will *quadruple* the power going to your motors for short periods of time, giving you twice the pushing power you usually have, assuming your tires can make use of the extra power. Think of it as a super-adrenaline Kaioken attack for robots.

By adding another relay, battery, and sensor switch to your mini-sumo circuit, we're going to build a voltage-doubling module. Think of this whole portion of the circuit as a substitute for the single battery in our original circuit. We're going to take two identical batteries and arrange them so that they're wired in parallel ("+" to "+", "−" to "−") most of the time. In this arrangement, you won't notice any difference in speed or performance until the opponent-sensing switch is activated. On activation, the relay changes the battery wiring from parallel to series ("+" to "−", "+" to "−"), which stacks up the voltage of the two batteries and gives you a surge of extra power.

Figure 12-43
The "I need more power, Scotty!" adrenaline-kick circuit schematic and installation

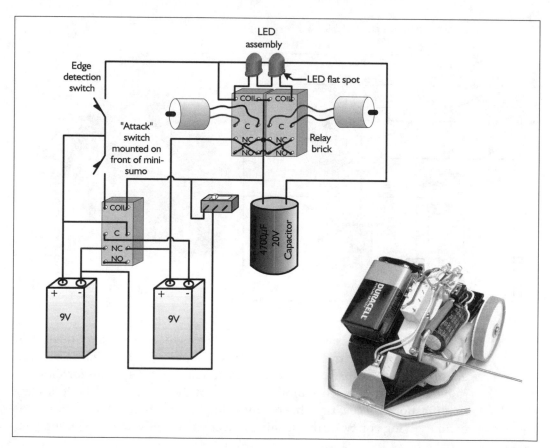

Of course, nothing comes for free, and your motor probably won't be able to handle that much power for extended periods. You don't want to abuse your motors for very long, or they might self-destruct. Use this technique if you're prepared to deal with damaged motors, or you are confident your motors can handle the power surges. We don't have to worry about the new spike in voltage affecting the reverse and turn capacitor, as it (and the touch sensors) are permanently wired up to only one of the batteries and will never see more than 9 volts.

The Robot Geek Says

Competition Mini–Sumo Wrestling

Build your mini-sumo with an eye on making *power* the top priority. A quick mini-sumo can't push an opponent out of the ring if it doesn't have any pushing power!

The secret to mini–sumo wresting success is *practice, practice, practice*. Build two different robots and face them off against each other to see what characteristics makes one better than the other, then improve the loser until it beats the champion. Then do it again.

Some motors can be run harder than their rating, if only in bursts, separated by cool-down periods. As a mini-sumo match rarely goes over three minutes, you might be able to run a 6-volt motor at 9 or 12 volts for extra power and speed.

Make your mini-sumo as heavy as possible, without going over the maximum weight limit. It's a scientific fact that the heavier a robot is, the more traction and pushing power its tires will have.

Soft rubber tires will always give more pushing power than hard plastic ones.

Clean your tires before each match. The dust that collects on them will decrease your traction and pushing power!

Put in a fresh battery before each competition. If you get to the final event, put in a fresh battery for that little bit of extra **OOMPH.**

Make *sure* your start-up timer doesn't start your robot too soon, which can get you disqualified. A fresh battery might make it start a bit sooner than it should, so test, tweak, and time your start-up circuit until you're positive it won't cause you trouble!

Use *good* batteries. Utility-grade carbon-cell batteries can't provide much discharge power, but alkaline batteries like Energizer, Duracell, and Ray-O-Vac are quite good. Nicad and nickel-metal hydride rechargeables are also very good at dumping power, but at slightly lower voltages than the alkalines.

Narrow-nosed robots like our mini-sumo example are better at deflecting robots away than pushing them out of the ring. A wide, flat front scoop on the nose of your mini-sumo will give much more satisfactory pushing ability than a narrow point.

Care and Feeding of Your Junkbot Mini-Sumo

You need a place to practice with your mini-sumo. If you don't have a suitable Viking shield or large bongo-drum, try using an upside-down pizza pan as a temporary mini-sumo platform, and put your mini-sumo robot against the scourge of all robots—a hockey puck! Well, a hockey puck isn't necessarily that evil, but it does make a suitable test opponent for a mini-sumo. If you can successfully find and shove a puck or a full soup can off the platform, your mini-sumo is ready for some competition. Get on the ball, salvage another set of parts, and build a new mini-sumo in a different configuration to fight against. It's more fun than watching your lonely mini-sumo push pucks and cans around!

Figure 12-44
Our playmate for our junkbot mini-sumo: Build a second robot to practice against!

Mini-sumo is becoming a standard event at many robot competitions, so search the Internet for upcoming events. There are some fine resources on-line, including http://www.robotroom.com/SumoRules.html, which does a very good job of explaining the competition rules. The Web site at http://www.robotgames.com has a great collection of videos from past competitions and an excellent photo archive. Check http://www.botlanta.org/superlinks.htm#sumo for a growing list of other worthwhile mini-sumo-related pages to visit.

Now that you have at least one mini-sumo robot under your belt, you may wish to expand your horizons by building more advanced versions. Our simple relay-using mini-sumo circuit can't be modified to do much more than it does now, so when you start building your next one, take some time and first learn about "H-bridge" circuits or ICs like the L283D and L298 that are specifically designed to power motors. These circuits and chips are very easy to use and connect to. Relays are great for powering motors but can be more difficult to connect to, especially when you want to introduce more custom control circuits to one. The site http://www.solarbotics.com has some schematics in their "circuits" page for smarter (but still simple) mini-sumo robots. If you're really gung-ho on more strategy, consider picking up a micro-controller like the "Basic Stamp" (http://www.hvwtech.com) and a free set of documentation from http://www.parallax.com, and start learning about programming more complex mini-sumo behaviors.

Chapter 13

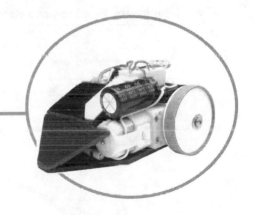

Project 7: The BEAM Walking Robot

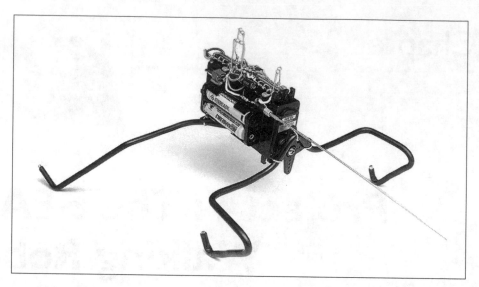

Parts List

- ❏ **3** × 74AC240 octal buffer chips
- ❏ **6** × Resistors
- ❏ **8** × Pin sockets
- ❏ **4** × 0.22μF capacitors
- ❏ **1** × 22μF capacitors
- ❏ **4** × AA (1.5-volt) batteries and holders
- ❏ **2** × Servos or suitable gear motors
- ❏ **1** × Stiff wire for legs
- ❏ **1** × Thick guitar string for sensors
- ❏ **1** × 13 mm (1/2") heat-shrink tubing that just fits over the thick guitar wire
- ❏ **1** × Ring crimp connector
- ❏ **1** × Leg centering spring

Optional Parts

- ❏ **5** × Bicore process indicating LEDs
- ❏ **5** × 470Ω to 1k resistors

The BEAM Walking Robot

One of the most important contributions BEAM has brought to the robotics community is the technique of building relatively simple walking robots. Historically, building a walking robot required a pretty intense effort and considerable mechanical and electronic knowledge. By using collections of simple electronic oscillators (clock circuits) connected together, practically any walking robot mechanics can be controlled without the need of a microprocessor or programming language.

Another benefit of using BEAM controllers is that there is a built-in "feedback" path that can help self-control the motor without any extra circuitry. It's a common behavior for a BEAM Bicore controller to change the duration of a control pulse to make an overloaded motor fight harder against an obstacle. In a walking robot, this means that a leg stuck in a hole will automatically be given more time during each step to help the robot power the leg out of the hole.

Although not strictly necessary in a BEAM circuit, adding a microprocessor as a "master brain" can be very useful to a BEAM-controlled walking robot. As described earlier with the "Headbot" project, a robot module that works well on its own and takes input from another separate module is something we call a "horse and rider" layout. With a BEAM walker as the horse, you can add a microprocessor rider to give it direction and behavior control when needed while the BEAM circuit takes care of the motor control signals and the "involuntary" reaction to collisions. This removes the burden of low-level motor control from the microprocessor and lets it do the things it's really good at—like advanced logic decision making, mathematics, and interfacing with communications modules and electronic compasses. If you have any sort of experience with microprocessors, you may find the integration of the two methods of robotics well suited to your application!

The walking robot we're going to build is simple in behavior, as it walks forward until it bumps into something, then kicks into reverse for a preset time, then resumes walking forward again. Having only two motors makes it simple mechanically but somewhat limits its ability to steer. We'll concentrate on building this simple walking platform, after which you can explore more advanced behaviors with a wide range of circuits available on the Internet.

Figure 13-1
Simple BEAM
two-motor
walker
schematic

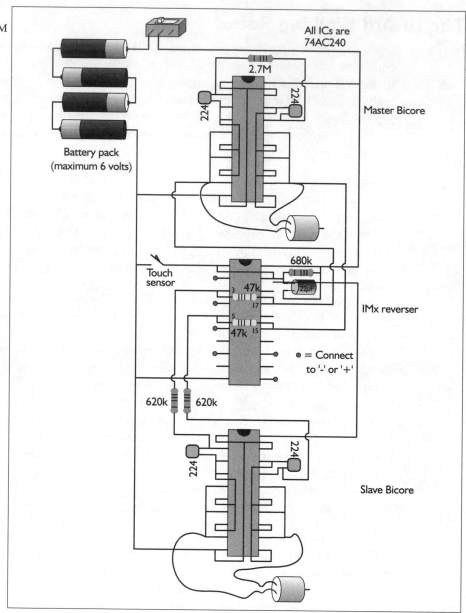

Battery pack
(maximum 6 volts)

All ICs are
74AC240

2.7M

224

224

Master Bicore

Touch
sensor

680k

47k

3

17

5

15

47k

22µF

IMx reverser

● = Connect
to '-' or '+'

620k   620k

224

224

Slave Bicore

Bicores for Walking Robots

To get a single motor to move back and forth, we need a single two-node Bicore circuit. You might recall from the single-motor Headbot project that the Bicore is a little clock circuit with two nodes that throw a "process" back and forth between them. We can delay or speed up the interval that each node holds onto the process before it gets thrown back at the partner node. With the walker circuit, we will use two motors and two Bicores.

One of these is the master Bicore, which sets the rhythm of the whole robot much as your spinal column has a "central pattern generator" that sets the rhythm of motion in your heart, muscles, and breathing patterns. We adjust the frequency of the master Bicore by using a resistor suspended between the inputs of the two nodes, turning it into something that we call a *suspended Bicore*. A suspended Bicore has a 50/50 duty cycle, meaning each node holds onto the signal for half the time, unless there's outside influence from sensors or motor loads in the Bicore chip itself. The master Bicore nodes control the back-and-forth motion of the front motor and also feed the signals to the second (slave) Bicore that controls the rear motor.

Bicore Master/Slave Relationships

No, this doesn't describe how a ruling class of Bicores overpowered a lesser type and forced them to build pyramids for their rulers—it's a way to make Bicores communicate.

We can easily chain Bicores together and make a signal from one cascade (or jump down) to the next by simply introducing a resistor from the output of one Bicore to the input of the next. This "master/slave" configuration lets a master Bicore set the rhythm, which the slave echoes after a specific time delay. The delay time is determined by the resistor passing the slave signal down from the master, with bigger resistors leading to a longer delay before the slave follows. If you simply want the slave to do exactly what the master Bicore is doing, use a wire. Using slave resistors that are the same value as the master Bicore's suspended resistor will give you a 180° phase angle difference, which means it will be timed exactly to do the reverse of what the master is doing. In this arrangement, when the master Bicore's node just turns off, the slave node will be just turning on. If you use a resistor *larger* than the master Bicore's suspended resistor, the slave Bicore "revolts" and begins not to listen to the master anymore.

Since master/slave relationships can be arranged with a single resistor (from one master output to one slave input), you can initially tune your circuit with a single trimpot (variable resistor). The walking motion of practically all multilimbed creatures is set by a time-delay relationship. With a four-legged quadruped (like a horse), the rear leg follows the same motion of the front leg after a set delay, which is very easy to see when a horse is in a slow walk. A millipede with its many legs also sets a delay between each leg and the one behind it, and the same applies to our BEAM walking robot.

A wide variety of walking behaviors can be explored by simply twiddling the trimpot knob, changing the time interval from when the front leg moves to when the rear leg copies that same movement. With a two-motor walker, it's pretty easy to start with an effective forward walk, which slows into a stationary "stomping" gait and then becomes a reverse walk—all by twiddling the knob on a single trimpot! When you like the robot's walking gait, take the expensive trimpot out, measure the resistance value, and replace it with a pair of suitably sized penny-resistors (one resistor for each output-to-input connection for better reliability).

In an alternative style of master Bicore known as a "grounded Bicore," each input has a different resistor value connected to ground, which lets you set up an *asynchronous* oscillator. This means each node holds onto the process for whatever amount of time the resistor connected to it determines, allowing for a Bicore that (for example) holds the process on one side for 70 percent of the time instead of the 50 percent ensured by the suspended Bicore. Although it is very useful, we won't be using the grounded Bicore in this application, but it's good to know about when you want to start doing strange things with motors.

Walker Motor Drivers

It's a simple task to use Bicores to generate back-and-forth signals, but it's not so easy to strengthen those signals enough to power a motor. By itself, each member of the pair of Bicore nodes can power a signal LED to show whether it is currently on or off. To get enough power to drive the motor, we're going to feed the output signal into three other nodes whose only purpose in life is to add their strength to the signal to the point that it can drive a significant load. That's where our 74AC240 chip comes in with its eight gates. Each gate can be configured as a Bicore node, *or* as a buffer that adds strength to the signal. We'll use two gates to create our Bicore oscillator, and the remaining six to strengthen the signal.

Reklaw Circuitry ("Walker" in Reverse)

Once tuned, your robot will be most adept at moving in a forward direction, but unfortunately it doesn't have the necessary tunneling equipment to burrow through a wall if it gets cornered. A much more reasonable solution is to make it back up and try a new direction. Fortunately for our robot, the difference between walking forward and walking backward is simply swapping the signals running through two wires.

In standard forward-walking mode, the front motor activates just before the rear motor does. Going in reverse means simply reversing this action, having the rear motor activate just before the front motor. Swapping the signals around so that this happens is done by a circuit called an *inverting multiplexor (IMx)*, which is a complex name for something that takes signals, turns them upside down, and sends them in a new direction. Fortunately, it's not a hard circuit to build.

The IMx circuit interferes with the signal pathway only when the IMx chip is turned on by the "enable" pins. These "enable" lines are easily controlled by a touch sensor, a resistor, and a capacitor. When activated, the resistor and capacitor make sure the IMx stays on for a set amount of time before turning back off again.

By default, the IMx simply passes the incoming signal straight through a 47k resistor to the output, adding a practically unnoticeable amount of resistance to the signal (compared with the slave resistors, which are 10 or 20 times larger). When activated, the IMx springs into action, taking the input signal, turning it upside down inside the chip, and sending it out the output line. Of course, the 47k resistor is still trying to pass its original signal through, but since the output of the IMx chip is much stronger than this signal, it overpowers it and makes the new inverted signal the one that is read by the slave Bicore. With this new inverted signal, the slave Bicore now activates before the front (master) Bicore, and the robot now walks in reverse!

Figure 13-2
IMx reverse
circuitry
explained

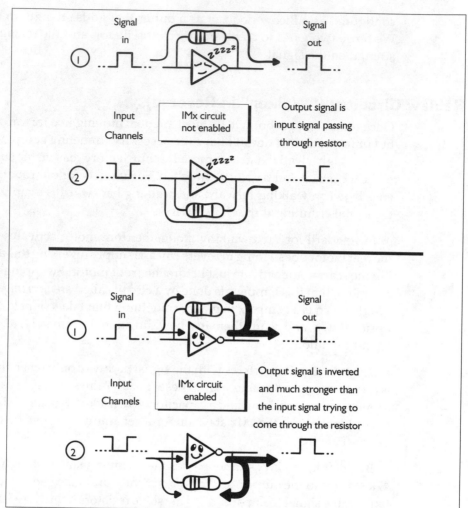

Walking Robot Parts List

Walking robots are among the most varied robot types. Given two identical sets of parts, two roboticists will turn them into two very differ-
ent-looking walking robots. With that in mind, don't strive to copy what
parts we've selected:

❑ **3** × 74AC240 octal buffer chips. We'll be using two in "Bicore" configuration, where they're providing a left/right oscillation to the front and rear motors. The third will be what is referred to as an "Inverting Multiplexor" reverser circuit.

❑ **2** × 47k resistors. These are part of the IMx circuit, and pass the original input signals to the outputs. When the IMx activates, it overpowers the signals passing through these resistors and swaps the signals around. These resistors can be anywhere in the 10k to 100k range.

❑ **1** × 2.7M resistor. This resistor is used on the "master Bicore" and sets the main time constant for the whole robot. Want it to move the legs faster? Lower this resistor value. Keep that in mind, because depending on what sort of motors you use, you will have to adjust the value of this resistor to make your walker function properly.

❑ **2** × 620k resistors. These are the values we found to work as our "slave resistors." The function of these resistors is to delay the signal to the "slave Bicore" circuit that drives the rear motor. Any walking creature (biological or mechanical) depends on timing to make sure things happen in the right sequence, and with our BEAM controller, these slave resistors are crucial to making the rear motor activate at the right time. The larger they are, the more time it takes the signal to activate the motor. Although we can technically do the job with just one resistor, using two ensures proper operation.

❑ **1** × 680k resistor. This value (in combination with the 22μF capacitor) sets the time your walker spends in reverse mode. Feel free to adjust this value to suit your own walker.

❑ **8** × Pin sockets (see Figure 13-3). These are immensely handy little devices, which allow you to easily insert and remove items like capacitors, resistors, and transistors. We'll be using them for changing out the resistors that set Bicore timing and slaving intervals.

Figure 13-3
Pin sockets, available in rails, individually, or in carriers

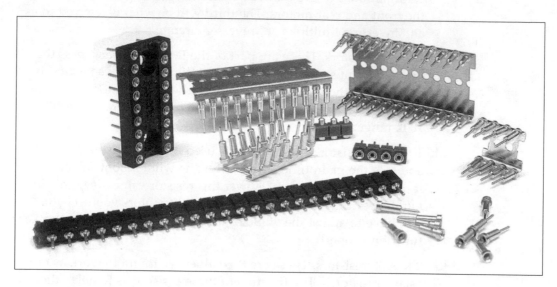

❑ **4 × 0.22μF capacitors.** You need two for each of the Bicore circuits you'll be building (one master, one slave).

❑ **1 × 22μF capacitor.** The size of capacitor (in combination with the 680k resistor) sets the time the walker spends in reverse mode.

❑ **4 × 1.5-volt batteries and holders.** You can use a four-pack of AA or AAA batteries, and if you think your walker is up to the task, saddle on C or D cell batteries for extra long life. Whatever you do, *do not* use any combination of batteries resulting in greater than 6 volts, as the Bicore chips will most likely burn out if you do so. Feel free to use rechargeables, as they also work well.

❑ **2 × Hobby servos or suitable gear motors.** It's tough to find suitable motors for a walking robot, because you have to be able to supply considerable torque to make the feet lift off the surface. This application is much like the mini-sumo project, where we need to trade off motor speed for the ability to twist the motor shaft. Not too many toys are suitable for this application (the Hasbro B.I.O.-Bug is a notable exception), but fortunately, the hobby industry has been making miniature gear motors for many years. These *servos* are actually gear motors with brains (which we'll need to remove) and are commonly available from most hobby stores for $9 to $40 each. If you need to use a servo, start with the cheapest ones you can find so that there's little loss if you destroy one while modifying it. Better yet, get a set of inexpensive gear motors that are practically ideal for the job from Solarbotics. Their GM2 and GM3 motors are almost impossible to destroy. You may also get lucky checking old photocopiers and printers for their precision gear motors—they're among the last things to wear out. Sometimes good gear motors are stripped out of dead machinery and sold at surplus outlets.

Figure 13-4
Suitable walker motors: Salvaged gear motors, hobby servos and toy walker mechanisms, and precision surplus gear motors

❏ **1** × Stiff wire for legs. You will most likely have a wire coat hanger in your closet (or on your neighbor's car as a substitute radio antenna) that can be used for the legs of your walker. The only problem with coat-hanger wire is that it's pretty springy, and if you fold it too many times, the bend point fatigues and breaks. A better solution is solid 8-, 10-, or 12-gauge copper wire used for wiring houses. If you can't find it individually, you will definitely find it as part of a multiconductor wire with black,

white, red, and possibly bare wires all in one bundle. It's very
easy to solder and pretty inexpensive, so buy a few feet and leave
that stuff in your wall alone—it's already busy carrying power to
your soldering iron.

❑ **1** × Guitar string. It is surprisingly difficult to find a sensor wire
that is solderable, holds its shape when bent, has adequate
stiffness, and is inexpensive. Practically all these requirements
describe metal wire-wound guitar strings. If you know any
musicians (especially an electric bass or guitar player), ask them
to hold onto their broken strings for you. The really fat strings
are ideal for sensors that will be knocked around lots (like with a
walker), and the thinner ones are great for small mobile wheeled
robots like Herbies and other photovores.

Figure 13-5
Guitar strings
of various
thickness
are useful as
touch sensors

❑ **1** × 13 mm (1/2") heat-shrink tubing. We'll be using this as an
insulator in our sensor. We need a way to securely mount our
sensor (guitar) wire to the body, but in a way that it doesn't make
electrical contact with anything until it bumps into an obstacle.
This heat-shrink will isolate the wire from the rest of the sensor
body until it happens to touch something.

❑ **1** × Ring crimp wire terminal connector #8 (16–14g). No, no—we're
not going to connect any wire to the wire terminal connector. This

is BEAM/Junkbot technology, and we *rarely* use something for what it's meant for! We're going to use the terminal connector (see Figure 13-43) as the mount for our touch sensor. Radio Shack carries these (part #64-3118, 16 for $1.69), as does Future-Active (part #80559, 20 for $1.99). Practically any place that has automotive parts will carry these as part of a wiring kit.

❏ **1** × Leg centering spring. In the particular geometry we're using for this walker, the rear legs do little more than give pure forward/backward thrust. Because of this, the rear legs don't have any method of feedback to keep them centered, so we use a medium-stiffness spring to pull the rear legs back into approximately the correct alignment. You'll most likely find a suitable spring in the parts left over from a VCR dissection.

Optional Parts

❏ **5** × Bicore process indicating LEDs. Blinky lights are always necessary on a robot—didn't you *ever* watch any science fiction movies? Besides, they're a good diagnostic tool, especially when you're figuring out the Bicore on a breadboard circuit, which is where we'll use ours.

❏ **5** × 470Ω to 1k resistors. Use one of these in series with each indicator LED to limit how much power the LED draws from the Bicore.

Figure 13-6
BEAM walking robot parts, ready to go!

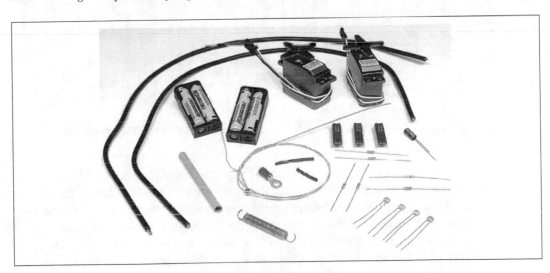

Breadboarding the Walker Circuit

Yes, we're going to breadboard our parts *again* to make sure they are compatible. Not even simulations on a computer will do the job—there's no other way to make sure a new circuit will work with the parts you have on hand. This is assuming that you have suitable gear motors to work with. If you haven't already done so, skip down to the servo modification section, fix the servos up, then come back here to the breadboarding section—it's important to test the circuit with the parts you'll be using!

We'll construct and test our breadboarded circuit in the three sections as used by the robot—the front Bicore, the rear Bicore, and the IMx reverser circuits. When (and *only* when) the first two circuits are functional, you'll add the reverser and test the whole thing as a complete unit.

Start breadboarding by placing all three 74AC240 chips down on the breadboard, leaving two or three empty rows between them. We'll use the top '240 for the master Bicore, the middle for the IMx, and the rear for the slave Bicore. Starting with the top '240, connect it up. With the optional LEDs installed and power applied, you'll see the two nodes pass the signal back and forth between them, just as planned. Hook the motor leads up to the two outputs of the Bicore, and now you have back-and-forth motion too!

Figure 13-7

Basic Bicore breadboard layout, common to both the master and slave Bicores. The layout on the right shows testing it with indicator LEDs and a suspended resistor across inputs 2 and 17.

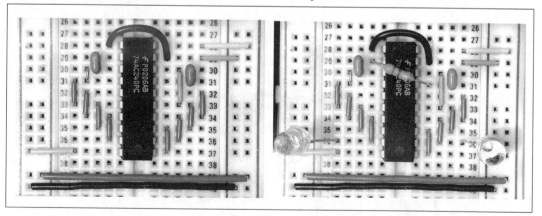

We'll skip over the second chip for now and build the second (slave) Bicore on the bottom '240 chip. It's almost exactly the same as the master Bicore, except it doesn't have the "suspended" resistor across the inputs. For now, let's make it a suspended Bicore (yes, just like the master Bicore) by dropping in a resistor larger than 470k in value (you can use lower, but the pulses start getting *quite* fast to watch) and make sure it oscillates just like the master Bicore.

It does? Good. Let's take out the suspended resistor and play a bit by install-ing the slave resistors from the outputs of the master Bicore and feeding one each into the inputs of the slave Bicore. When it's powered up, you'll see that the slave follows the patterns set by the master Bicore. For fun, moisten your fingertips and pinch the leads across the master Bicore suspended resistor, temporarily lowering the resistance. The master Bicore will speed up in fre-quency, and the slave will try to keep up to the change, but if the change is too drastic, they'll fall into a strange pattern as the slave syncs and de-syncs with the master. As a guideline, a slave resistor shouldn't be more than twice as large in value as the master oscillator suspended resistor; otherwise, it'll lose synchronization with the master too easily.

With both Bicores functioning properly, let's work on the IMx reverser cir-cuit layout. Compared to the Bicores, it's an easy circuit, with just a capacitor and three resistors.

When your circuit is functioning properly, you'll have two gear motors spinning left and right, with second motor echoing what the first motor is do-ing after a short interval. When the wires representing the sensor wire are temporarily crossed, the motors should reverse their behavior, with the sec-ond motor leading the first motor in the back-and-forth motions for several seconds. With the optional indicator LED and resistor, you'll see when the re-verse circuitry activates, and when it times out.

Figure 13-8
Walker
circuitry
breadboarded
for testing

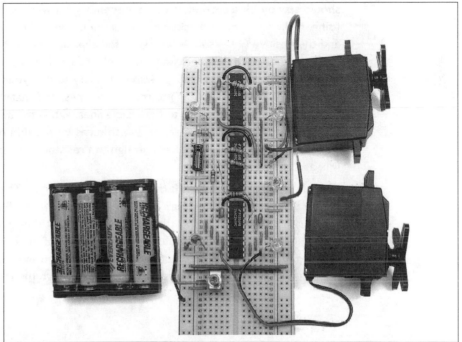

The Robot Geek Says

Troubleshooting Your Breadboarded Walker Circuit

✖ **Bicore LED indicators not lighting up.** A very common mistake is to connect the two enable lines on the chip together (pins 1 and 19) and forget to connect them to a ground ("−") line. If you don't do this, the chip won't turn on. It's also easy to mix up inputs and outputs on the chips. Make sure the timer capacitors and suspended resistor are in the right pin locations. Umm, you *did* remember to plug the batteries to the breadboard, right?

✖ **Bicore LED indicators have an unsteady flicker.** Again, that could be an enable line problem. Make sure both enables are wired to a ground line, or otherwise the chip is snapping on and off very quickly, as there's no proper signal to tell it to be on or off.

✖ **Bicore LED indicators are steady and dim.** The Bicore can run at pretty high frequencies, so the indicator LEDs may be being turned on and off very quickly. To get a steady, strong blink, make sure your timing capacitors are in the 0.1μF to 0.47μF range, and the suspended resistor is in the 470k range or higher.

✖ **IMx reverser circuit staying on only while sensor is activated.** It should stay on for a second or more, depending on what values you're using. Make sure your capacitor is connected between both enable lines and the positive ("+") supply line, with the capacitor cathode on the enable line side. If it's in backward, it won't take a charge properly, and the IMx won't stay on very long. Also check to see that your resistor is connected from positive ("+") to the enable lines, and that the switch is connected from ground ("−") to the enable lines. When the switch closes, it snap-charges the timer capacitor, which turns on the IMx reverser. The power then slowly equalizes through the resistor and turns off the IMx again.

✖ **The slave Bicore isn't oscillating, but the master is.** The slave Bicore takes its cue from signals received from the master Bicore. If there isn't a signal path for it, the slave Bicore will sit there with the process stuck on one node for an extended period of time. Follow the path from the master Bicore outputs and make sure it eventually gets to the input of the slave. This may mean tracing it through the IMx resistors, then the slave resistors. Make sure the slaving resistors eventually go to the inputs of the slave Bicore (pins 4 and 17).

✖ **Your motors don't have much power.** You did remember to wire up the buffers to the Bicore nodes, right? The pins alternate inputs and outputs, so be careful that you're not accidentally ganging up the wrong pins. If this isn't the problem, it simply could be that your motor is too powerful for the Bicore chip to run. Try stacking another 74AC240 chip on top of the first, as we suggested in the Headbot project.

Modifying Servos

Unless if you have gear motors ready to go, we'll have to find and modify a pair of hobby servos to do the task for us. Practically any servo can be modified into a simple gear motor, and the fact that we don't need the motor to spin all the way around (the legs go back and forth, remember?) removes a messy step involving removal of a mechanical stop. We recommend using a "standard"-style servo that is commonly used in the hobby industry, in our case a "Hitec 422" servo. If you're planning a tiny walker or a big brute, there are suitable servos on the market for your application that can be modified in much the same way.

Don't worry if your servo doesn't look the same as ours—the basic steps are pretty much identical, if not easier. A really easy-to-modify servo is the Tower Hobbies TS-53 / Futaba S3003 servo (they're identical), available from Tower Hobbies ($8.99/ea). If you're not interested at all in performing servo modifications, Solarbotics is announcing a less expensive, even stronger servo in a clear plastic case, *without* the electronics (contact Solarbotics for details).

Let's start by removing the bottom plate of the servo. The servo is split into two halves, so don't let them fall apart! If you do, the servo gears may come out, and you'll have to figure out how to reinstall them again. Not a terribly hard task, actually. Perhaps even fun. Okay, if you *really* want to, take a peek at the gears, but don't blame us if you spill them out and can't get it back together again!

With the bottom plate removed, you'll see the bottom of the motor, and a circuit board. We'll be removing this circuit board and running a simple pair of wires to the motor instead.

Figure 13-9
Removing the
servo bottom
plate

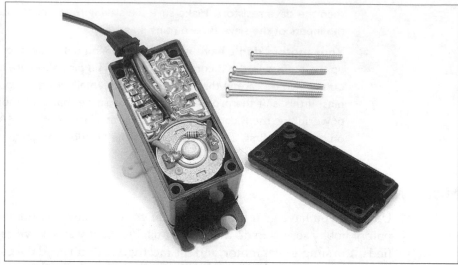

With a bit of prying with a screwdriver (which by the way, *isn't* the proper use of a screwdriver, but I won't tell the Safety Geek if you don't), the circuit board will pop loose, revealing a mess of wires. We're going to snip or desolder these wires, remove the circuit board, and save it for later. There's other uses for these nifty controllers, so don't throw them out—you may need them for another project. If you're working on the TS-53/S3003 servo, the whole motor and trimpot assembly will pop out with the circuit board. Either desolder the motor contacts from the circuit board before prying or yank the whole works out, desolder the motor from the circuit board, and slide it back into place in the servo cavity.

Figure 13-10
Exposing
the servo
internals,
most of which
we'll remove

Snip the wire off the edge of controller board you just removed from the servo, and clip off the end with the plastic connector. Strip off the one wire that *isn't* red or black, so you're left with a two-conductor wire. We're going to use this fine piece of wire as our power lead to the gear motor, so solder the red wire to the motor contact closest to the dot, and the black to the other contact. This last contact *may* have a metal clip that connects this contact to the motor body, which is done to help keep the electrical noise generated by the motor to a minimum. This connecting of one motor contact to the motor body is acceptable practice, although not all servo manufacturers do it. Just make sure your solder connection to the other motor lead is very compact—you don't want it to accidentally touch the motor body, or the motor will be shorted out!

When your motor soldering is finished, lay the wire down so that it exits the same area of the servo where it did before, and use the rubber support grommet if you still have it. This grommet supports the wire where it exits the motor body and helps keep it from breaking.

Figure 13-11
Wiring up
servo motor
leads and
laying down
the wire with
the rubber
grommet

When you're done soldering and arranging the wire and grommet, screw the bottom plate back onto the servo. It should look like it did before, except missing one wire. If everything went correctly, you should be able to grab the output shaft of the servo and give it a twist left and right. It should turn fairly easily and then stop as it hits the internal rotation stop. If it takes considerable effort to twist, then it's likely that you shorted out the motor contacts, which means getting out the screwdriver again....

Figure 13-12
Finished
servo
modifications
with bottom
plate
reinstalled

Walker Body Construction

With the servos ready, let's progress to building the robot body. We aren't going to do anything too extreme like framing up a full body shell, as we find a simple 90° arrangement gives one motor lots of lift ability and the other lots of thrust ability. Feel free to experiment with different motor geometries, as each has different abilities. The 90° angle we're using with our robot makes for a walker with good climbing ability but slow forward speed. If you want even better climbing ability, arrange your motors so that both have a lift component to their motion. For speed, lower the angle of both motors so that there is more forward motion than lift motion.

Figure 13-13
Walker motor
geometry
determines
speed versus
climbing
ability.

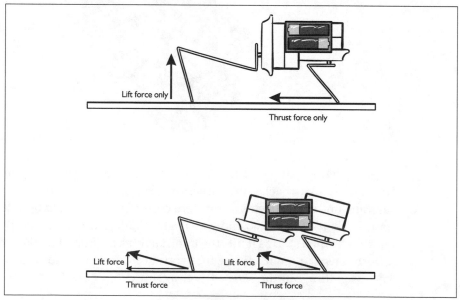

You may need to trim off one of the servo mounting tabs to make them nest together so that there's a flat surface across the top of the robot body, which is nice for mounting your circuitry to. We used double-sided sticky-tape to glue the two servos together, but feel free to use epoxy, or even hot glue (if you must). Don't worry if it seems a bit flimsy at the moment, as we'll reinforce this mechanical connection later when we attach the battery packs.

Remove the X-shaped output arm from the servo, so that we can attach our legs to it without fear of damaging the servo itself. Although you can use coat-hanger wire, we're using more of our favorite leg-shaping material, 10-gauge solid copper wire. Since the servo output arm is made of plastic, we're going to bend the middle portion of the leg wire into a *V* shape and twist-wire it to three of the output arms with some finer solid copper wire. When done, use a bit of super glue to keep the fine twist-wire from coming loose. One solution that works particularly well for attaching legs to servo arms is the Solarbotics "leg mounting pads" that come in two grades (LMP1 and LMP2—see the Solarbotics Web site for details). Solder your metal leg wire to a leg mounting pad, and screw the pad to the servo output arm—that's it.

Figure 13-14
Attaching leg wire to the servo output arms, front and back views

With the legs attached to the servo arms, push the assembly back onto the servo, but don't screw them on yet. Spin the servo shaft left and right and try to center the servo arm/leg assembly so that it is about midway between the left and right stops with the walker in an upright position. We don't want the legs to be hitting the servo's internal stop during normal walking operation. When you think you have it about right, put the servo screw back in to hold the servo arms/legs to the servo. Don't worry about the leg shape yet, as we'll tune that aspect of the robot later.

Figure 13-15
Servo arm/
leg assemblies
reattached to
the walker
servo body

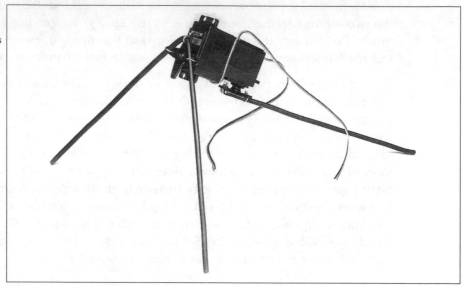

Free-Form Bicore and IMx Reverser Construction

We'll build our Bicores in "deadbug" fashion (legs up), using exactly the same technique we used with the Bicore headbot project. Refer back to Chapter 10 if you need a step-by-step approach. The following images show the two main steps to Bicore construction: forming the leads and soldering on the necessary connections.

Figure 13-16
Bicore
"deadbug"
leg forming
and soldering

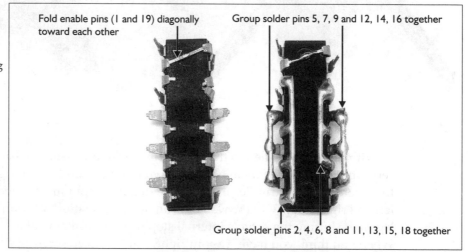

Fold enable pins (1 and 19) diagonally toward each other

Group solder pins 5, 7, 9 and 12, 14, 16 together

Group solder pins 2, 4, 6, 8 and 11, 13, 15, 18 together

Just to recap the Bicore free-form building process, let's not forget to add the timing capacitors and the ground wire from the enables (pins 1 and 19) to the 74AC240 ground pin (pin 10).

Figure 13-17
Bicore
free-form
capacitor
and enable
line soldering

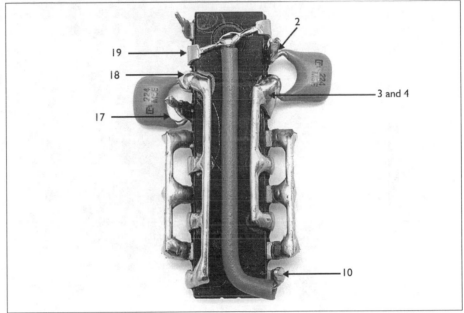

We're going to add one new feature to these free-form Bicores that wasn't included in the headbot project: pin sockets. Using pin sockets to remove and replace components is vastly easier than desoldering/resoldering. They're a pretty common part, available in a 24-pin carrier (SPin24) for $1 from Solarbotics. You can also clip them out of "SIP" and "DIP" (standing for single/dual inline packaging) sockets, which are commonly used for plugging chips into. Both Radio Shack and Future-Active carry a variety of these SIP/DIP sockets to select from. *Note:* You want the sockets with the round holes, not the square ones, as the square ones don't hold the round leads of resistors very well. Then again, you just might be the type of person who *likes* to try to put round pegs in square holes.

We're going to solder a pair of these sockets each to the inputs (pins 2 and 17) of the master and slave Bicores.

Figure 13-18
Adding pin
sockets to
the inputs
of the Bicore

Now that you've finished building your Bicore, go back and do it all one more time. Remember, we need one for each motor in our design, that being two! When you've finished the second Bicore, we'll do the IMx circuit.

Done yet? We can wait. We'll just watch another rerun of "The Simpsons" while you work. Finished already? Excellent—let's continue (it wasn't a good episode anyway).

The IMx circuit is very easy to free-form. Start the same way as with the Bicore by taking a 74AC240, folding the two enable lines together (pins 1 and 19), and soldering them together. Then we'll take our 47k resistors and install one across pins 3 and 17, and the other across pins 5 and 15. These resistors are the pathways the Bicore slaving signals will travel through when the IMx circuitry isn't active.

Figure 13-19
IMx free-forming: Adding the 47k resistors, and tying the enable lines together

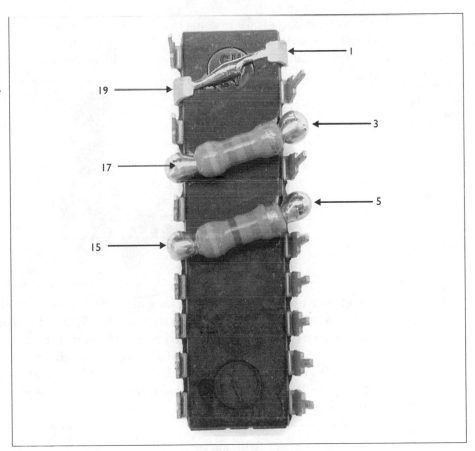

Take your 22µF capacitor and solder it to pins 19 and 20 of the 74AC240 chip, with the capacitor cathode (near stripe) going to pin 19.

Figure 13-20
Soldering the 22µF capacitor to pins 19 and 20

The four pin sockets we're going to add to the IMx circuit are for plugging a backup time-out resistor (on pins 1 and 20) and for connecting the slaving resistors (pins 3 and 5) to the second free-form Bicore.

Figure 13-21
Adding the four pin sockets to the IMx circuit at pins 1, 3, 5, and 20

Let's take a break from soldering for a moment and just lay out the three modules we've been working on. The front module will be the master Bicore and drive the front vertically mounted motor; the middle module is our IMx reverser, and the rear module is our slave Bicore that will drive the horizontally mounted motor. It's looking good! If we keep this general layout in mind when we glue the chips to the robot, we'll have a good idea of how the wiring will progress.

Figure 13-22
Taking a break to see how the chip layout is going to look

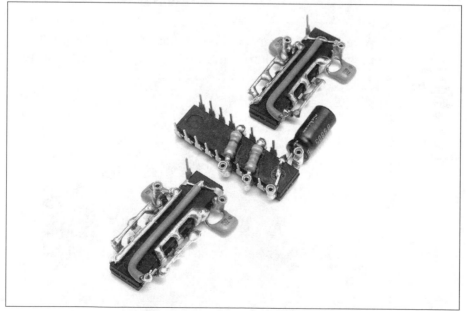

This step is all about *preventing problems*. The chip we're using for our IMx has pretty sensitive input lines, and it doesn't take much of a signal to cause a change to happen on the output, and these changes can occur thousands of times a second. This "floating input" creates noise on the output pin that can play havoc with the rest of the chip, causing it to use up more power and affect the performance of the other input and output lines.

The way to fix this is to give all the inputs a signal to listen to. For sake of convenience, we're going to tie two of the spare inputs to one of the signal channel outputs of the IMx (pins 2 and 4 connecting to pin 3) and the other three spare inputs to the output of the other signal channel output (pins 6, 8, 11, and 13 connecting to pin 5). These changes make the unused inputs "listen" to the output of the two channels we're using for the IMx reverser. This can be useful, because now we can use the outputs of these spare channels to connect an indictor LED to the circuit. When activated, the IMx will be able to use an indicator light to show that the IMx is passing a process through, reversing the signals to the slave Bicore. If this seems a bit confusing, you can ignore all the previous wiring suggestions and just simply wire all the unused inputs (pins 2, 4, 6, 8, 11, and 13) to the negative or positive power pins (pin 10 and 20, respectively).

Figure 13-23
Preparing and soldering the unused inputs to the two channel outputs of the IMx circuit

Note how we've trimmed back the unused output pins so that their long leads won't cause any short circuits, but we can still solder to them if we need to.

Installing Bicore Brains to Your Robot Body

Now is the time to copy the chip layout in Figure 13-22 and super-glue the circuit modules to the topside of the walker body. Don't worry about connecting the wires yet—just make sure that the chips are securely in place, with a bit of space between each module.

Figure 13-24
Gluing the
Bicore brains
and IMx
modules
to the
robot body

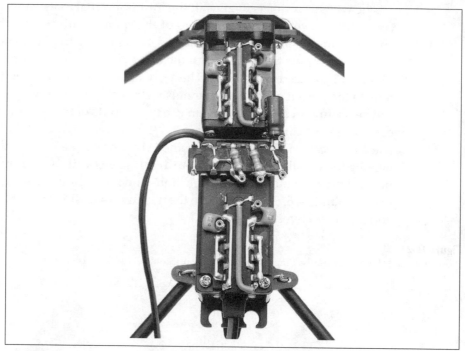

Find your battery packs, and epoxy, hot-glue, or tape (using double-sided sticky-tape) one to each side of your servo body. Super glue will most likely *not* work in this application, as you want something that will absorb some bumping and twisting, which super glue can't do very well (but it still *does do* fingers up noses very nicely—ouch). Make sure that the battery packs don't interfere with the rotation of the servo and that they have their wires or pins poking out at convenient places for you to solder to. Insert the batteries temporarily to make sure that everything fits well, then take them out again until you're ready to power your robot up.

Figure 13-25
Mounting the battery packs to the robot body

While we're dealing with battery packs, let's start wiring up the power. One of the first things to add is your power switch, so find a convenient location near one of the battery pack's "+" terminals and glue your switch down. Then run a red wire (red is nice to identify "+", remember?) from that battery pack "+" terminal to the bottom post of your switch.

Figure 13-26
Wiring the power switch to the battery pack "+" terminal

From the middle post of the switch, run a wire to each of the Bicore power pins (pin 20). Don't worry about the IMx module yet! We're going to first be sure that each Bicore module works properly before adding the IMx into the mix.

Figure 13-27
Running "+" power connections to the Bicore modules

Leave that first battery pack alone and jump over to the other battery pack not near the power switch. Locate the negative terminal on this pack and run a wire (black for "–" is ideal) from this terminal to one of the Bicore ground pins

Figure 13-28
Connecting the other battery pack "–" pin to the Bicore ground pins (pin 10)

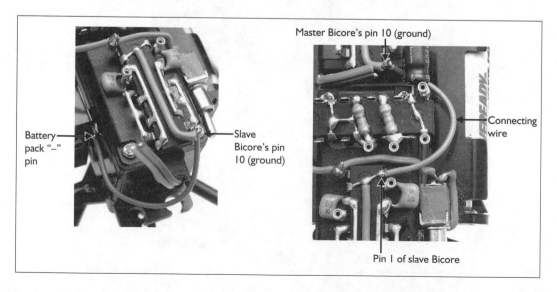

(pin 10). Since the ground pin is also connected to the enable lines (to keep the chip on), we can tap off one of these enable pins and run another "−" wire to the other Bicore's pin 11.

The Safety Geek Says...

Don't Work With Live Power

We're not going to solder the connecting wire between the two battery packs until we're *absolutely* ready to do so. It's a bad idea to work on a robot with live power. Although 6 volts may not be deadly to you, it can melt down parts of a robot and cause a burn! Of course, this doesn't matter if there are no batteries in the battery holders, but some people like to build robots with preassembled battery packs in place.

Now let's wire up the servos to the Bicores. We're going to take the servo wires and wire them to the output of the Bicore above it. Remember that the Bicore outputs are the *outside* set of pins, and that (at this point) it doesn't matter which motor wire gets connected to what side of the Bicore.

Figure 13-29
Wiring the servos to their respective Bicores

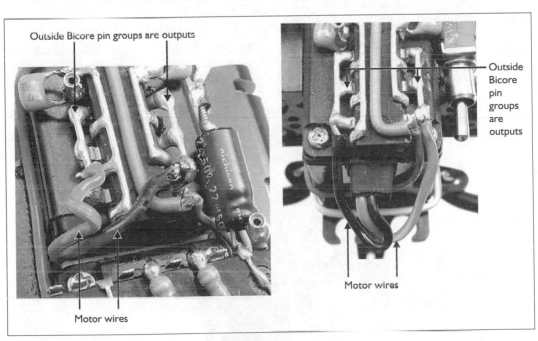

Outside Bicore pin groups are outputs

Outside Bicore pin groups are outputs

Motor wires

Motor wires

With the servos wired up to the Bicores, let's add a suspended resistor across each Bicore's inputs, turning them both into two fully operation Bicores. It really doesn't matter what resistor values you use, as practically anything larger than 100k will cause a noticeable shaking when we power up the robot.

Figure 13-30
Making the Bicores self-oscillating by adding a suspended resistor to each

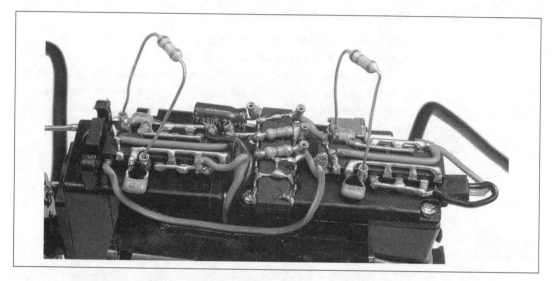

We're ready to solder on the wire that connects the two battery packs together. Best to do this with at least one of the batteries popped out, so your robot doesn't start flailing about unexpectedly. Locate the remaining "+" on the one battery pack, and the remaining "−" on the other pack, and solder the wire between them.

Figure 13-31
Connect the battery packs together only after removing at least one of the batteries.

Left battery pack "+"
to right battery pack "−"

Ready to insert the battery and throw the switch? Exciting time, isn't it! Remember the battery-powered robot procedures we've already used with the other projects—be ready to quickly turn it off, and watch for any tell-tale signs of smoke! (Robotics can be so *exciting!*)

Flip the switch on, and see what happens—you *should* have a pair of motors flailing about left and right, totally out of synchronization with each other. At this moment, they're two totally different circuits, with no way of influencing each other. We'll fix that next when we wire up the IMx reverser circuit and add the slaving resistors.

 The Robot Geek Says

Troubleshooting Your Walking Robot Bicores

At this stage, all we're doing is powering up the two separate Bicore circuits that are connected to two separate motors. Each troubleshooting tip applies to each Bicore equally right now.

✘ **The motor isn't turning at all.** Make sure power is getting to pins 10 and 20 of the chip by using a voltmeter to check for the presence of 5 or 6 volts (the output of the batteries). Make sure the enable lines are connected to negative ("–"); otherwise, the chip is working but just not activated. Your motor wiring may be at fault. If there's an accidental short circuit when you soldered on your motor wires, the chip is dumping all its power to nothing! Desolder the motor from the chip, and see if you can get any action out of it by tapping the wires against the power terminals of the battery.

✘ **The motor is turning only one way.** Make sure the suspended resistor is connected in across the two Bicore inputs. If there isn't a resistor installed, the Bicore will default to one side and make the motor spin in only one direction.

✘ **Absolutely *nothing* is going right.** That's why we're testing now. You may have a hard-to-locate wiring bug, a burned-out gate in the chip, or some other frustrating minor ailment. When push comes to shove, build another Bicore unit and substitute it in for the troublesome one. Sometimes it's simply easier to rebuild than to repair. Long-time BEAM roboticist Mike Trzecieski came up with the acronym "FIBA," which stands for "Forget It! Build Another!" Build another circuit, this time taking a bit more time and care. Rewards come to the patient roboticist.

Now that your tests have proved successful, remove one of the batteries and wire in the IMx reverser circuit. Remove the suspended resistors from the Bicores, and get some wire (white or green is good)—we're going to connect the front master Bicore to the IMx. Let's start by adding short wires from the same outputs that the master Bicore uses to drive the front motor to the input lines (pins 15 and 17) of the IMx, where the 47k resistors are.

While we're at it, let's also connect another negative ("−") ground wire (should be black!) from the slave Bicore's enable line (pin 19) to the IMx ground pin (pin 10).

Figure 13-32
Connecting the master Bicore's outputs to the inputs of the IMx reverser circuit, and making the ground connection to the IMx reverser chip

Wires from master Bicore outputs (outer rail) to pins 4 and 6 of the IMx

Ground "−" connection from slave Bicore pin 19 to IMx pin 10

We just gave the IMx chip a ground connection, so now we need to provide positive ("+") power as well. Run another wire (red) from the middle pin of the switch to pin 20 of the IMx chip, which also happens to be where the 22μF capacitor is connected.

Figure 13-33
Feeding a positive ("+") line from the switch to pin 20 of the IMx chip

We're getting close to being able to test the forward walking motion of our robot. Insert the 2.7M master Bicore suspended resistor into the pin sockets across the inputs of the front motor master Bicore.

Install the pair of 620k resistors, one each from the outputs of the IMx, to the inputs of the slave Bicore.

While we're at it, let's add the 680k resistor to the pin sockets at the front of the IMx chip where the 22µF capacitor is connected. We're not quite ready to use this part of the circuit yet, but let's put the resistor in and be done with it for now.

When installing these resistors, leave the leads nice and long. It's doubtful that the exact resistor values *we're* using will work for you, so don't trim them down and make them fit flush until you're happy with the way your robot is walking.

Figure 13-34
Installing the master, slave, and reverse time-out resistors into their respective pin socket locations

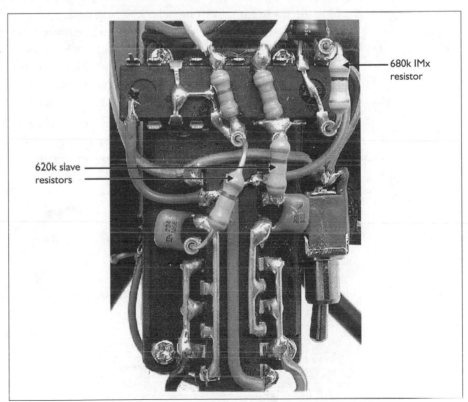

680k IMx resistor

620k slave resistors

Walking Robot Leg Geometry 101: The Basics of Leg Design

We'll take a break from electronic construction for a while, and work on leg design. When your legs are suitably shaped, we'll return to the process of finishing the electronics.

Let's take your creation to a nice open spot of floor, put it down, and fire it up. We'll bet that one of the first things it'll do is "turn turtle" and roll over onto its back. What you're seeing is a situation where your legs are totally out of tune to the body shape. Leg shape is the *single hardest aspect* of this project. Motor strength, leg length, and weight distribution all play a factor in this equation, and when you adjust one, it most likely will throw one of the others out of kilter.

The first question you have to ask yourself when tuning a walker's legs is "What is making the legs return to a normal position?" There *has* to be something helping the legs remember where they are supposed to be. With any biological creature, there's a pair of muscles tugging on a bone, and when both muscles are at rest, that's the normal position for the limb. Ever see video of the astronauts sleeping on the space shuttle? When they are asleep, their arms float up until they're almost shoulder height, in a bike-riding position. In this position, your arm muscles are in balance with each other. You have to make sure your robot's limbs have the same sort of "normal position" memory.

With the front motor and legs, it's not that hard a task. The robot is continually pushing against gravity every step, with gravity acting as a natural "pull back down to normal" force. Knowing this, you can tweak the front legs to take advantage of gravity to help the bot remain stable.

Figure 13-35
Vertical stepping legs can use gravity to pull them back to the normal position.

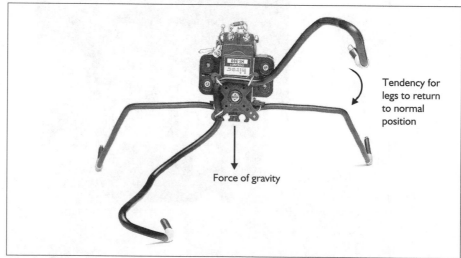

Tendency for legs to return to normal position

Force of gravity

The rear motor and legs are a tougher problem. Since the legs are swinging sideways across the surface, gravity doesn't work to return the legs to a normal position. To give the rear legs a centering force, we have to introduce an artificial pull from a spring. You may have to experiment a bit before you find the best spring, but remember, you can always clip down a too-long spring to make it have more force on the rear legs.

Figure 13-36
A spring is necessary to pull the horizontal-stepping legs back to the normal position.

Let's start with the leg shape. Simply said, we really don't care what shape the leg is. Make it a giant spiral or jaggy shape—it doesn't ultimately affect how the robot walks. What *does* matter is where that leg touches the ground—specifically, *how far* from the motor output shaft does the foot touch the ground. This direct "line of string" distance is really the only leg measurement that counts, so when we talk about leg length, we're referring to this length: the distance from the motor output shaft to the point where the leg hits the ground.

Figure 13-37
Leg shapes don't matter: It's where the leg touches the ground that counts!

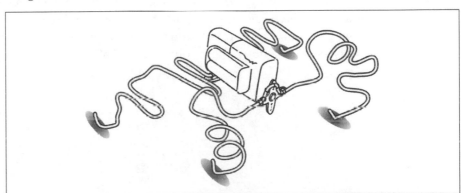

A walker's leg length is best determined by the torque strength of the motor, which is the ability of the motor to twist a load. The more torque a motor has, the longer the legs of your walking robot can be, and the better it will be able to step over obstacles. A good rule of thumb is that if you grab your robot by one foot and dangle it in the air, the motor should still be able to vigorously twist the robot body around. If the robot barely moves, the leg is too long, so bend it back so that the foot is closer to the motor shaft. With most hobby servos, we find that leg lengths of 8 – 13 cm (3" – 5") from foot to motor shaft are about right.

Use leg length as the way to add or reduce the force of gravity for the return to normal position. The longer a leg is, the easier it is for gravity to pull the walker back down to the normal position. A shorter leg resists gravity better and won't fall back down as easily. This is an engineering concept called "torque-arm distance," which is worth looking up in any senior physics textbook. Keep this concept in mind when you're trying to get both of your robot's front feet to rise and fall equal distances.

Walking robot geometry is largely about the relationship between the four contact points of the robot (the feet), and the center of mass of the robot (the point where it balances). We can get a good start on determining our leg shapes by drawing a large cross on a piece of paper, or by sitting down on a tiled floor surface (lots of squares)—we're going to use the lines as a guide.

Try to pick up your robot with only two fingertips where you think it'll balance flattest. That is, pick it up so that it doesn't tip forward or backward at all. You want it to hang between your fingertips so that the top of the robot is lying as horizontal as you can manage it. Draw an imaginary line between your fingertips, and another right down the middle of your robot, front to back. Where these lines cross is the *center of gravity (CoG)* of your robot. Arrange your robot on the surface with the CoG sitting right above the crossing point of the X on your floor, so that the X shoots off from the CoG starting at a 45° angle from the front of your robot. You want your robot's feet to touch the surface only at points along these four lines shooting out from beneath your robot.

Figure 13-38
The walking robot leg layout starts with *X* marking the spot!

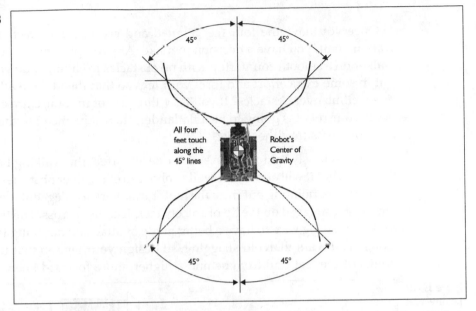

The front legs or rear legs can slide up and down these lines *as a pair*, as long as they remain the same distance out from the CoG to each other. That is, you can have a front set of legs close in to the robot's body for strong lifting capability, as long as both feet measure the same distance out on the diagonal lines from the robot's CoG. The rear legs can be farther out to give a greater distance per push, as long as both rear feet measure the same distance out from the robot's CoG. As soon as you start straying from these lines, you're bound to have tuning trouble.

Figure 13-39
Close front legs and far rear legs can work, if you keep the foot distances the same for each pair of feet.

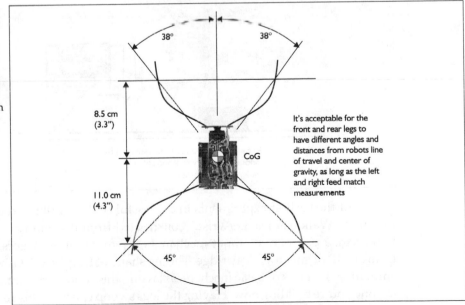

Once you have the four feet aligned and creating an effective forward walking gait, you have a decision to make: Are you planning on using your walker on a smooth countertop with no obstacles to climb, or do you want to put in some extra effort and form your legs so that they'll be ready to effectively climb over obstacles? If you're willing to put in some extra effort, read on. If your robot is going to be a flatlander, then skip ahead to the IMx wiring—no pressure either way.

We previously said that the shape doesn't affect the walking behavior of the robot, but it will affect how well a robot can climb over obstacles. A simple piece of wire pointing out from the motor *will* work as a leg, but it will immediately get snagged on the lip of any obstacle it comes across. The trick here is to shape the leg wire to have a better angle of attack on anything that comes along. You want to avoid snagging, so design your legs so that the contact points of the feet trail from behind a higher, more forward knee.

Figure 13-40
The direction from which the shin meets an obstacle determines how well the foot will handle it.

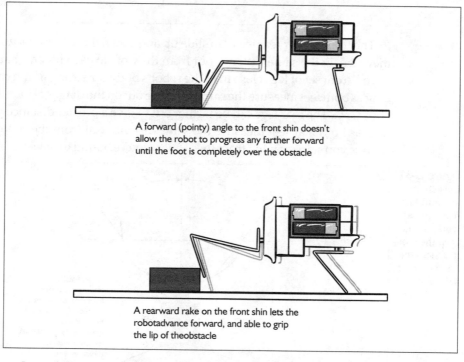

A forward (pointy) angle to the front shin doesn't allow the robot to progress any farther forward until the foot is completely over the obstacle

A rearward rake on the front shin lets the robotadvance forward, and able to grip the lip of theobstacle

One of the earliest experiments in successful BEAM walking robot design was "Walkman Daggerwrist," constructed from the remnants of a Sony Walkman, a pair of oven timer mechanisms, two vibration pagers, and wire from an HP printer toner cartridge. The leg shape of Daggerwrist is well worth emulating, in terms of basic mechanical layout, this robot is the grandfather of the one you're building now. Having the legs swoop considerably forward and then taper backward again to where the foot meets the ground is a very effective way to create legs that can tackle considerable obstacles.

Figure 13-41
Walkman
Daggerwrist:
An excellent
example of
legs shaped
for climbing
obstacles,
with close-up
of heat-shrink
"climbing
shins"

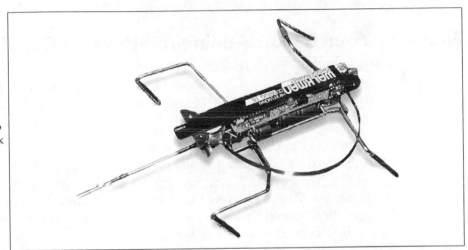

Besides originating the leg shape, Walkman Daggerwrist was one of the first BEAM robots to use multiple layers of heat-shrink tubing overlapping each other on the legs, so that if the "shin" of the leg rubbed against an edge, the lip of the tubing would catch and lift the robot over the top. This idea of having a serrated edge on the front of the robot has been reproduced successfully in the B.I.O.-Bug line of robot bug toys. The front legs of each toy have these teeth that help them get a grip on the obstacle they're trying to climb. You may want to try to duplicate similar teeth by bending your leg wire in step-shapes, gluing on a piece of step-shaped plastic, or soldering on a dull saw blade to the front "shin" of the legs.

Figure 13-42
B.I.O.-Bug
front shin
serrated
climbing
teeth

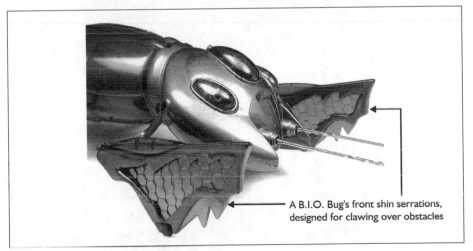

A B.I.O. Bug's front shin serrations, designed for clawing over obstacles

No matter what the final shapes of your legs are, remember the golden rule: Make *sure* that the feet end up touching the lines of the X that radiate out from the robot's CoG, that the front feet are parallel, and that the rear feet are parallel.

Finishing Your Robot: Adding the Reverse Capability

We're practically finished, with just the reverse sensor to be added. We didn't bother with the sensor *before* doing the legs because the touch sensor is a pretty tweaky device and would most likely add to the confusion when shaping the legs.

We're going to build what's called a "Scotty sensor," named after Scott Martin, who developed this easy and robust sensor layout. Being a musician, Scott has lots of spare thick metal guitar wire, and he correctly concluded that it'd be a great material for a touch (or *tactile*) sensor. Scott found that a layer of heat-shrink tubing on one of his guitar strings would fit almost ideally into a ring crimp connector, and that it would hold up to considerable abuse. Sounds like an ideal tactile sensor for a walking robot!

Start by shrinking your 13 mm (1/2") length of heat-shrink tubing over one end of the sensor wire, leaving enough wire poking out of the backside to solder to. Then prepare the #8 ring crimp connector by prying apart the collar apart at the rear.

Figure 13-43
Applying the heat-shrink tubing to the guitar wire sensor, and prying open the crimp connector

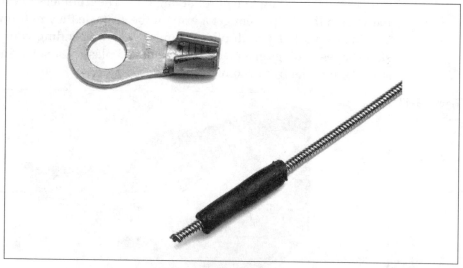

Slide the sensor/heat-shrink sleeve assembly into the collar so that the sleeve is about halfway in. Squeeze the collar closed again so that it securely clamps around the sleeve, and *only* the sleeve.

Figure 13-44
Inserting and clamping around the sleeve and sensor assembly

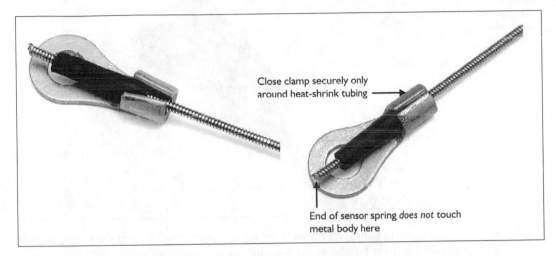

Close clamp securely only
around heat-shrink tubing →

End of sensor spring *does not* touch
metal body here

The way this sensor works is on the principle of *deflection*. When nothing is touching the sensor, it stays centered in the middle of the collar, supported by the insulating layer of heat-shrink tubing. When the sensor is deflected off to the side in any direction, it contacts the collar, making an electrical connection that is passed back to the reverser circuitry.

Figure 13-45
The sensor operates by passing a signal only when it's deflected enough to touch the metal collar around it.

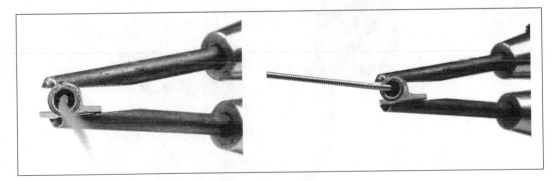

Depending how stiff your sensor wire is, you may not be able to get enough deflection to make the sensor touch the collar. The solution to this is to solder a brass sleeve around the front of the tubing, closing the distance between the sensor wire and the collar. It will take much less movement from the sensor now to touch the collar.

Figure 13-46
Using a brass
sleeve to
make your
sensor more
sensitive

We're going to mount our sensor up high, near the front of the robot, so that it doesn't get hit by the front legs in normal walking mode. We tucked the large part of the ring crimp connector between the servo and one of the battery packs, and we used super glue to keep it firmly in place. If you're ambitious, you may consider mounting a sensor on each of the front legs, so that the robot will go in reverse when the legs hit an obstacle rather than when the forward-poking sensor hits something.

Figure 13-47
Mounting the
tactile sensor
to the robot
body

To wire the sensor into the circuit, connect a wire from the ring crimp connector body to a ground connection—for instance, anywhere you wired up with black wire, in this case the master Bicore's enable pin (pin 1). Solder another wire from the end of the spring poking out of the back of the heat-shrink tubing to pin 1 of the IMx module. Note that this is also the same pin to which the 22µF capacitor's cathode (near the stripe) is attached. When the sensor closes, it connects the capacitor cathode to ground, letting it quickly charge up and activate the IMx reverser. When the capacitor finishes discharging, the IMx turns off, and the robot goes forward again.

Figure 13-48
Wiring the tactile sensor to the root of the robot's electronics

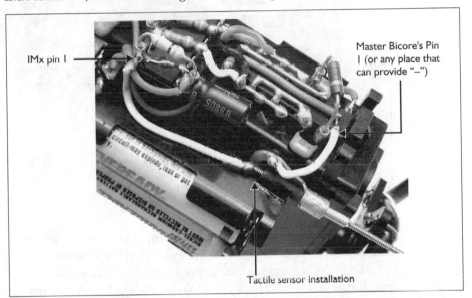

IMx pin 1

Master Bicore's Pin 1 (or any place that can provide "−")

Tactile sensor installation

As designed, this backup sensor will cause the robot to kick into reverse the instant it touches an obstacle. Although a good idea at first, having a robot instantly respond to its sensors doesn't make for the most robust behavior. Sometimes it's good to let the robot struggle against what is in its way, as it may be able to shove the obstacle enough that it can progress past it. Fortunately, it's pretty easy to add this modification to the sensor circuit. If you simply add a series resistor to the signal line to the IMx reverser, the sensor will have to be held on for a while until the signal is strong enough to activate the IMx. We added a 10k resistor between the sensor output and the IMx signal input, and this introduced a quarter second delay in activation time. It doesn't sound like much, but it made a considerable behavioral change in our robot, making it less "twitchy" and less sensitive to accidental activations of the sensor. The sensor would occasionally activate just because of the up and down motion of the front legs swinging the sensor around, but after installing this single resistor, it is much more reliable.

Figure 13-49
Adding a signal-smoothing resistor to the touch sensor installation

Break line and insert 10k resistor

Whatever resistor you select, make sure that it is no more than 1/10th the size of the reverse time-out resistor. As our IMx is using a 680k resistor, we could have made our resistor as big as 68k, but that would have made our robot charge an obstacle for a good two seconds before it decided to back up (too long, in our opinion).

Care and Feeding of Your Walking Robot

The *X* you used when doing your initial leg layout is adjustable for different designs, as long as the angles are the same front-to-back. For instance, the angle between the front two feet and the CoG in our first leg layout is 90° (each line being 45° from the front of the robot). You can narrow or widen that angle, as long as the angles are equal and used for both the front and rear sets of legs. Make the angle between the legs really wide (say, 120°) for a fast robot, or narrow (around 60°) for better maneuverability. In both cases, you'll need to speed up your Bicore as you stray from the baseline 90° alignment *X*.

Figure 13-50
Different angles of the alignment X give different walking abilities.

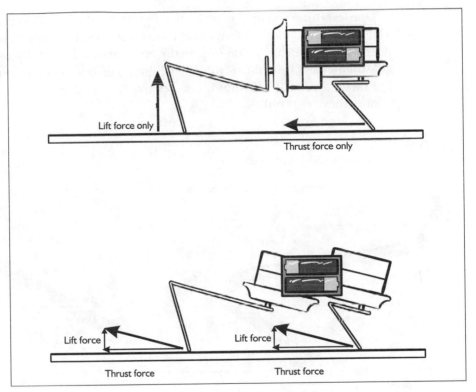

The motor arrangement used for this project happened to be one of convenience, where we simply glued the flat face of one servo to the flat face of another. One motor gives lift; the other, thrust (forward motion). There's no reason not to experiment with different motor geometries where both motors are slightly angled upward from flat, or with the front motor at 30° from horizontal, giving lift *and* thrust—there's many, many experiments to do on *just* the motor geometry in regard to lift and thrust parameters. Consider building a variable-geometry walker that changes the angle between the motors as it travels—that'd be a very interesting project!

Feel free to play with the alignment of the walker in respect to ground. That is, when you view your walker side-on (when, for instance, you put it on a table and view it from right alongside), you can form the legs so that the nose dips down and the rear lifts up. A nose-down attitude will make this robot add a bit of forward thrust to the front motor legs and a bit of lift component to the rear motor legs.

One last thing you may want to do for your robot's feet is to give it booties. The plastic insulation on the leg wire we used is fairly slippery, so the robot doesn't have much traction (especially on linoleum floors). By using a suitable diameter of heat-shrink tubing, we shrunk on booties to the points where the robot touches the ground. Use several layers, if possible; as with any bootie, they wear out over time.

Figure 13-51
Robot booties, on the front and rear feet of our robot

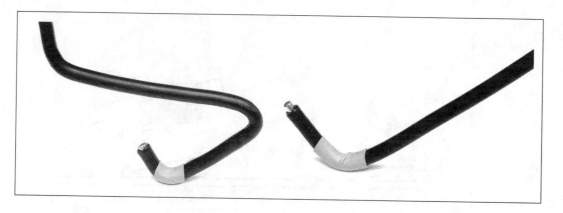

How ambitious are you feeling? Think you can tackle one more modification to your walking robot? As is, your robot will go forward and backward but not do much else. Here's a simple modification to the circuit that will make it turn while backing up, making it much more able to go in new directions, and all it requires is another 620k resistor: Once you have that installed and working well, the next step is to add a backup and turn for each side of your robot, triggered by two different tactile sensors. At this stage, you should be able to figure it out on your own, but if you need a hint, it requires separating the two "enable" lines on your IMx chip and adding two resistors and one capacitor.

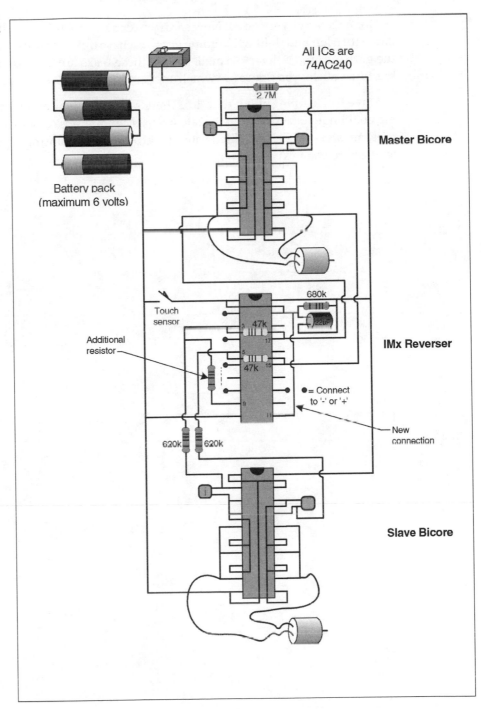

Figure 13-52
Final
challenge:
Adding a
turn to the
reverser
circuitry

Done already? Very good! Now see if you can successfully modify your robot to turn left and right while going *forward*, chase light, scare the cat, take out the garbage, and deliver the mail. Not all these tasks are immediately possible, but we'll let you figure out which ones are (perhaps you'll surprise us!).

Have fun learning about robotics. There's always a new and more interesting challenge to tackle when the latest one is conquered. As shown by all the great masters of the ages, life is about learning and exploring. Always look forward to the next challenge!

Chapter 14

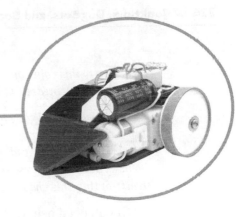

Biomech Motor Bridges and the Adaptive Bicore

U p to this point, our projects have been spelled out, fully detailed, and completely documented. Ready for a challenge?

Now that you've got your feet wet in the wading pool of robotics, it's time to take a jump off the high-diving board into the deep end under the care of your new lifeguard, Mark Tilden. If after reading this you think you're drowning, take a breather and visit some of the BEAM resources listed in Appendix A. They'll prepare you better for reattempting this chapter at a later date.

(If you need help with the nomenclature and symbols used in this chapter, shame on you. Go back and read the rest of this book.)

This chapter introduces the reader to the basics of minimal H-bridge motor driving and introduces a few unstable biomech twists to some old favorites. Though there are many other DC motor drivers on the market, many are difficult to configure or handle for the low-power, variable-load operations biomech devices require. The following circuits are based on an SCR-like current amplifier arrangement that, when biased correctly, works quite well for most push-pull inductive actuators, from solenoids to stepper motors. The advantages are

❑ Low parts and connection count

❑ Operable voltage range 1.7 V–60 V (or whatever your transistors will do before the smoke pours out)

❑ Standby current: microamps

❑ Reasonable efficiency, losing only about 1 volt across the drive transistors

❑ That most fold elegantly into a tight physical package

❑ Easy variable gain on either half of the bridge (to compensate for motor inequalities)

❑ CMOS or TTL drive compatibility at very high impedance, so the motor can even be driven by the weakest controller signals

❑ Positive or negative control edge reconfigurability, so they can work on either high or low signals

❑ Low cost, such that they can usually be hacked from spare electronics

❑ Operation with most complementary transistor sets (the always available 2N3904 NPN and the 2N3906 PNP, for example) up to about a watt

For all the following, we assume a motor with an average static impedance of six ohms, about 50 percent efficiency (typical for hobby or toy servo motors), and a power supply between three and seven volts DC. Given this, the smallest reliable motor bridge driver is based on this minimal power-mode amplifier:

Figure 14-1
A minimal high-gain one-way motor driver, positive signal trigger (+ve)

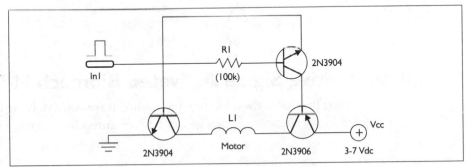

Basic Positive-Signal Activated Module for our Biomech H-Bridge

When the input goes high, current flows through the respective drive transistor bases, biasing them into an active state and allowing current to flow through the motor. When the input goes low, the motor current shuts off, creating a very high impedance across the circuit. That is, the only current that flows is in transistor leakage normally too small to worry about. The advantage here is that the activating control input signal can be very low current, provided its voltage is kept close to Vcc. This circuit is useful for pulse-driving a motor in one direction from, for example, CMOS logic control outputs in solar-style designs, where a high-impedance off-state is critical to save power. The real advantage, though, is that the drive impedance R1 is so high that very little signal can "leak back" to the control circuitry, even if the motor is overstressed, back-geared, or electrically noisy.

Basic Negative-Signal Activated Module for our Biomech H-Bridge

The complement to this circuit uses a PNP in place of the trigger transistor, so now the motor moves on a negative instead of a positive signal at In1.

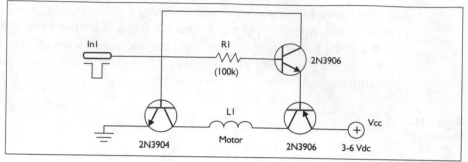

Figure 14-2
A minimal
high-gain
one-way
motor driver,
negative
signal trigger

Complete Positive-Signal Activated Biomech H-Bridge

By doubling the first of these circuits and folding it appropriately, an active-high triggered biomech motor H-bridge can be configured like Figure 14-3.

Figure 14-3
A basic biomech motor bridge (positive trigger)

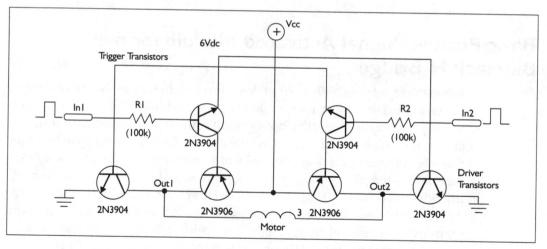

It's called an "H Bridge" because the array of driver transistors forms a *H* structure where current direction switches across the motor depending on which of the two inputs is triggered. It's different from many other H-bridges in that it doesn't use limiting and pull-up resistors around the driver transistors, normally used to limit gain saturation. Though adding these resistors is a good idea, they're not necessary here as it turns out that so long as R1 and R2 are greater than 50,000 ohms (50k), most transistors can take the load well. When saturation does happen, the drive transistors heat up and motor efficiency drops drastically. This is usually not a fatal problem, but power is wasted as heat, not motion. The solution is to increase R1 and R2 to the next higher resistance value and reapply power.

At the other extreme, R1 and R2 can be as high as 20 megohms and still allow enough current to spin most hobby and toy motors, though the output current drops linearly with the increase in bias resistance. Exact bias equations vary depending on transistors used, but even high-power drive transistors can be controlled from small bias transistors, typically 2N3904s or 2N3906s. Of special note is that the inputs of the biomech H-bridge are so electrically sensitive that just touching them usually generates a motor response.

A further advantage is that this circuit is not just "bang-bang," the common term for all-power-forward, all-power-reverse, or nothing circuits. The motor power profile can be set at the driver itself by varying R1 and/or R2 accordingly. For example, on a multilegged walking robot, while a leg is raised and unloaded it needs very little power to move forward (R1 = 5 meg typical), but while on the ground and driving the robot, it needs the maximum motor power (R2 = 68k) to travel the same distance while under load. That is, the bridge can be easily biased to deliver a best-guess full-power leg-drive force, but only a minimal-power leg-return force. Such biasing can also linearize the action of motors with a forward-reverse rotational discrepancy. Often gearing or internal friction can give a gear motor uneven forward-backward motion, which a careful biasing of either R1 or R2 can reduce. Furthermore, uniformly high values of R1 and R2 can further reduce the maximum motor torque to where it is unlikely to damage itself from unexpected external forces, like the unexpected trauma of falling off a table. The biomech bridge can serve as a "variable suspension" to reduce power requirements and back-gearing damage without the need for complex mechanics. This is its one major advantage over all-or-nothing FET-based H-bridge drivers and set-point servo controllers, and it makes the biomech bridge invaluable during debugging and fine-tuning of complex mechanical designs.

It's also dead cheap and buildable pretty much anywhere.

Complete Negative-Signal Activated Biomech H-Bridge

To drive the same motor from negative, or active low-logic signals, you'll need the circuit shown in Figure 14-4. With the only change being the bias transistor type (PNP) and orientation, this is the circuit most commonly used in biomech designs to take advantage of standard nervous net (Nv) negative logic control.

Figure 14-4
Biomech motor bridge (negative trigger)

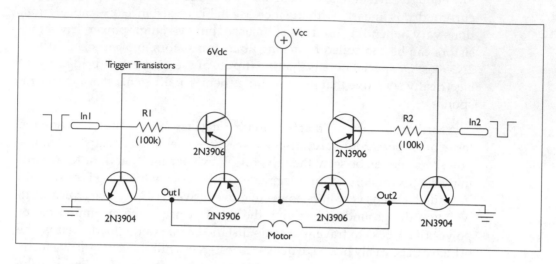

Single Control Signal Biomech H-Bridge

And of course, the bias transistors can also be mismatched to make an alternate input polarity driver. This design is fine for straight push-pull from a single control source if desired, the only caveat being that the motor can never turn off while power is applied.

Figure 14-5
The single-input biomech motor bridge

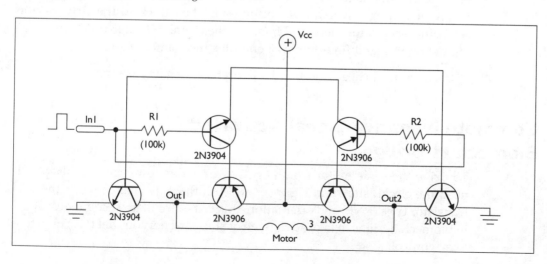

Safety Biomech Motor Bridges

The difficulty with the two-input H-bridges is that they can "smokeshow" if both inputs are triggered at the same time. Activating both sides directly shorts your power to ground across all your driver transistors, and smoke is usually the result. A simple way around this is to add a pair of diodes connected to a "safety" control signal.

Figure 14-6
A "reset" input added to a motor bridge (+ve trigger)

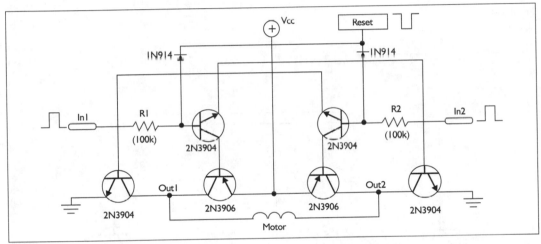

Or better yet, install a safety, antismoke transistor to disable one side of the bridge if both inputs ever go high.

Figure 14-7
Position of the anti-smoke transistor

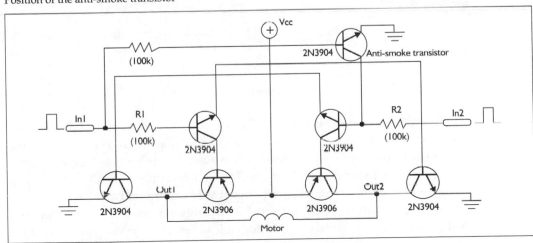

Contrary to the command "turn left *and* turn right," your motor will move in one direction, and your transistors will live as well.

The Decoded Safety Motor Bridge

For a more stable, elegant motor controller, Figure 14-8 does the job of isolating the decoded inputs so that a controller's two-bit digital output can never fry the circuitry, provided the control signals are kept below 30 Hertz (this is so the backward electromotive force [back EMF] from the motor doesn't overload the drive transistors due to dynamic loading).

Figure 14-8
The safety motor bridge

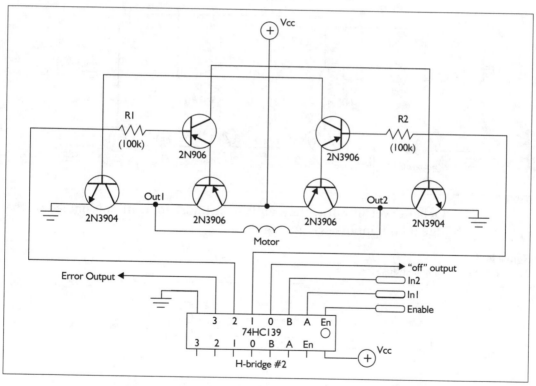

The fairly common 74xx139 (where *xx* represents LS, C, HCT, HC, or whatever logic family specification is cheapest, or available) is a symmetrical dual one-of-four decoder that can handle two such motor bridges elegantly from one chip. The Error output from the 74139, if put into an LED, for example, would indicate if an inappropriate input was generated by the driving controller; such output is often useful in debugging control code in processor-based designs. The decoder's active low "enable" input will turn off the bridge, restricting all Input signals; however, it does make the H-bridge susceptible to electrical noise. If this driver is in an electrically noisy environment, or driven over long control lines (six inches or more), two 1 meg pull-up resistors to Vcc on the outside edges of R1 and R2 will keep the bridge from picking up strays and starting the motor unexpectedly.

The logic table for the safety motor bridge is as follows:

In2	In1	Enable	Result
Doesn't matter	Doesn't matter	High (positive)	All signals high
Low (negative)	Low (negative)	Low (negative)	"off" output –ve
Low (negative)	High (positive)	Low (negative)	Out1 –ve, Out2 +
High (positive)	Low (negative)	Low (negative)	Out1 +ve, Out2 –
High (positive)	High (positive)	Low (negative)	"Error" output –

Dynamic Braking Safety BioMech H-Bridge Controller

A further use for this Error output is as a dynamic brake, as shown in Figure 14-9.

Figure 14-9
The full-featured motor bridge

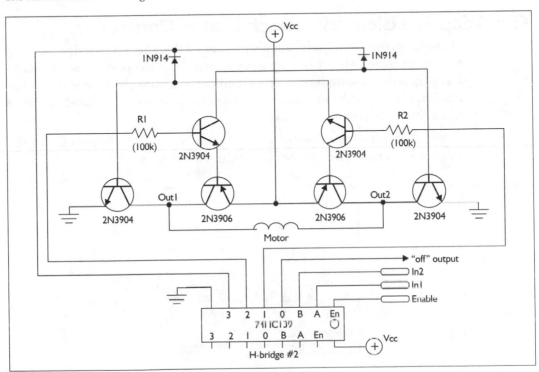

The two additional diodes mean that when both Reverse and Forward are triggered (1, 1), the motor shorts across the connecting Vcc rail. Not as good as a relay short, but effective, simple, and a solid state implementation of "back-EMF braking" to quickly halt the motor and assist in holding its position. This design features all four useful control states for a motor: Free-wheel (0,0), Forward (0,1), Backward (1,0), and Brake (1,1). Furthermore, as this type of dynamic breaking does not shunt across Vcc and ground, the electrical noise generated is significantly reduced, making this circuit safer, if not ideal, for sensitive digital controllers.

For motors up to two watts (standard hobby and toy motors), these circuits have shown themselves quite capable using common switching transistors. For more powerful motors, larger transistors with built-in shunt diodes are recommended to keep back-EMF spikes from blowing out the base-emitter junction couplings. The problem with such designs is that these spikes are dumped on the Vcc-ground rails and can severely destabilize any sensitive control circuitry that shares this power. Analog designs are resistant to such effects, but strong bypass caps (1000μF or better) are recommended across the Vcc-ground rails on every bridge.

In other words, when in doubt, try a cap across your rails.

The Adaptive Bicore Biomech Motor Controller

H-bridge drivers are dandy, but the problem is that they still need something to control them. Also, you may have noticed that the parts count tends to creep up with these bridges, making them less palatable for the die-hard minimalist. If we're willing to take some chances, however, the following circuit has a lot of interesting features.

By adding a diode-shunted capacitor for feedback to both sides of the Biomech H-bridge, we get the circuit shown in Figure 14-10.

Figure 14-10
The basic adaptive Bicore (ABc) schematic

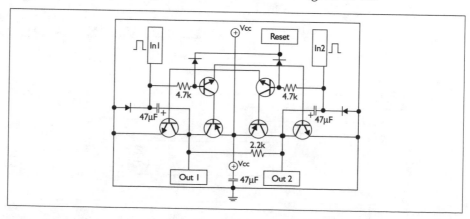

The addition of the 47uF capacitors and diodes turns the bridge into an unstable two-mode oscillator, either off or bouncing back and forth approximately every four seconds. The advantage is that the signal fed back into the circuit is directly dependent on the degree of motor load. What this means is that any reasonable motor attached to it will start to move backward and forward spontaneously at its own rate but reverse if it encounters an unexpected overload. Because it's a pair of differentiators in a loop, very much like conventional chip-based nervous network circuits discussed elsewhere, we call this an adaptive Bicore circuit, or ABc.

Its features are

- ❏ Operating voltage, 1.5–15 volts, but prefers 3–7 volts with these bias resistors
- ❏ Output current, 1–500 mA (3 watts max, 1 watt nominal)
- ❏ Input impedance, 47k ohms (adaptation), 1000 ohms (direct drive)
- ❏ Self-starting oscillator, adaptive to most motor impedances higher than 4 ohms
- ❏ Drive inputs through 47k resistors to use as antishorting H-bridge motor driver with adaptation

The ABc offers considerable flexibility to the user, such as

- ❏ For a quick conversion, drive the inputs through 27k resistors to use as an antishorting H-bridge motor driver without adaptation. Higher resistor values start making the ABc act as a slave, with the associated operation phase delay. Lower resistor values risk melting down the input transistors.
- ❏ For a better conversion to a standard H-bridge driver, simply remove the 47µF capacitors, and drive the inputs through resistors between 47k and 100k.
- ❏ The ABc can be "suspended," which means that a resistor can be placed between the inputs to increase the output frequency from the default oscillation period. A 47k value is typical to get an unloaded one-second period, for example.
- ❏ "Reset" (active low) shuts off the outputs. Using the "reset" line for more than a few seconds kills the self-starting feature.
- ❏ Insert a 0.1µF capacitor across each of the diodes on the "reset" line for self-starting after an extended reset (requires toggling reset line from low to high).

❏ The adaptive reverse mode depends on the 4.7k resistors; it is currently set at 80 percent of maximum load. What this means is that the reverse threshold is directly proportionate to voltage and is nominal at 6 V. Pulsing the "reset" input at about 2 Hertz will cause the circuit to restart in the opposite phase to which it powered down in.

❏ Replace the 4.7k internal biasing resistors with CdS photoresistors for phototropic oscillations (ideal for headbots). No further electronics required.

❏ "Headbot" behavior can also be accomplished using back-to-back IR photodiodes (*not* LEDs) across the inputs.

❏ Substitute PN2222 for 2N3904 transistors and PN2907 for 2N3906 transistors for generally improved behavior.

But basically, it's an H-bridge with a mind of its own. The symbol for it appears in Figure 14-11, which also shows some typical ways in which it can be hooked together to make behaviors.

A full schematic is shown in Figure 14-12.

Figure 14-11
Symbol for the ABc showing a simple coupling example

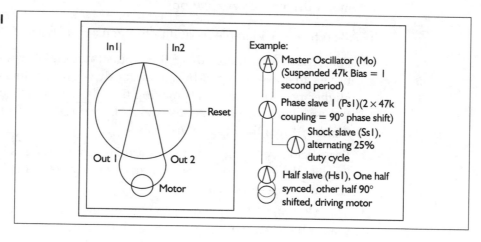

Figure 14-12
A full ABc 4.2 schematic diagram showing bias points, power and output LEDs, and the reset input

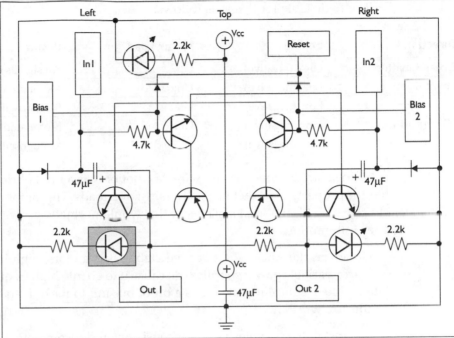

The additional LEDs make using the ABc very convenient, as you can never be sure when it's oscillating, especially if your motor load is exotic enough to shut the ABc down.

Experiments in Adaptive Bicore One-Wire Control

I'll leave experimentation to the reader, but Figure 14-13 offers one example to show the versatility of this little beast. It's the circuit for a "one-wire" H-bridge adding just three components to the ABc circuit just described.

Figure 14-13
Symbol schematic for the "one-wire" ABc H-bridge

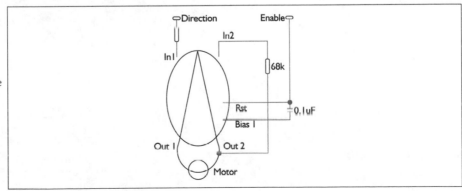

The logic table for this is as follows:

Direction	Enable	Motor Load	Result
Doesn't matter	High (positive)	Off	All signals off
Low (negative)	Low (negative)	Unloaded	Motor spins left
Low (negative)	Low (negative)	Loaded	Motor oscillates
High (positive)	Low (negative)	Unloaded	Motor spins right
High (positive)	Low (negative)	Loaded	Motor oscillates

So in six transistors, the one-wire ABc not only is a full H-bridge but also has the property of ratcheting itself against overloads. The motor never has to shut off or stall, and so a lot of energy that would normally get wasted as heat goes into motion.

However, the ABc is still not predictable. Bad motors, high-inertia gearboxes, or variable power supplies can cause it to go into high frequency oscillations like a squealing cat. Takes a bit of biasing to make it stable, but the results are worth it.

It's unstable. It's explosive. It's inconsistent and incomplete. I like it a lot. Hope you have fun with it.

Appendix A

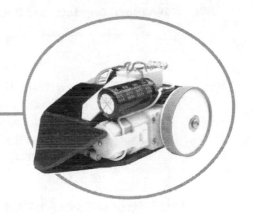

Resources for More BEAM Information

Congratulations on making it all the way to the end of the book! That deserves a reward: For a free bonus project, visit http://www .solarbotics.com and click on the Special Projects link. What is it? Well, it's special…. and it's a *project!* We guess you'll just have to come on by and find out, won't you?

Internet-Based Information

There's a tremendous explosion of information on the internet regarding robotics, and the following is just a short list of sites we particularly recommend. Some have already been mentioned in earlier chapters, but they're worth relisting here. Don't have Internet access? Try visiting a local library; most have free Internet access now, and bring a pocket full of quarters to print stuff—there's information on the Web that's simply not available anywhere else.

Information Sites

- ❑ **Solarbotics.net (http://www.solarbotics.net)**   This Web site is the "BEAM Community Server," sponsored wholly by Solarbotics Ltd. as a service to the BEAM robotics community. No SPAM, no banners, no pop-up advertisements, just raw, unpasteurized BEAM information, coming mainly from the skilled hands of BEAM veteran & webmaster Eric Seale (aka "Conan, the Librarian"). Besides the main technical page of BEAM circuits, definitions, photographs, and comparison charts, Solarbotics.net also offers free Web site hosting for BEAM-related pages, with more services being added all the time. Please note that Dave Hrynkiw is the founder and president of Solarbotics Ltd. and, even so, Solarbotics is a resource well worth investigating. Really. Honest!

- ❑ **The BEAM Robotics mailing list at Yahoo.com**   Visit the group page at http://groups.yahoo.com/group/beamrobotics/ for full details. The central purpose for the mailing list at Yahoo! is for people interested in BEAM to share their ideas. With over 800 members, it's quite active, so expect between 5 and 25 e-mail a day from this list alone.

- ❑ **BEAM-Online (http://www.beam-online.com)**   One of the oldest BEAM Web sites still in existence, and although its author, Ian Bernstein, has had to ignore it in favor of his academics, it's still a very worthwhile resource to visit.

❏ **The Robot Room (http://www.robotroom.com)**   David Cook's excellent robotics page, including a fairly comprehensive list of robot clubs around the world. His listing of projects (both robotic and nonrobotic) is a fun read.

❏ **Robots.net (http://robots.net)**   This is a great general news site regarding robots in the media, upcoming robot competitions; it also has listings of linked robotic projects.

❏ **GoRobotics.net (http://www.gorobotics.net)**   Similar to robots.net, this focuses on book reviews and project tutorials.

❏ **COMP.ROBOTICS.MISC**   A healthy usenet newsgroup that has discussions on all aspects of robotics, but focuses mainly on the hobby and personal robot aspects. As with all newsgroups, there's the occasional flare-up of nastiness, but don't let that put you off from reading it. If you have any non-BEAM–related type of robotics question, post it here for a good answer. For BEAM questions, stick with the Yahoo! mailing list, as some members of the COMP.ROBOTICS.MISC newsgroup have, uh, disapproving points of view regarding BEAM technology, regardless of how successful it is. If you have a strong constitution, post away!

Commercial Websites

❏ **Solarbotics.com, "Your BEAM Robotics Resource"**   Yup, the people who brought you Solarbotics.net also have a commercial site too. But don't let that put you off, as Solarbotics.com has one of the largest image collections of BEAM robots available. Plus, all the documentation for the kits is available as a free download. Make sure to check out the technical documentation for the "Bicore Experimenter's PCB," as it has many circuits you can build on your own.

❏ **Mondo-Tronics (http://www.robotstore.com)**   This has the most comprehensive assortment of robot-related goods in the known universe. These guys have almost all the really cool robot stuff gathered together into one big Web site They also carry a whole bunch more of cool no-robot stuff. It's hard to place a small order here, so expect to spend money at this Web site. Lots of it.

❑ **Robot Books.com (http://www.robotbooks.com)**   A specialty Web site dealing mostly with robot books. There are titles and reviews for books for every aspect of robot construction. Carlo Bertocchini (of Battlebot "BioHazard" fame) has done an excellent job of compiling detailed listings for books with similar themes. If you are weak in one area of study, RobotBooks.com definitely has the textbook for you.

❑ **Digikey (http://www.digikey.com)**   One of the largest, most complete electronics suppliers in the world, they also have a Canadian branch (http://www.digikey.ca), deliver quickly, and a really killer Web site with loads of technical data. Well worth visiting first when you're trying to locate information on a part.

❑ Other worthwhile sites for datasheets on ICs and transistors are Fairchild Semiconductor (http://www.fairchildsemi.com) and Texas Instruments (http://www.ti.com).

❑ If otherwise stumped, the Datasheet Locator Web site (http://www.datasheetlocator.com/) has a large collection of datasheets and links, as does the Semiconductor Datasheets on the Web site by Bertrand Gros at http://www.bgs.nu/sdw/full.html.

Surplus Goods Websites

❑ **PrincessAuto.com** has an interesting banner on the top of their page: "The Unique World of Princess Auto," which pretty much sums them up. There's farm-implement machinery, surplus goods, car parts, and ancient computer equipment all in the same catalogue. If you have the opportunity to visit one of their 20 stores, do so! Based out of Canada, they've got a splendidly inexpensive domestic shipping program to bring your order to a store near you. They also ship to the internationally, so the Web site is worth visiting by all.

Warning From Dave

Do not visit these pages unless you have money to spend. Otherwise, you're just frustrating yourself paging through all the neat stuff thinking about what projects you could do!

Although there are a great many surplus stores, the following are our favorite surplus-dealing Web sites in the U.S. These are well worth visiting on a monthly basis, just to see what's in the "What's New" pages.

- ❏ All Electronics (http://www.allelectronics.com)
- ❏ Marlin P. Jones & Associates (http://www.mpja.com)
- ❏ Electronic Goldmine (http://www.goldmine-elec.com)
- ❏ B.G. Micro (http://www.bgmicro.com)
- ❏ American Science and Surplus (http://www.sciplus.com)

Printed Resources

There are a few *excellent* companion books we recommend getting to compliment this book.

- ❏ The top of our list is practically anything written by "Forrest M. Mims III." Particularly, his book *Getting Started in Electronics*, which is available only from Radio Shack, is an excellent primer in electronics, and will be the best $5 you'll spend on a book. Pick one up at your local Radio Shack dealer.

- ❏ Next on our list is a relatively new book by David Cook (yup, the "Robot Room" guy) called *Robot Building for Beginners* (A Press, 2002). Written for the absolute newcomer to robotics, it goes into great detail regarding the tools and techniques for building a single line-following robot. With this singular task in mind, the book covers practically any question related to the project.

❑ Where *Robot Building for Beginners* goes over a single project in very close detail, **The Robot Builder's Bonanza, Second Edition** (Tab Books, 2000) by Gordon McComb, is a wide-ranging collection of projects. Subtitled "99 Inexpensive Robotics Projects," it covers many small-to-large projects dealing with various electronic and mechanical aspects of robotics. Definitely worth adding to the bookshelf.

❑ *Nuts and Volts Magazine* is a very long-running electronics publication that has a robotics column. If you want exposure to different technologies in the industry, this is the magazine to read! We recommend getting and reading the other books before starting with this magazine, as it can be a bit advanced at times. Pick up an issue or two from your local bookstore before deciding on a subscription.

❑ *Vehicles: Experiments in Synthetic Psychology* by Valentino Braitenberg (MIT Press, 1986) is a great read if you want to get "inside the head" of a BEAM robot. The first ten chapters are of particular interest, as Braitenberg delves into how seemingly advanced behaviors can be generated from essentially simple sense/reaction responses. If you're craving a bit more of a robot psychology book, this paperback is worth picking up.

❑ *Robosapiens* by Peter Menzel and Faith D'Aluisio (MIT Press, 2000) is a great book of photos about the state of the art in robotics. There's a feature on BEAM robotics as well, so that alone makes it a worthwhile read.

Appendix B

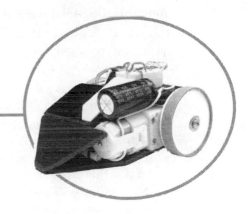

Materials and Techniques of BEAM Robotics

Robotics is a very wide-ranging field of study, where a brilliant scientist's robot can flop miserably because of simple mechanical failure, and a machinist can build stunningly fabulous but functionally inept robots. To be a successful roboticist, you need to wear the hats of a mechanical engineer, electronics guru, computer scientist, and even a philosopher. We've tried to make this book as "hands-on" as possible, and the following tips and techniques will further round out your mechanical and practical skills as roboticists. As for the other characteristics of being a successful roboticist, we suggest you crack open a few more books and build, build, build!

Little-Known Motor Testing Procedure

❏ Want an easy way to test DC motor efficiency when you don't have a power supply? Twist the motor shaft and see if you can feel it "bump" from one position to the next. Good motors have very little, if any, "bumping."

❏ Another test is to short out the motor leads and see how hard it is to turn. Good motors will take more effort to spin when shorted out, and will spin easily with open contacts.

❏ If you have access to two of the motors, hook the terminals of one to the terminals of the other (doesn't matter which), effectively turning one of the motors into a *generator*. Give the first motor a good strong spin, and see how well the second motor spins. The higher the motor efficiency, the more turns you'll get out of the second motor.

Little-Known Gear Motor Testing Procedure

❏ The best motors are usually made by Escap, MicroMo, and Namiki. They can be recognized by their cases—they are usually encased in a steel sleeve, not plastic. There are lesser, but adequately good, motors that are encased in plastic, like Nihon and Omron, and some in metal, like Copal.

❏   A quick manual test is to give the output shaft a spin and listen to it. The quieter the gears, the better made it is. Try wiggling the shaft back and forth—the less slop (movement), the better.

❏   Not sure what voltage that gearmotor is designed to work at? Connect the leads to a 100uF capacitor so it charges through a diode, and manually spin the gearmotor output shaft as quickly as you comfortably can. Measure the voltage stored on the capacitor, and that will be approximately the voltage that motor was designed to run at.

Optical Sensors

Besides the standard IR sensors we've already been using, you may find these more advanced sensors worth investigating. They all have some sort of electronic or physical preassembly done to them that makes these sensors a worthwhile addition to your electronics supply list.

The Sharp IR Ranger Module

As shown on the minisumo robot, the Sharp series of "IR ranging modules" read the reflected angle of a focussed beam of infrared light to calculate the distance to an object as far as 76 cm (30") away. The really impressive quality these sensors have is that it doesn't matter what the color of the object is, and that they're so easy to work with. They come in three flavors: threshold-set binary output (GP2D15); analog output (GP2D12); and serial output (GP2D02).

With the binary output GP2D15, the sensor uses a fixed "threshold" value of 24 cm, or about 10". The sensor detects any object at that distance or closer and will generate an active low output you can use in a similar way that a tactile switch is used to react to obstacles in the path of a BEAM robot. The GP2D12 Analog output version uses a changing voltage output between 0.6V and 3.1V to indicate how close an object is. The closer the object, the higher the voltage climbs.

Figure B-1
Advanced optical sensors, like the Sharp IR ranging module, Fairchild QRB1114 opto-reflectors, and the Sharp IS1U60 IR decoders are commonly used in hobby robotics.

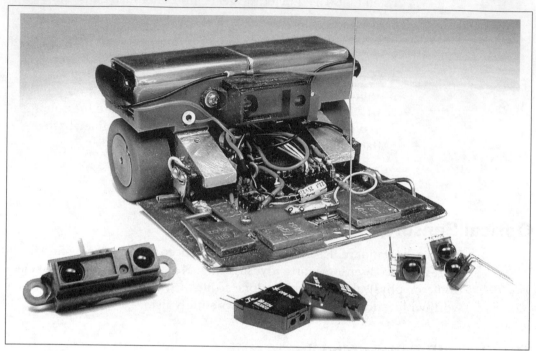

The GP2D02 serial output version would return the distance as numbers transmitted in serial data to be read by a microcontroller to determine the distance. It seems that this version of the sensor is getting displaced by Sharp's analog-output versions, as most microprocessors can get the distance information quicker by simply reading a voltage level.

For more information on these Sharp modules, visit:

❏ The Sharp Web site at http://www.sharpsma.com/sma/ products/opto/OSD/distance_measuring_sensors.htm

❏ Acroname at http://www.acroname.com/robotics/info/ articles/sharp/sharp.html

❏ HVW Technologies at http://www.hvwtech.com/sensors.htm

The Opto-Reflector Sensor

The small truncated triangle is the Fairchild QRB1114 opto-reflector style of sensor. These are not electronically complex, but they are convenient in that they have an IR emitter and receiver molded into one easy-to-mount module. They're arranged so they both are looking at the same point in space (focal point), and when a reflective surface comes into the focal point range, the transmitted IR beam is picked up by the IR receiver and generates a signal. These opto-reflector sensors are *very* common in robot sumo wrestling, where they're tuned to pick up the white line on the edge of the competition platform. As the focal point is no more than a fraction of an inch away, this sensor can only be used to detect objects in very close proximity—and nothing else!

You can find information on it (or it's little brother, the QRD1114) from:

❑ Fairchild Semiconductor at
http://www.fairchildsemi.com/pf/QR/QRB1114.html

❑ HVW Technologies at
http://www.hvwtech.com/sensors.htm#qrd1114

The Sharp IS1U60 IR Decoder

The last sensor doesn't do any active sensing, and requires a pulsed signal of 38kHz to look for. In fact, it's *specifically* tuned to the frequency used by many IR remote controls, such as the ones used for TVs and VCRs. There have been many hacks done to these so that they can be used to detect reflected IR light and use that information for obstacle detection for robots. Practically any toy or consumer piece of electronics that used a remote control will have this (or a similar) sensor in it, and they're worth holding on to for either remote-control purposes or IR sensor purposes.

Find more information on the IS1U60 from:

❑ Sharp Electronics at
http://www.sharp.co.jp/ecg/opto/products/

❑ HVW Technologies at
http://www.hvwtech.com/sensors.htm#is1u60

A Closer Look at Soldering

Generally, experience will tell you whether solder will stick to a material: watch for materials that are shiny and metal. This section covers what materials will solder and good structural materials to use for general robot building.

There are two main types of solder—lead based and silver based. A typical lead-based solder will contain 60 percent tin and 40 percent lead—this is the most common type of solder. Silver solder comes in two grades—jewellers and consumer. The jewellers-grade solder is typically 30–85 percent silver, and consumer-grade silver solder contains about 2–3 percent silver. The consumer solder will melt with a regular soldering iron, much like lead solder does. The jewellers solder will require a torch to melt, and there are many precautions to observe when using this much heat, but that could be an entire chapter by itself. In short, *do not* use jewellers solder unless you're already familiar with the techniques and procedures.

A ball bearing is solderable, but the sheer mass of what your trying to solder will cause a problem. Steel acts as a great, big heat sink and sucks away the heat you're trying to melt the solder with. The way around this is to use a bigger gun (we like bigger guns…), one with sufficient wattage that can bring the whole metal mass up to the point of melting solder. Alternatively, a small butane soldering torch works well, but use this with *extreme* caution, as *house on fire* equals a *bad thing*.

It's good practice to clean the surface that will be soldered with a scour pad or sandpaper, and, if possible, use a paper towel and rubbing alcohol (the 99.953 percent pure stuff is best) to remove any dust and dirt. A clean, shiny surface is the easiest to solder to.

Solderable Structural Materials, in Order of Preference

Bronze Brazing / Welding Rod

Welding supply stores have a surprising variety of metal alloy rods. After examining and testing a fair variety of rods, the best we've found so far is bronze rod. In many respects, it's half as strong and stiff as steel, which is still considerably good. It takes solder very well and is slow to build an oxide layer. Bronze lasts a *very* long time, as proved by recovered bronze artifiacts dated at over 3,000 years old. Another nice characteristic about bronze is that it is self-lubricating, making it ideal for bearings and sleeves.

Heavy Copper Wire

As already mentioned in several of the projects, 10-gauge solid copper wire used for electrical wiring is an excellent material for forming, soldering, and inexpensive availability. However, the flexible nature of this wire can make for wobbly walker legs that can deform easily after an accidental drop to the floor. In many cases, we'll use this "Gumby" wire to get the initial geometry of the part we want (like legs), then copy that shape into something more permanent, like bronze or steel rod.

Printer Cartridge Rod

Printer cartridge rod *seems* to be a stainless-steel rod with very high nickel content, giving it the unique characteristics of acting like stainless steel, *and* still being solderable. The only real disadvantage is that the rod we find is 2 mm in diameter, which makes it difficult to find a suitable size of brass tubing to create a brass bushing or bearing for this wire. We haven't had any luck in determining the exact composition or source of this material—if you find out, let us know!

Copper Clad Welding Rod

Unfluxed copper-clad welding rod can be found at nearly any welding supply store, and is fairly inexpensive (sold by the pound). The rods come in standard imperial sizes (1/16", 1/32", 1/8") in three-foot lengths. The copper cladding takes solder better than the bare steel, and copper takes longer to corrode than bare steel. Unfortunately, the cladding has a bad habit of tearing off at the solder joint when subjected to any substantial load.

Stainless-Steel Welding Rod

Stainless-steel welding rod offers both excellent and disappointing qualities. The good news is that it's very tough, readily available from most welding shops, and looks great. The bad news is that lead solder techniques will not work on most kinds of stainless steel. This material can be soldered with high-content silver solder, making for a much stronger connection than with lead-based solder, but it means dealing with a blow torch and a special flux designed for high temperatures. Again, leave silver soldering for those with the proper tools and techniques.

Metal Clothes Hangers

To use metal clothes hangers, simply sand off the paint and straighten the coat hanger as best as possible. *Voila!* You have a fairly sturdy structural rod that can be soldered to. Two problems to be aware of:

1. Bare steel rusts rather fast.

2. Mom won't like you leaving clothes on the floor.

Material Soldering Characteristics

❏ **Copper**   Probably the most common type of metal used in electronics, copper is the second best conductor of electricity, and solders very well.

❏ **Gold**   Solders very well. Some expensive PCBs are gold-plated as well as some audio and video connectors, due to fact that gold does not corrode. Gold is the third best conductor of electricity.

❏ **Silver**   Also solders well, but tends to build up a black oxide layer that solder will not sick to. Some copper wires are silver-plated, as silver is the best conductor of electricity. Silver-plated wire is fairly common in very thin-gauge wire—for example, 30 gauge and higher.

❏ **Steel**   Most steel alloys will solder reasonably well, excluding stainless steel. For best solder joints, really scuff up the surface of steel with a file or sandpaper before soldering to it.

❏ **Chrome**   Solder flows well onto chrome, but since most chrome pieces are just chrome *plated,* you can tear off the chrome if the joint is subjected to too much force (much like the copper-clad welding rod). Magnets and ball bearings are common examples of chrome-plated surfaces.

❏ **Bronze**   Excellent soldering characteristics, structurally stiff, a good electrical conductor, and self lubricating for mechanical joints make bronze a good general building material.

❏ **Brass**   Another easily solderable material, and easily found as brass tubes and rods at most hobby stores, brass tubes are very handy for creating bushings, sensors, and a multitude of other mechanisms requiring low mechanical strength.

❏ **Tin**   Common as a plating on electrical components, tin is cheap, protects the copper from oxidizing, and solders very well.

❏ **Aluminium**   Although technically possible, soldering to aluminium is very difficult, due to the oxide layer that rapidly forms on the surface of the aluminium during the process. Not generally recommended as a solderable structural material, aluminum is otherwise excellent for sawing, drilling, riveting, and screw-fasteners.

❏ **Stainless Steel**   Generally, lead-based solder will not stick to stainless steel, although some stainless steels with a high nickel content will solder. Stainless steel isn't as commonly available as brass and aluminum stock.

Appendix C

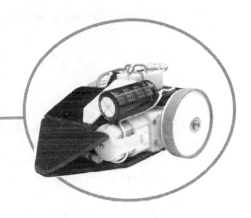

Technical Schematics

In the project chapters, we used a circuit layout drawing that showed how to layout and connect all the components. The following schematics of each project show the circuit drawn using standard electronic symbols and standards for the benefit of readers with a more technical background. If we included these in the project chapters, people new to electronics would find them more confusing than helpful.

The Flashing LED (FLED) Solarengine

This particular solarengine tends to lock up under bright light conditions and go into a high-frequency oscillation, which you may hear as a high-frequency buzz. One way to counter this is to cover the FLED with heat shrink or a felt marker so that light won't affect the triggering of the FLED.

Figure C-1
The FLED solar engine technical schematic

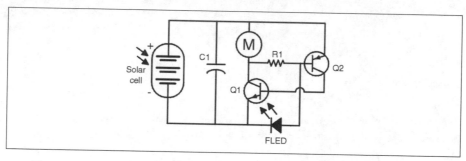

- ❏ **R1** 1KΩ to 10KΩ
- ❏ **C1** 1000μF to 10F, main storage capacitator
- ❏ **Q1** 2N3904 / PN2222, NPN type transistor
- ❏ **Q2** 2N3906 / PN2907, PNP type transistor
- ❏ **FLED** A regular flashing LED, red works well
- ❏ **M** Motor rated 1 to 6 volts (power efficiency important)
- ❏ **Solar cell** Minimum of 1381 trigger value + 1 volt, 1mA

The Miller Solarengine (or MSE)

The Millerengine is one of the best solar engines to date, is simple and easy to free-form, has a low quiescent current draw (low leakage), and has no known lockup issues. The variety of component values may be confusing to a new BEAM roboticists, but the benefits of this solarengine outweigh the potential confusion. The following Miller solarengine 1381 trigger voltage values are compiled from a circuit using a 4700μF storage capacitor, a 0.47μF timer capacitor, a regular standard signal diode, and a 2N3904 as a driver transistor.

Figure C-2
The Miller
solarengine
technical
schematic

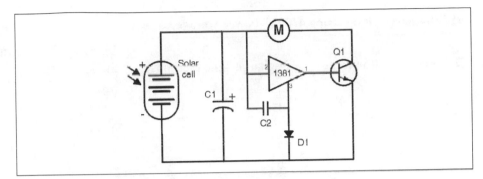

- ❏ **C1** 1000µF to 10F, main storage capacitator
- ❏ **C2** 0.1µF to 22µF, timer capacitator
- ❏ **Q1** 2N3904 / PN2222, NPN type transistor
- ❏ **D1** 1N914 regular silicon diode
- ❏ **M** Motor rated 1 to 6 volts (power efficiency important)
- ❏ **Solar cell** Minimum of 1381 trigger value + 1 volt, 1mA
- ❏ **1381 trigger** Value determined from Table C-1

1381 Trigger Letter	Trigger Voltage of the MSE
C	2.51
E	2.63
G	2.99
J	3.22
L	3.66
N	4.07
Q	4.36
S	4.94
U	5.36

Table C-1
The Miller Solarengine Voltage Trigger Table

The Miller Solarengine uses the C2 capacitor to determine how long it stays on when activated. Tables C-2 and C-3 give these values for two common-sized capacitors, the 4700µF and 0.33F capacitors. These measurements were taken using a Solarbotics SC2433 solar cell, 1381-G, driving a 25 ohm motor load.

MSE Discharge Times Using 4700μF Power Storage Capacitor

C2 Timer Capacitor Value	Discharge Time (Seconds)	Discharge Time with Motor Stalled (Seconds)
.22uf	0.168	0.240
.47uf	0.150	0.150
1.0uf	0.560	0.540
4.7uf	2.9	2.9
6.8uf	4.0	4.0
10uf	5.8	5.9

Table C-2
Miller Solarengine Discharge Times Using a 4700μF Capacitor

MSE Discharge Times Using 0.33F "Panasonic AL Gold" Power Storage Capacitor

C2 Timer Capacitor Value	Discharge Time (Seconds)	Discharge Time with Motor Stalled (Seconds)
.22uf	1.88	0.180
.47uf	1.84	0.260
1.0uf	1.98	0.620
4.7uf	3.72	3.08
6.8uf	4.48	4.0
10uf	6.7	6.2

Table C-3
Miller Solarengine Discharge Times Using a 0.33F Capacitor

The Herbie Photovore

The Herbie circuit is a clever example of using minimal parts for maximum performance. The design is improved with a relay that swaps the power feed polarities to the motors, causing a reverse behavior.

Figure C-3
The Herbie
photovore
technical
schematic

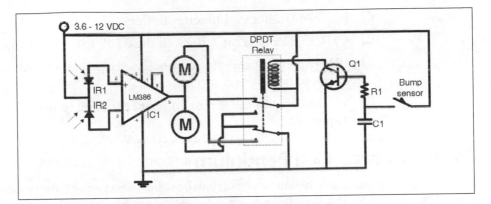

- ❏ **IC1**   LM386 Audio Operational Amplifier
- ❏ **R1**   1kΩ to 47kΩ, sets reverse time
- ❏ **C1**   10µF to 100µF, also used to set reverse time
- ❏ **IR1, IR2**   Identical infrared photodetectors, IR LED emitters, or photodiodes
- ❏ **Q1**   2N3906 / PN2907 PNP transistor
- ❏ **DPDT**   5 to 9 volt Double-pole, Double-throw (DPDT) relay
- ❏ **M, M**   Identical motors rated 1 to 6 volts (power efficiency important)

Bicore Light-Seeking Headbot

This simple circuit controls a light tracking "head," but is also the basis for many phototropic beam critters. Optional resistors can be added to take care of extreme bright and dark conditions.

Figure C-4
The Bicore
light-seeking
headbot
technical
schematic

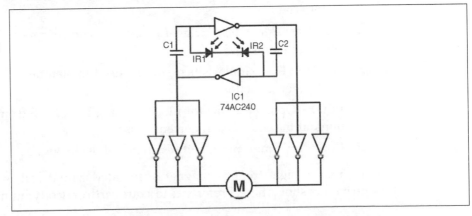

❏ **IC1**   74AC240 Octal Inverter Buffer

❏ **C1, C2**   Identical capacitors, in the 0.1µF to 0.47µF range

❏ **IR1, IR2**   Identical infrared photodetectors, IR LED emitters, or photodiodes

❏ **M**   Motor with minimum 3:1 gear reduction (power efficiency important)

Magbot Force Coil Pendulum

This particularly unique circuit can be solar-powered or battery-powered via a 4.7k to 10k resistor and, when properly mechanically aligned, is self-starting. A magnet suspended by a 24.84 cm (9.78") line gives a period (back and forth swing) of *extremely* close to one second.

Figure C-5
Magbot force coil pendulum technical schematic

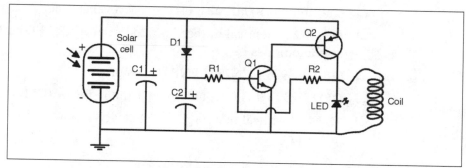

❏ **R1**   10kΩ to 100kΩ, sets voltage trigger point of circuit

❏ **R2**   10kΩ to 100kΩ, sets voltage trigger point as well as maximum current to coil

❏ **C1**   1000µF to 4700µF main storage capacitor, sets initial power kick to coil

❏ **C2**   1000µF to 4700µF trigger capacitor keeps trigger voltage near activation threshold

❏ **D1**   1N914 or similar silicon diode, used to maintain charge on the trigger capacitor

❏ **LED1**   Optional indicator LED, utilizing back-EMF from coil to blink at the end of each current pulse

❏ **Coil**   1mH minimum, coil resistance of 3Ω to 30Ω

Note that a high-strength magnet suspended above coil is required, though it is not shown here. Preference to a rare earth or neodymium magnet.

Mini-sumo Edgebot

This robot uses an effective, robust, electromechanical "brain." The maximum voltage that this circuit can utilize is only limited by the voltage ratings of the relay, backup capacitor, and the motor.

Figure C-6
Mini-sumo edgebot technical schematic

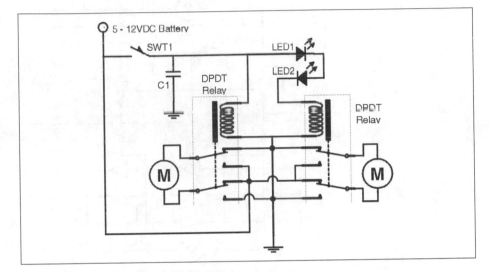

- ❏ **C1**   1000µF to 10,000µF reverse timing capacitor
- ❏ **DPDT, DPDT**   5 to 9 volt Double-pole, Double-throw (DPDT) relays
- ❏ **LED1, LED2**   Standard LEDs
- ❏ **SWT1**   Edge detecting sensor, normally open, closes on edge detection
- ❏ **M, M**   Gear motors in the 25:1 to 200:1 reduction range, rated 3 to 12 volts, drawing 200 to 500mA nominal under load
- ❏ A 5 to 12 volt DC power source

BEAM Bicore Walking Robot

One of the simplest basic walking robot designs that is functional and expandable is shown next.

Figure C-7
Bicore
walking
robot
technical
schematic

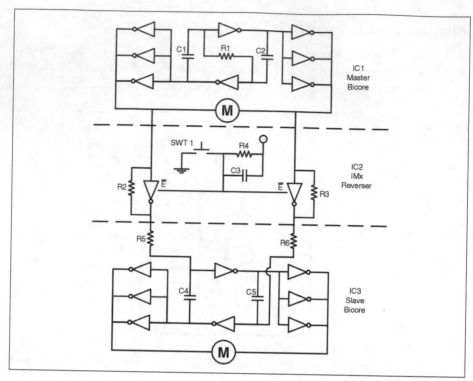

- ❑ **IC1, IC2, IC3**   74AC240 octal inverting buffer
- ❑ **R1**   470kΩ to 10MΩ master suspended resistor, sets rhythm of entire walker
- ❑ **R2**   10kΩ to 100kΩ IMx bypass resistor (R2 and R3 should match)
- ❑ **R3**   10kΩ to 100kΩ IMx bypass resistor (R2 and R3 should match)
- ❑ **R4**   10kΩ to 300kΩ backup timer resistor. Increase value for longer reverse time
- ❑ **R5, R6**   470kΩ to 10MΩ slave resistors that set delay between front and back Bicores
- ❑ **C1, C2**   0.1µF to 1µF master Bicore capacitors
- ❑ **C3**   1µF to 100µF backup timer capacitor. Increase value for longer reverse time
- ❑ **C4, C5**   0.1µF to 1µF slave Bicore capacitors
- ❑ **M, M**   Gear motors in the 100:1 to 200:1 reduction range, rated 3 to 12 volts, drawing 200 to 500mA nominal under load
- ❑ **SWT1**   Normally open tactile sensor, closing on obstacle impact, which triggers reverse circuit

Index

Note: Page numbers in *italics* refer to illustrations or charts.

Numbers

74AC240 chip
    Bicore circuit and IMx reverser
      construction, 298
    Bicore Headbot project, 168,
      174–176, 183–185
    walking robot, 283, 288–289

A

adaptive Bicore controller, 334–338
    See also Bicore circuit; Biomech
      H-Bridge
    diode-shunted capacitors, 334–335
    experimental options, 337–338
    features, 335
    flexibility features, 335–336
    "one-wire" H-Bridge, 337–338
    schematics, *334, 336, 337*
aesthetics, BEAM robotics
    overview, 6–7
agility, mini–sumo wrestling edgebot, 268
anodes, 42
    See also diodes; identifying
      electronic bits
"appropriate technology" concept,
    robotics, 9–10
aprons, safety considerations, 21
armor, mini–sumo wrestling edgebot, 266
Aronson mouse, Symet project, 109

assembling electronics. *See* gluing;
    soldering
asynchronous oscillators, Bicore circuit,
    280

B

balancing considerations, Magbot
    Pendulum project, 230–232
batteries
    Bicore Headbot project, 176,
      182, 194
    Herbie Photovore project, 134, 138,
      144–145, 152
    installing Bicore circuit in walking
      robot body, 302–307
    Magbot Pendulum project,
      207, 230
    mini–sumo wrestling edgebot, 240,
      252, 258, 264
    power sources for BEAM devices,
      14–15
    safety considerations, 23
    walking robot, 284
battery-powered devices, garbage
    reclamation, 87
BEAM robotics, 5–15
    See also projects; robotics
    aesthetics, 6–7
    "appropriate technology" concept,
      9–10

361

overview, 53
safety considerations, 21–22
sponges and, 56
stands, 55
wire strippers/cutters and, 54–55
solid-core wire, solder and, 60
SPDT (single-pole, double-throw) switch, mini–sumo wrestling edgebot, 269
sponges, soldering irons and, 56
springs, leg design and, 311
start-up timer circuit, mini–sumo wrestling edgebot, 264–265
Strider robot, Bicore Headbot project, 195
sumo wrestling edgebot. *See* mini–sumo wrestling edgebot
SunSeeker headbot, Bicore Headbot project, 170, *171*
super glue, mechanical tools, 71
supercaps, 38–40
See also capacitors; identifying electronic bits
internal impedance, 39–40
supermagnets, Magbot Pendulum project, 204–205
support tools, 75–77
See also tools
bins, 76
boxes, 76
drawers, 76
plastic baggies, 76–77
power bars, 76
surplus goods web sites, Internet-based information, 342–343
surplus sources, 83–85
See also scavenging parts
suspended Bicore, Bicore circuit, 279
suspension point, Magbot Pendulum project, 206
switches, transistors as, 42
Symet project, 91–109
See also projects
Aronson mouse, 109
bases, 99
BEAM robotics, 92–93
behavior, 95
"Behemoth," *108*
build procedure, 98–107
capacitors, 102–104
collectors, 99

emitters, 99
FLED (flashing LED), 97–98, 101–102
gluing wires, 105, *106*
heat-shrink tubing, 108
maintenance, 107–109
parts list, 92, 96–97
pinouts, 99
power storage capacitors, 102–103
solar power, 92–93
solarengines, 93–95, 102–107
tips, 97–98
transistors, 99–100
wire loop, 104
wiring, 104–107

T

tantalum capacitors, *35*
See also capacitors; identifying electronic bits
technical schematics. *See* schematics
Tilden, Mark
Biomech H-Bridge, 326
history of robotics, 4, 5–8
laws of robotics, 10–12
timer-based solarengines, 94
See also solarengines; Symet project
timers, delay. *See* delay timer
timing capacitors, Bicore circuit and IMx reverser construction, 297
toner cartridge wire
consumables, 78
garbage reclamation, 86
tools, 67–79
consumables, 77–79
electronics, 72–75
mechanical, 68–72
safety considerations, 18–26
support, 75–77
tips, 79
"torque-arm distance," leg design, 312
touch sensor extension, Herbie Photovore project, 161
touch switches, Herbie Photovore project, 140, 147–148
transistors, 42–45
See also identifying electronic bits
as amplifiers of signals, 42

INTERNATIONAL CONTACT INFORMATION

AUSTRALIA
McGraw-Hill Book Company Australia Pty. Ltd.
TEL +61-2-9415-9899
FAX +61-2-9415-5687
http://www.mcgraw-hill.com.au
books-it_sydney@mcgraw-hill.com

CANADA
McGraw-Hill Ryerson Ltd.
TEL +905-430-5000
FAX +905-430-5020
http://www.mcgrawhill.ca

**GREECE, MIDDLE EAST,
NORTHERN AFRICA**
McGraw-Hill Hellas
TEL +30-1-656-0990-3-4
FAX +30-1-654-5525

MEXICO (Also serving Latin America)
McGraw-Hill Interamericana Editores S.A. de C.V.
TEL +525-117-1583
FAX +525-117-1589
http://www.mcgraw-hill.com.mx
fernando_castellanos@mcgraw-hill.com

SINGAPORE (Serving Asia)
McGraw-Hill Book Company
TEL +65-863-1580
FAX +65-862-3354
http://www.mcgraw-hill.com.sg
mghasia@mcgraw-hill.com

SOUTH AFRICA
McGraw-Hill South Africa
TEL +27-11-622-7512
FAX +27-11-622-9045
robyn_swanepoel@mcgraw-hill.com

**UNITED KINGDOM & EUROPE
(Excluding Southern Europe)**
McGraw-Hill Education Europe
TEL +44-1-628-502500
FAX +44-1-628-770224
http://www.mcgraw-hill.co.uk
computing_neurope@mcgraw-hill.com

ALL OTHER INQUIRIES Contact:
Osborne/McGraw-Hill
TEL +1-510-549-6600
FAX +1-510-883-7600
http://www.osborne.com
omg_international@mcgraw-hill.com

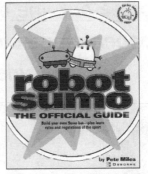

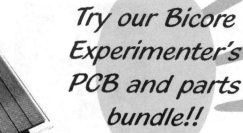